Crossing the Street in Hanoi

Crossing the Street in Hanoi
Teaching and Learning about Vietnam

Carol Wilder

intellect Bristol, UK / Chicago, USA

First published in the UK in 2013 by
Intellect, The Mill, Parnall Road, Fishponds, Bristol, BS16 3JG, UK

First published in the USA in 2013 by
Intellect, The University of Chicago Press, 1427 E. 60th Street,
Chicago, IL 60637, USA

Copyright © 2013 Intellect Ltd

All rights reserved. No part of this publication may be reproduced,
stored in a retrieval system, or transmitted, in any form or by
any means, electronic, mechanical, photocopying, recording, or
otherwise, without written permission.

A catalogue record for this book is available from the
British Library.

Cover designer: Ellen Thomas
Cover photo: Carol Wilder
Copy-editor: MPS Technologies
Production manager: Tim Mitchell
Typesetting: Planman Technologies

Print ISBN 978-1-84150-735-4
ePUB ISBN 978-1-78320-148-8
ePDF ISBN 978-1-78320-149-5

for Elissa and Casey
my life teachers

"God save us always from the innocent and the good."

Graham Greene
The Quiet American

Table of Contents

Foreword by William Logan		xi
Introduction		1
Chapter 1:	The War That Won't Die	11
Chapter 2:	*Hoa Lo* Prison Museum: "The Fury Burning Within"	29
Chapter 3:	*Bac Ho*: "Casting Pearls before Swine"	61
Chapter 4:	*Life* on Vietnam: "A Glory Preserved in a Wilderness Valley"	75
Chapter 5:	Reading Graham Greene: A Promise to the Dead	99
Chapter 6:	*Vietnam Love Songs*: "Rode Hard and Put Away Wet"	125
Chapter 7:	Reinventing Rambo: *Flooding with Love for the Kid*	147
Chapter 8:	Murder on May 4th: The Case of the Missing Mob	169
Chapter 9:	*Long Bien Story*: Giving and Taking Away (with Douglas Jardine)	201
Afterword:	A Note on Theory	221
Acknowledgments		233
References		237
Index		247

Foreword

What a delight it is to read Carol Wilder's perceptive book on Hanoi. It's a city I know very well and recognize so clearly in Carol's book, although she presents fresh and refreshing new perspectives. It was in January 1990 that I first visited Vietnam's capital city, not many years before Carol's first foray into Hanoi in 1993. I went there on a UNESCO mission to help local planners identify and protect the city's built heritage before the American embargo on foreign aid and investment ended and development pressures would impact on the city's historic precincts, streetscapes, and buildings. Little did I know then that Hanoi would be the focus of much of my heritage work as university scholar, educator, and consultant.

Back in January 1990, Hanoi was capital of a state that had been locked in civil war and foreign invasion for half a century and was still tied to the Soviet bloc politically and economically, though not culturally. There had been little building in the city during that time and the late nineteenth- and early twentieth-century streetscapes were still mostly intact. It was a silent city, apart from the loudspeaker system that still woke the citizens each morning with rousing tunes. Hardly a motor vehicle was seen—only the occasional Russian-made jeep—and the French colonial tramway system was in a state of collapse. People moved around the city on foot or in swarms of bicycles.

I wish I had taken more photos of the city as it was then: hardly any shops or motor vehicles, no advertisements—a quiet city. But that city is long gone, transformed economically, socially, and physically in the most dramatic ways imaginable. The Sixth Congress of the Vietnam Communist Party in 1986 officially introduced a set of *doi moi* (renovation) policies that opened up Vietnam to the world. The American embargo ended in 1994 and Vietnam was admitted to ASEAN year the following year. Foreign investment was through joint ventures and focused on manufacturing, tourism, and urban development. High-rise office and apartment buildings now dominate much of the colonial French Quarter, but mercifully have mostly been kept out of the Ancient Quarter—the market town of shop-houses and narrow streets—or around Hoan Kiem, the little lake at the city's heart.

While the traffic in those days was quiet, there were still some distinctive noises—pigs being herded through the Ancient Quarter to market in the middle of the night, the wake-up music broadcast across the city on the war-time PA system, and, of course, the fireworks at Tet. The foreigner from more sedate cities enjoyed the overload of sensory stimuli—and the constant bustle of people everywhere. In 1990 the intense overcrowding of Hanoi dwellings meant domestic life spread onto the footpaths—cooking, relaxing with friends, washing clothes and children. My own writing on Hanoi has largely focused on the built environment, although always with the aim of showing how architectural design and urban planning reflected the values of the state and its people. Carol Wilder brings in the people in a much more satisfactory way, delving into the attitudes of Hanoians and opening up new dimensions for teaching and learning about Hanoi and Vietnam.

By the late 1990s motorbikes started replacing bicycles; then came the fleets of taxis and installation of traffic lights. The footpaths have become motorbike parking lots, pedestrians are now forced to walk on the street itself, often weaving in and out of the traffic, and crossing streets is a nightmare. Carol Wilder has chosen one of those defining Hanoi experiences to represent the city's and Vietnam's rapid economic and social transformation. But it's also an apt metaphor for the difficulties that outsiders—especially those coming from the "advanced West"—have in understanding what makes Vietnam tick. How are the country and its capital city run, who are the key players and where do the people fit in? What do Hanoians think about current political, social, and environmental issues impacting on their city and their lives?

The metaphor extends to the attempts by foreigners to understand their history, especially the place of the two wars of independence, the first against the French (1945–1954) and the second against the United States and its allies (1955–1972). It's again like cutting through the traffic of vehicles coming from the left and right, with the aim of getting to the other side intact—with a coherent set of notions about how contemporary Vietnam was formed. In fact, many Vietnamese also have difficulties in understanding their country's history. From the 1940s ideological pressures in the North put blinkers on the way the past could be understood, or at least discussed in public forums and taught in schools.

With regard to the war of independence, Vietnam is the exception to the rule that it is the victors who write the history. Much research and writing has been done by French and American scholars, some infused by Cold War attitudes but some remarkably independent. By contrast there has been little critical work published in Vietnam but a considerable output of state-sponsored books running the official line on Vietnam's history. This will change as the ideology softens; but in the meantime we are left wondering how major events such as the Vietnam War persist in memory and popular culture.

This is where Carol Wilder's book comes to the fore. Drawing on her background in communication and media studies, she probes into what the past means to the Vietnamese today, what is passed from one generation to the next and how, and what has been the role of the media in shaping consciousness of the war and its aftermath. She sees the Vietnam War as an "undead war" that simply refuses to lie down because it doesn't fit with the American national narrative in which the United States is the good guy and the winner. By contrast, she finds that, in Vietnam, it is only one of many wars and relegated to the distant past by many, if not most young Vietnamese today.

In America, Vietnam is treated as a commodity in the popular culture of books, films, memorials, and tourism and that war is the dominant focus. She was surprised to find,

Foreword

therefore, that the Vietnam War was only a very minor feature in Hanoi's Ho Chi Minh Museum. A visit to the Revolutionary Museum in the old colonial customs house would have given a different impression, as did, in fact, her visits to and research on the Hoa Lo Prison Museum. But the general point that she and others, including President Clinton, make is fundamental—that Vietnam is more than a war. In Vietnam, memories of the wars of independence survive among those who lived through them and who are now in old age, of course, but there has been a dimming of passions. The overseas Vietnamese—the Viet Kieu—are on the whole an exception: living in the United States, France, Australia, and Canada, they maintain their rage. Again, this will fade as the generations pass.

Carol Wilder's book comprises a set of stories that tease out what the Vietnam War still means to a selection of Vietnamese and Americans who were touched by it. Her aim is to put a human face on what was an inhuman experience, and she succeeds wonderfully. The chapter on the Hoa Lo Prison Museum demonstrates Carol's multidimensional technique. She describes the museum site as a microcosm of the contradictions and tensions in contemporary Vietnam between protecting war heritage and encouraging new development, and explores the personal memories of Nguyen Thi Phuc Hang, who was imprisoned there by the French because of her nationalist activities, counterpoised against those of John McCain, downed U.S. pilot and presidential candidate, who was jailed there by the Democratic Republic of Vietnam.

The book is thoroughly researched and draws on a wide variety of primary and secondary sources. Additionally, there is a fascinating autobiographical aspect in which Carol uses her own experiences from memorializing the Vietnam War and reading Graham Greene's *Quiet American* to her year in Hanoi funded by a Fulbright award in 2007–2008. Her personal reflections and diary entries become an integral part of the exploration. Carol is to be congratulated for achieving such a fine balancing act, effectively getting her to the other side of the street. I hope readers will enjoy Carol Wilder's book as much as I did.

William Logan
Melbourne
January 2013

Introduction

Nobody gives way to anybody. Everyone just angles, points, dives directly toward his destination, pretending it is an all-or-nothing gamble. People glare at one another and fight for maneuvering space. All parties are equally determined to get the right-of-way—insist on it. They swerve away at the last possible moment, giving scant inches to spare. The victor goes forward, no time for a victory grin, already engaging in another contest of will.

Andrew X. Pham, Catfish and Mandala

I long resisted writing about the traffic in Vietnam because it is a cliché to anyone familiar with Hanoi or Saigon, but at the same time I have been haunted by the first entry in my journal the first time I arrived there in 1993:

Crossing the street in Hanoi !!??!!

I remember sitting on the lumpy mattress in our forlorn Hoan Kiem hotel stumped by how to put the terrifying walk I had just tried to take into words. Despite the existential immersion of the pedestrian experience, I have never succeeded in doing so. What moves me to return now to the subject is the fact that Hanoi traffic persists as an omnipresent challenge, and successful pedestrian navigation does indeed stand for moving forward hopefully and unscathed in many aspects of life in Vietnam. When friends say *"Crossing the Street in Hanoi,* what a great metaphor!" I say "Thanks, but it has more meaning as a metaphor if you have survived it in the material world."

Extreme Walking, Hanoi Style

Consider the case of artificial intelligence luminary Seymour Papert, in Hanoi to deliver a keynote address at the 17th annual conference of the International Commission of Mathematical Instruction when he was struck and critically injured by a motorbike while crossing the street near his hotel. The 78-year-old Papert was also studying Hanoi's gridlocked traffic patterns. Papert's colleague and companion at the time, Uri Wilensky, said that when Papert was hit he was following the prevailing wisdom that instructs one to walk across the traffic slowly at a steady pace. Papert had become fascinated with Hanoi's traffic as an emergent self-organizing system and with the mind of a mathematician he most likely discerned some pattern and intentionality in the smoggy swarming hordes. What he may not yet have realized was that the predictability that anchored the "walk steady" wisdom is no longer operative, the more apt advice being what I learned from riding a motorcycle myself: assume that most drivers do not see you, and those who do are trying to kill you. Vietnam records about 1,000 traffic fatalities each month, a figure thought to actually be much higher. Even so, it is nearly twice the U.S. annual per capita rate and one of the highest in the world. Hanoi has seen a thousand-fold increase in motorbikes in the past 15 years, and I think I could have given Professor Papert better advice.

The "walk steady" school of thinking is based on the old Hanoi of not much more than a dozen years ago where bicycles were the norm and traffic lights were nonexistent. The sight of 12 lanes of bicycle traffic going north/south and 12 lanes going east/west meeting and flowing through each other at an intersection without missing a beat was a marvel of human choreography: intuitive, lyrical, organic. Bicyclists were all riding to the same rhythm. Crossing the street and weaving through them yourself was heart stopping but the "slow and steady" advice put you in their flow and they could avoid you using the same undulating movements they used to avoid each other. No more.

Today it is a different world of almost all motorbikes and new stoplights at most major intersections. The helmet law that went into effect in December 2007 has resulted in eggshell head protection, diminished sight and hearing and a lot of bad hair days in the tropical heat. Lights are obeyed about 75 percent of the time, which is worse than not at all. The result of this has been a cultural forgetting of the complex bicycle protocols. Changing material conditions (motorbikes, helmets, lights) have disrupted the learning of a choreography deeply ingrained over decades. Most riders are young enough to barely remember when bicycles predominated on the streets. The idea of pedestrian right-of-way that is sacrosanct in U.S. cities is turned on its head; right-of-way is a function of horsepower—trucks, then cars, then motorbikes, then cyclos and bicycles—which pretty much leaves pedestrians at the bottom of the food chain. As a consequence, you have the worst of all possible worlds: riders who do a pretty good job of avoiding each other, but have no memory of the code that kept pedestrians from getting flattened. What once behaved like a beehive now behaves like a beehive having a nervous breakdown, with rogue bees flying every which way, wearing masks to protect from the choking smog and headgear that would not save a melon.

"Slow and steady" has become "run for your life." (And whatever you do, do *not* go backward!) Or at least *walk* for your life, but I can attest that no one is looking out for you except yourself. Drivers are careless and often aggressive. I have never seen one of the plentiful policemen make a traffic stop. One night I was crossing Hang Bai Street with ample space for an oncoming bike. Instead of continuing smoothly, he accelerated, leaned on his horn, and swerved to miss me at the last second, in what I could only conclude was a macho little hostile way of amusing himself. It is these moments that make negotiating traffic a truly daunting and unpleasant part of the Hanoi experience. I heard the story of an

Introduction

American diplomat who was asked what she thought her last words would be: "Don't worry. It's perfectly safe to go now. Come on, I'll show you."

Even Wikipedia has weighed in on the subject: "Hanoi's traffic is chaotic, with seemingly perpetual traffic jams, and a large number of almost suicidal motorcyclists and pedestrians. As such, driving yourself around is not recommended, and you should leave your transportation needs in the hands of professionals" (2012).

If Seymour Papert had left his transportation needs in the hands of professionals and had enough time to observe carefully, he might agree that entropy is a better model than self-organizing systems for Hanoi traffic, which is poised between the past beauty of organic cooperation and some imagined future of orderly traffic patterns. Meanwhile, the status quo is a state of semi-controlled chaos, with an emphasis upon the chaos, reflecting the more general state of development in Vietnam, which reveres the past while sustaining a blurring pace of change—"developing at the speed of a Polaroid," said Pico Iyer way back in 1993 (117). Having secured independence from a long and familiar list of invaders, it remains to be seen if the invasion of capitalism and development can conquer a culture that great armies could not.

Princess or Nurse?

As a girl growing up in the tidy U.S. Midwest of the 1950s, I never in my wildest imagination conjured a place on earth with the beauty, intensity and complexity of Hanoi. The idea that there was life that was not regulated, safe, clean, affluent, and conforming at all times was barely imagined on the inside of the silken threads of my cocoon. It was like growing up in a coloring book where you might get to pick your page from a narrow set of choices (princess or nurse?), but from that day forward were expected to stay within the lines. Vietnam came out of nowhere and exploded the lines with colors brighter than any I had ever seen.

Almost everyone I have met with a deep connection to Vietnam has not lived life coloring within the lines. It is, in the first instance, geographically unlikely that an American and Vietnamese resident would have much contact or awareness of each other, literally half a world away. Only 30 percent of Americans have passports even today, and the number is no doubt lower for Vietnamese. The American War in Vietnam was a catastrophic blind date set-up by the French and fueled by a toxic fear of communism and a near-psychotic avoidance of losing face. While the stories in this book were first brought to my attention because of the war, for the most part they are stories that look toward the future. I can count on one hand in many trips to Vietnam the times that I have heard a sustained conversation about "the war," and even then the subject is usually raised by a first time (American) visitor, making it a kind of rookie topic. The American War is long over in Vietnam, except for when it isn't. This book is a collection of stories that tell the ways it persists in the people whose lives it touched on both sides of the planet.

A Narrative Collage

Crossing the Street in Hanoi began as a series of historical and critical essays of Vietnam in popular American culture: film, literature, media, art and architecture. Somehow that always seemed an abstract and dry approach for such a charged and poignant subject, and eventually the project evolved into a narrative collage that is now as much about people as about artifacts. Fragments from my journals crept into the text slowly with the encouragement of early readers who to my mild consternation claimed in some cases to like the personal digressions better than the subject at hand. Each chapter now takes a historical and critical view of some artifact or event—for instance, Hoa Lo Prison Museum—but the story is told as it relates to the first-person account, in that instance, of a woman who spent five years incarcerated at Hoa Lo in the 1940s. The chapters that follow also braid the history of various media texts with those who lived them. In the end, the book is about their stories as enduring histories of Vietnam and of the American War that bound together such unlikely bedfellows. I think of myself like the stage manager in Thornton Wilder's *Our Town*, weaving the disparate story threads into whole cloth by offering commentary and continuity.

An introductory chapter "The War that Won't Die" (long the working title of this book) considers why so many of us still care about Vietnam as well as how I became deeply attracted to the subject. How does the Vietnam War persist in history, memory and popular culture both in the United States and Vietnam? How does the media environment create consciousness? What was the mediated world of the war years that shaped government policy and public opinion? Vietnam is also introduced as a commodity that has been successfully monetized in American popular culture—books, films, memorials, cuisine, and now tourism.

"Hoa Lo Prison Museum" is where we meet the remarkable Mme. Nguyen Thi Phuc Hang, jailed by the French in Hoa Lo for her nationalist activities only to find herself six decades later still watched by the government for which she gave most of her life. The story of Hoa Lo is a microcosm of the contradictions and tensions in contemporary Vietnam between heritage and development. I explore Hoa Lo's various incarnations as an ancient craft village, as a French prison built to hold Vietnamese revolutionaries, as the site of incarceration of hundreds of American pilots during the war, and today as a museum and mammoth commercial and apartment complex. I look at the galleries in the museum devoted to the experience of the American pilots in Hoa Lo, including John McCain, contrasting them to an exhibit of 14 Vietnamese nationalist women incarcerated by the French.

Bac Ho, Uncle Ho, Ho Chi Minh, the man of many names—the mysterious hero of Vietnamese independence, looked to the West and to the United States in particular for support of his country's freedom. Surely, the nation that fought and died for liberation from colonial subjugation would want the same for others? On 2 September 1945, Ho Chi Minh delivered a speech that marked what DeCaro has called "an extremely important event in world history—perhaps the most important event since the 1917 October Revolution in

Introduction

Russia" (2003: 16). Modeling his speech after the U.S. Declaration of Independence, Ho spoke to half a million ecstatic countrymen in Ba Dinh Square, and Mme. Hang was there.

"*Life* on Vietnam" tells how I came into a cache of *Life* magazines about Vietnam in a box that also held letters home from Marine Lt. Stephen Tace. This chapter blends the story of Lt. Tace and his family with a look at *Life* magazine coverage of the Vietnam War. It argues for *Life's* importance as a visual medium and its unique role in American middle-class media culture. The chapter subtitle "A Glory Preserved in a Wilderness Valley" comes from *Life's* 1960s door-to-door sales pitch, which I delivered many times myself during a brief summer job. The box contained other memorabilia including a letter to President Lyndon Johnson written by the soldier's mother. I locate the soldier and his family and learn the bittersweet ending.

Nguyen Ngoc Hung, the subject of a 1989 *60 Minutes* profile "The Enemy," was a North Vietnamese war hero I met when he toured the United States. It was not until later I learned that for four decades his brother was one of 300,000 Vietnamese missing in action in the American War until a spirit medium led the family to his remains in a remote corner of Quang Tri province.

"Reading Graham Greene" tells about my initial forays into teaching in Vietnam, which Hung was instrumental in arranging. Tom Wolfe wrote a celebrated 1965 essay on Marshall McLuhan asking "What If He's Right?" referring to McLuhan's general premise that media transforms everything. This is the point of departure for writing about teaching and setting up a media lab in Vietnam, a country with no history of media education, critical thinking, or open expression. I write about the classes I taught, or tried to teach, with their baffling, comical, awkward, and moving moments. Hung frames the chapter in his role as director of an English language institute and later as a ministry official. Finally, we encounter Graham Greene's *The Quiet American*, a book peddled for years on Hanoi street corners, to share media and filmmaking and criticism across the cultural divide. My students and I read the book and view both versions of the movie with surprising results.

"Vietnam Love Songs" looks at images of combat veterans in film, from Erich Maria Remarque's pioneering World War I drama *All Quiet on the Western Front* (Milestone, 1930) to the great story of three World War II veterans in *The Best Years of Our Lives* (Wyler, 1946) to the Vietnam classic *Coming Home* (Ashby, 1978) to the Iraq-related story *In the Valley of Elah* (Haggis, 2007). I learn a lot about PTSD from these films, but the story takes an unexpected turn when John Rambo comes down off the screen and into my life. Mike was a poet, a wanderer and, as it turned out, an addict. From him I learned the hard way about the dangers of life with a combat veteran suffering from PTSD.

Rambo has cast a long shadow over subsequent decades, and like the annoying cultural meme it has become, surfaces on a regular basis. Zachary Oberzan was not even born during the Vietnam War, but as an artist he reframed it for a new generation on stage as *Rambo Solo* and on film in *Flooding With Love for the Kid*, featuring Oberzan's reinvention of Rambo, the quintessential war icon. I consider the power of the history of the symbol and the story, looking back at several of the Rambo films. Bringing Rambo up to date, I write about the 2008 British film *Son of Rambow* where two young kids act out the story, and the recent stage and film performances by Oberzan, whom the *New York Times* Charles Isherwood, one hopes affectionately, dubbed "Rambo Nut." Oberzan's feature length film adaptation of the *First Blood* novel with him playing all the characters (dogs included) was shot entirely on location in his 220 square foot New York City apartment. *First Blood* author David Morrell called it "wildly creative and energetic." Rambo lives on in American popular culture as well as in American foreign policy.

Thomas M. Grace was a dutiful catholic boy from Syracuse who emerged as an antiwar activist at Kent State, becoming a casualty of Ohio National Guard gunfire on 4 May 1970 and a reminder of that terrible day ever since—the day the Vietnam war came home. "Murder on May 4th: The Case of the Missing Mob" looks back at the Kent State killings from the perspective of the fortieth anniversary commemoration ceremonies in May 2010. Since I was a student at Kent in 1970, I was invited to be a speaker on several subsequent memorial occasions including this one, where I participate in a public conversation with Tom Grace, whose personal odyssey frames the chapter. As a lesson in memory and representation, I compare various maps of the May 4th shootings that suggest very different interpretations of the events. A recent decision to place 17 acres of the campus on the National Historic Register adds a timeless feel to the somber site. I take in the atmosphere of an SDS gathering that may qualify as the strangest college reunion ever. Back home with my brother on the camera I organize some do-it-yourself cartography using the local high school football field in an attempt to represent the shooting distances.

"Long Bien Story" tells the tale of a group of our young filmmakers who set out to capture the magic of Long Bien Bridge and environs in digital video projects. Long Bien is a rich and beautiful site where architecture, politics, poverty, and hope intersect on a monumental scale. I share authorship of the chapter with my late colleague Douglas Jardine, incorporating some of his unpublished historical writing. Doug's passion about Long Bien, teaching, photography, and filmmaking inspired our documentary film project, and the fine results are a testimony to his influence. I also document the ongoing journey of our new generation Vietnamese filmmaker, To Mai Lien, in her travels to the United States to attend graduate school in order to return to Hanoi University to bring the Media Lab to life.

Some indication of the complexity of getting things right about Vietnam is apparent in the mere act of spelling, let alone pronunciation. Out of consideration for Vietnamese convention, I first drafted this book writing "Viet Nam," minus tone and vowel marks. This felt politically correct but grated against the many quotes herein that use the Western "Vietnam" spelling, to which I eventually succumbed. Further, using the single syllable Viet Nam—all words in Vietnamese are single syllable—would have also suggested using the spelling Ha Noi, Sai Gon, and so forth. Of course then come the tone and vowel markers—Viet Nam ("Viets of the South") carries one marker over the "e" that indicates a short vowel sound, and a dot under the "e" that indicates a period-like tone that are essential to the language as spoken. Are you with me? It is a little odd to think of it as "Vietnamese" spelling at all, since the historic language was transliterated from the Chinese characters using the

Portuguese alphabet by a French missionary who himself observed that the spoken language "resembles the singing of birds." It certainly does not resemble anything that can be captured in print. The only source I quote at length who consistently uses the Viet Nam spelling is the young marine writing home from Vietnam in 1967, so maybe Americans had it right once upon a time. Nonetheless, I resigned myself to "Vietnam" as the least obtrusive if not the least hegemonic choice.

Each chapter of *Crossing the Street in Hanoi* is written to stand alone, but I hope the wider arc that emerges for the reader who persists contributes some measure of understanding and healing while at the same time honoring the loss that underwrites the lessons. This is a layered project that embraces multiple points of view and levels of analysis, yet it is a work with no particular ideology except perhaps for Martin Luther King Jr's teaching that the arc of the moral universe is long, but it bends toward justice.

Chapter 1

The War That Won't Die

In 1988 with a small grant from San Francisco State University, where I taught, my colleague Hank McGuckin and I brought the "Moving Wall" to campus, a half-sized replica of the Vietnam Veterans Memorial in Washington D.C. We were all taken by surprise by the power of this 252-foot-long work of plexiglas on plywood. Over the course of three days, our students and Bay Area veterans read aloud all 58,148 American names on the wall and a team of volunteers helped visitors find specific names, listed in chronological, not alphabetical, order per architect Maya Lin's inspired design. Thousands of visitors came through over the week leaving poems, flowers, teddy bears, and hundreds of other mementos. This simulacrum provided an "as if" experience of its granite parent, which is in turn a ghostly echo of the dead. The Moving Wall was affecting and undeniably authentic if not strictly speaking real. This was the decade of Jean Baudrillard's (1982) writing about media, simulation, and hyperreality, and the Moving Wall embodied all of those emergent expressions of postmodernity. Of course, erecting a similar monument or reading a list of the three million Vietnamese dead in that war, if such a list existed, would span a mile and take three or four months, not days. School would have been recessed for the summer well before we were done. As it was, I had imagined what it would be like for someone walking across campus on Monday to the cadence of the roll call, and then taking the same path on Wednesday while the names were still being read. One person that unintentionally happened to was me, and I was stopped in my tracks.

The first time I was actually able to visit Hanoi in 1993 it was still illegal for an American to visit Vietnam as a tourist, so I traveled as an official visitor sponsored by the Vietnam Ministry of Labor, Invalids, and Social Affairs. It was love at first sight in Vietnam and the first of many visits to follow for research, tourism, and once even escorting a blind baby for adoption by Mia Farrow, a mission that did not turn out as expected. I liked the idea of being "illegal" in Vietnam—I mean, wasn't the war undeclared and thus illegal? I was now illegal in the eyes of the U.S. government for visiting a country where American soldiers were jailed if they refused to go. Confusing? Maybe because of a multitude of such ironies, Vietnam appealed to my politics and aesthetics and to a subversive streak that had animated me and bedeviled my elders since I was a kid.

I am not sure where my troublesome sense of righteous indignation was born, but as a third grader, I became engaged in an argument with my teacher over when it was safe to cross at the corner light. "Question Authority" was not even a concept to me at the time, nor to hardly anyone in my generation in the post-WWII complacent Midwest of

Figure 1.1: Vietnam veteran reading names of dead at Moving Wall, San Francisco, 1988.

America. Mrs. Foltz, my teacher, taught that we should cross when the light was green. I insisted that it was safe when the light was red. This was her last straw with my persistent interrogations. My mother was summoned to school and the three of us marched to the nearest intersection presumably to show once and for all who was right. It became apparent we had been looking at different lights, she at the one in the direction of the cross, myself at the signal controlling the perpendicular traffic. I lost the argument on the basis of sheer power, a valuable lesson in its own right, while privately maintaining my belief in the superior safety of crossing on red. After all, it is the cross traffic that runs you over. Clearly, I am still having the argument.

I may have lost the battle at the intersection but I won the war in my own mind by learning two lasting lessons: reality depends upon one's point of view, and while "might makes right" is catchy as an axiom, it is wrong as moral practice. I grew up in a suburban Republican family, where very little of political sophistication broke through the consciousness cocoon spun around us, but by a young age I had a keen sense of equality and justice as well as a full-blown hypocrisy detector. Nothing upset me more than if I believed something was not fair. For instance, I did not think it was fair that Jews were prohibited from living in our manicured enclave of Forest Hills, developed as a subdivision restricted to white protestants by Standard Oil (later Exxon) founder John D. Rockefeller in the 1920s. This was especially awkward since my high school was 95 percent Jewish. Of course, within weeks of starting at the school nearly all of my friends were Jewish and I was lobbying my parents for a Seder and regaling them with my memorized version of the prayer that blesses the wine. It became even more awkward when I acquired a Jewish boyfriend. We nearly had a Romeo and Juliet ending when both sets of parents discovered the forbidden relationship and went ballistic. Butchie told me recently that he gave me a Jewish name for his parents and he remembered our daring prank of smuggling him into the private Forest Hills Swim Club. I reminded him of the time we sneaked over to his house for lunch and I used one of the wrong pots, not even knowing what Kosher *was* let alone how to keep it or that it had to be kept.

The Cleveland Heights Jewish community was at least prosperous and the families were close and could not care less about Mr. Rockefeller's murky legacy or precious housing development. The situation was predictably worse when it came to the black residents (this was pre-"African American") who heavily populated Cleveland's East Side. When the progressive young Associate Pastor of Forest Hills Presbyterian Church started bussing black parishioners up from East Cleveland, my parents were among the many well-heeled donors who withdrew their support from the church. I knew that these things were not right and not fair, but I had no context for interpreting or acting upon them. I am sure I had never actually heard the word "hypocrisy." The Civil Rights Movement was no more than an abstraction in a life where I was discouraged from even having friends who were Catholic, an outcome that was easily accomplished because they had their own schools where it was rumored that regular beatings and brainwashing occurred and the girls were really fast. My own cocoon was not only literally unenlightened, but it was lined with the silk thread of middle class comfort that made the vague unease I persistently felt seem ungrateful. Historian Marilyn B. Young calls this state the "twilight sleep" induced by the drone of the government and media disinformation machine. In an interview with Bill Moyers, talking about Condoleeza Rice's manipulation of Iraq information delivered with a tone of unshakable authority, Young said:

Look, people in Iraq know what's going on. People in Europe know what's going on. People in the region, as she calls it, the neighborhood—they know what's going on. It's this country that is often kept in a kind of twilight sleep. I wouldn't say the dark. It's just sort of twilight. It's a little hard to see what's going on. Every now and then it becomes more clear, and people are really angry (2007).

And that fugue state was never more pervasive than during the early years of the American War in Vietnam.

Twilight Sleep

I did not begin to put any of the pieces together until following President Kennedy's assassination in 1963, which I learned of while walking across the serene campus of Miami University. The world changed on that day, which marked the start of what we now think of as the 60s, though it took until 1970 for my world to catch up. By the time the 60s were in full bloom in 1968, I was home with a baby and my nose pressed to the windowpane of the revolution. It took decades for me to recognize that not every location or generation experiences revolutions in culture, music, politics, ecology, human rights, spirituality, and pharmacology within a secure economic environment. How lucky we were. I was especially lucky to be growing up just before drugs entered the mainstream, or I might be dead now or writing this from prison.

Vietnam was at most a marginal part of my consciousness during the 1960s. I am not from a military family, unless you count the celebrated/notorious Civil War General William Tecumseh Sherman said to be on my paternal grandmother's side. My father was 4F in World War II because of a punctured eardrum, so he joined the U.S. Coast Guard and spent the war "chasing rats off the East Ninth Street Pier" in Cleveland. Most of what I knew about Vietnam had to do with the increasing lengths young men were going to in an attempt to be deferred from being drafted or to secure the sought-after 4F status—"not qualified for service under established physical, mental, or moral standards." Teachers qualified for deferral, fathers qualified, students qualified, but it got harder to get out with every military escalation. In 1965, there were 184,000 U.S. troops in Vietnam; by 1968 there were 538,000. Stories abounded about the insane things draft-eligible males would do to ensure failing the draft physical, foremost among them the ingestion of whopping quantities of drugs. Speed was a favorite, since it was still legal in many diet pills and widely prescribed. Rocker Greg Allman, high on speed and whiskey, shot himself in the foot, literally.

My door to Vietnam opened wider with another incident of inequity when I was prohibited from returning to my college teaching job after a maternity leave not because the job was unavailable but because my husband had taken a position at the same college and they had an anti-nepotism policy that prohibited both spouses from being on the faculty. He could not leave his teaching position for fear of being drafted. I do not remember even blinking an eye at this determination since it was about a year short of my being hit over the head by feminism. Since I could not return to my job as a teacher, I decided to do the only other thing that I knew how to do by that time and return to being a student working on a Ph.D. It was an unlikely path. I had been such a terrible student in high school I was disqualified as my homeroom's pick for homecoming queen because my grades were so bad. It wasn't cool for girls of my generation to be smart, and being cool was all I cared about, a shallow goal at best, not attainable by trying. College was not much better until I stumbled across a debate class and discovered my latent killer instincts. I never lost a debate. After that, school was easy and so satisfying that I have never left.

There were two Ph.D. programs in communication within commuting distance, one at Case Western Reserve University and one at Kent State. While Case Western would have been a better line on my resume, especially on the status conscious East Coast, and was closer to my house, the Kent program was new and innovative and offered a blend of humanities and social sciences that appealed to me. They also offered me a Teaching Fellow appointment, and I started classes in the summer of 1969 with a seminar on "Aristotle's *Poetics*" and another on the "Psychology of Communication," which typified the range of the program, a breadth that has held me in good stead throughout my career.

At Kent, I stood out only for my conventionality as a suburban wife and mother. Credit or blame for the first few degrees of the 180 degree change I made that year goes to my officemate Jim Crocker, a radical hippie Students for a Democratic Society (SDS) member I viewed with anthropological fascination and alarm. A hundred hours of talks with Jim and the charged air on campus began to break through my drowsiness. I began to wonder why all the smartest people around me were "radical." Everyone had always told me I was smart, in fact "too smart for my own good," but I was apolitical. It did not make sense except in terms of the cognitive dissonance theory I learned from the "Psychology of Communication" class. Dissonance theory would predict change in one of my attitudes to reduce the tension between conflicting cognitions, and indeed change came swiftly. Even before the May 4th shootings that marked the end of my first year of graduate studies there was no turning back from the political awakening that came to consume me, first in the women's movement and ever since in issues having to do with the media, war, and peace. My first publications were a feature series in a local Cleveland newspaper chain on "Issues of the Women's Movement," which my mother greeted with "We're proud of you, Sis, but did you have to write about *that*?"

My dissertation on *The Rhetoric of Social Movements: A Critical Perspective* (1974) was the first opportunity to explore at length the relationship between media and social change. While there was some attention given to television at the time, the concept of media as ubiquitous and transformational was in its infancy. The role of media made virtually no appearance in the communication or sociology literature, and the strange new thinking of Marshall McLuhan was so out of the box it was not taken seriously except in a few tiny enclaves like John Culkin's Center for Understanding Media established in 1968 in New York, the forerunner of the pioneering New School Media Studies Program which became my future home.

Where the 60s Lasted Through the 70s

My first long-term faculty job was at San Francisco State, which had experienced a polarizing faculty strike in 1968 and was one of the most politicized universities in the country. During one of my job interviews a senior colleague literally took me into a broom closet to coach me that I had best know who was on what side of the strike when talking to the faculty. Colleagues in the department had led the strike (though some had "stayed in"), so I moved from the frying pan of Kent into the fire of San Francisco. During the first ten years at SFSU, I commuted from Palo Alto, where my husband was a computer scientist at Xerox Palo Alto Research Center, an organizational culture that would turn out to be even more revolutionary than San Francisco. The learning curve was steep at both ends of Interstate 280.

My first SFSU officemate was the celebrated radical lesbian feminist Sally Gearhart, who was tall and charismatic and kind and scared me to death. She was very close to Harvey Milk, who was assassinated in 1978 along with Mayor George Moscone, just days after the massacre of 918 mostly Bay Area residents at Jonestown, Guyana. It was my second year on the faculty and it still felt like the 60s, which as a decade continued far into the 1970s, certainly in San Francisco. It was the catastrophic toll of HIV/AIDS in the 1980s that ended the 60s for good.

My other San Francisco State officemate was Hank McGuckin with a Stanford Ph.D., a fierce intelligence and integrity to match. His father was noted Wobbly Henry E. McGuckin Sr. who passed along his radical sensibilities as well as priceless memoirs (1986). Hank also had such a fine operatic baritone that literary lion Kenneth Burke wrote music for the man he dubbed *da voce*. The office next door was occupied by writer and activist Kay Boyle, who would have intimidated me even more had she acknowledged my existence, which despite multiple introductions she did not. I guessed that with 40 books and six children she had plenty on her mind.

The Department Chair (later Dean) Nancy McDermid, with a law degree from the University of Chicago, never saw a wrong she did not want to right. Under the wing of these extraordinary colleagues, my passion for politics and media deepened and grew. After several years of establishing my own niche I was delighted to be invited to team-teach a course on "Communication and Social Process" with Hank and International Affairs Professor Ted Keller. They had previously taught together with Kay, so there were some big shoes to fill. It was my first experience presenting an academic production number with more than 100 students filling a classic raked-seating lecture hall. McGuckin and Keller were good friends and great classroom performers who loved to argue at length about the issues at hand, so we seldom had time for guests.

We made an exception for one class in about 1982, where Vietnam was the subject. I arranged for the visit of four guest speakers through an organization new to us called the Veterans Speakers Alliance, whose mission was to send vets to schools to talk about their personal experience. That was nearly ten years after the end of the Vietnam war, and while Vietnam movies were coming out (*First Blood, Coming Home, Apocalypse Now, Deer*

Hunter), I had never heard an actual combat veteran tell his story, let alone heard a nurse tell hers, nor had hardly anyone else in the room. You could hear a pin drop as one after another former soldier told a raw, compelling, heartbreaking story. We were all speechless in this wounding moment.

Some years later the "veteran narrative" became virtually its own genre as more and more Vietnam veterans exposed their wounds both physical and psychological. As hard as it is believe today, even in the early 1980s the actual experience of the Vietnam War for the warriors, let alone for the Vietnamese, was a mystery to the overwhelming majority of Americans. For the most part combat veterans did not want to talk about the war and few people wanted to listen. There seems to be a lag time of at least ten years between combat experience and the ability or interest in talking about it to someone who did not share the trauma. This helps to account for why I do not recall anyone in my Jewish high school talking about the holocaust that had taken place little more than ten years earlier. It was just too soon.

I became preoccupied with learning everything I could about the Vietnam War both from reading and from listening at length to combat vets. As part of this Vietnam fascination I even deconstructed frame-by-frame Peter Davis' 1975 Academy Award winning documentary *Hearts and Minds* trying to find out what made it tick as a powerful rhetorical argument. It was like taking apart a Swiss watch. I later wrote it up in a comparison to Michael Moore's film *Fahrenheit 911* (Wilder 2005). A few years back I ran across those extensive logging notes and presented them to an astonished Peter Davis, by then a friend, who thought he had seen everything from the film's many aficionados. No detail about Vietnam was too small for my unwavering attention, a condition that persisted for years.

From the mid-1980s Vietnam was the focus of my interest both personal and academic. I am still not certain how that came to be, unless it was a need to peek behind the curtain of an America I had become convinced was more mythical than real. I read everything I could get my hands on and talked to anyone who would talk to me. I got involved with the Veterans Speakers Alliance by coaching combat vets and nurses who wanted to speak in the schools. I eventually joined the board of the highly regarded veterans rights organization Swords to Plowshares, where I remain to this day. In a moment of grace or synchronicity or both, the speaker at our opening divisional meeting in 1984 was an old friend of Nancy McDermid's, Professor (later Congressman) Walter Capps from UC-Santa Barbara. At the time, Professor Capps taught the largest class in the University of California system with 1,400 students. It was a class on the Vietnam War. I had no idea professors were teaching such a thing, and in fact fewer than 200 across the country did, almost none of them yet in history departments, for whom the war was not yet sufficiently historical. (Capps was in Religious Studies.) Following Professor Capps lecture I shared my until then private Vietnam fascination with Nancy, who promptly bought me a plane ticket to visit Capps' class and in doing so changed the course of my career. It may take knowing that the travel budget for the average SFSU professor was about $200 per year to understand that her gesture was generous beyond measure. Adding to the long-term consequences of the visit was the fact that the guest speaker in Capps' class the day I visited and at the small lunch that followed was then-Nebraska Governor Bob Kerrey, who came to loom large in my life much later as president of The New School for ten tumultuous years beginning in 2001.

The San Francisco State class that resulted in 1985 was "Vietnam: Rhetoric and Realities," team taught by McGuckin and myself along with a Vietnam combat veteran. Hank taught most of the history, I looked at representations of Vietnam in media and popular culture, and the veteran (we worked with several) organized narratives of personal experience of the war. The course was an immediate oversubscribed success and attracted local news coverage. One of the best known local television anchormen, the late Pete Wilson of KRON, had himself been a combat medic, and he was so pleased that we were interested in the treatment of veterans he helped in many ways.

It was during the ten years of teaching the Vietnam class that we brought the Moving Wall to campus. It was also during those years that the United States inched toward rapprochement with Vietnam and we eventually became more inclusive in the class with Vietnamese speakers, nearly impossible to find when we started. A heady roster of guest speakers joined us over the years: David Harris, David Dellinger, Michael Blecker, Paul Cox, Vu Duc Vuong, Nguyen Qui Duc, Country Joe McDonald, Le Ly Hayslip, Lily Adams, Douglas Pike, Trinh Minh-ha, Chuong Chung, Duc Nguyen, Nguyen Qui Duc, Hal Muskat, Jack McCloskey, Harry Haines, Barbara Sonneborn, Tama Adelman, Peggy Akers, Winnie Smith, Phil Reser, Keith Mather, Ralph Webb, Major Edward Palm, John Wheeler, Daniel Ellsberg, and S. Brian Willson.

It was our classroom, but they were the teachers.

For a few years in the 1980s Brian co-taught the Vietnam course before the horrific incident where he lost both legs and nearly his life being run over by a train at a 1987 anti-war protest at Concord Naval Weapons Station (Willson 2011). Before Dan Ellsberg could remember my name, he called me "the woman with the Harley in her living room," which tells you something about that period. Some pieces of this book—*Rambo*, veterans on film, *Life* magazine—began as lectures prepared for that class. The analysis of *Life* coverage of Vietnam is a good example of the serendipity that touched many parts of this project, since it was through the unlikely coincidence of my acquisition of the box of old *Life* magazines including letters from a young marine that I was able to write that story and return the letters to his family.

During the years of the Vietnam class, many small delegations of Vietnamese officials passed quietly through San Francisco. The visitor who would shape my future arrived in 1989, sponsored by *60 Minutes*, which had featured him in a piece called "The Enemy." Nguyen Ngoc Hung was a North Vietnamese war hero and a celebrated teacher of English in Vietnam. His soft voice, impeccable English and perpetual Buddha smile enchanted everyone who met him. Hung was received by the Bay Area veterans peace community with awe because such encounters with Vietnamese outside of combat had been rare. Hung was the perfect living olive branch. We exchanged business cards as is the custom if not compulsion of Vietnamese, but it was this connection that led to the opening of a new world for me several years later.

After 1995 when I moved to New York, Hank and I continued to teach "Vietnam: Rhetoric and Realities" online for The New School Media Studies M.A. program and during one especially ambitious term in 2002 attempted to cross-list the course with Hanoi University. Despite rather elaborate preparation, including a month I spent in Hanoi to set it up, a combination of technical problems and cultural disconnects led to what can most generously be described as an inconclusive experiment. I understood how the technical problems could be solved, but it was not until I lived and taught in Vietnam five years later that I began to understand the magnitude of the cultural divide I was attempting to navigate. Good intentions do not always equal good results, especially where language and culture are the elephant in the room and you are one of the blind men. I am sure colonialists and missionaries encountered the same obstacles but were fortified by their true believer ideology and zeal. During most of my years of interest in Vietnam I did not clearly understand my own intentions. I was running on instinct, fueled by an inchoate desire to make any amends possible for the hardships and losses that have been visited upon the Vietnamese people and the many U.S. veterans who had been virtual hostages because of the draft. This was not truly clarified until my Fulbright year in Hanoi as a "cultural ambassador" in 2007–2008, a designation that rang true in every way. If the wonderful Fulbright Program ran the world, we probably would not need the Fulbright Program.

During the 1980s when the occasional unofficial Vietnamese delegations traveled through the Bay Area, I would usually host one or two members at my home. Had there been Vietnam—U.S. relations they would have had much fancier accommodations, but I was pleased for the opportunity to meet some actual Vietnamese people. Since the language barrier between us was nearly complete I had no way of knowing until I went to Vietnam in 1993 that most of them were high-ranking officials in one ministry or another, and I received gracious treatment throughout the country. One of my guests was Mr. Nguyen Xuan Tue, Deputy Minister for International Relations for the Ministry of Labor, who arranged my itinerary since it was necessary to be escorted virtually everywhere you traveled. One memorable example of this was when I was met at Tan Son Nhut International Airport in Ho Chi Minh City by one of my "boarders" who turned out to be a ministry chief bearing red roses and being driven in a Mercedes. You have to conjure up a country with an average annual income of under $500 a year to fully appreciate that image.

Crossing the International Dateline

Even with this official support, getting into Vietnam in 1993 was a long and arduous process. The visa had to be secured in Bangkok, and my traveling companion Sue Collins and I had carefully planned to arrive on a Thursday evening in order to pick it up on Friday before flying out to Hanoi as scheduled Monday morning. This being my first trip to Asia, a factor like the International Dateline had never crossed my mind, and we lost Friday somewhere over the Pacific Ocean. Saturday morning we walked through the heat and stench for an hour to the Vietnam Embassy:

CLOSED
Hours 8:30–1:00 and 1:30–4:30 Monday-Friday
Closed Saturday and Sunday

We pushed warily on the "Closed" sign, coming to another door and giving another nudge, on the other side of which I miraculously found myself in the visa office with half-a-dozen other anxious souls. I leaned near the window and waited while the clerk performed an endless round of paper shuffling. This was my introduction to the fact that there is no such thing as waiting in a queue in Vietnam. There is no such thing as a queue at all. It is more like a squirming huddle surrounding the counter, where you somehow eventually wiggle yourself to the attention of the person on duty, who is appearing to ignore you even when she is not.

When my lucky turn came, I learned that despite multiple assurances from the Ministry of Labor in Hanoi, my name was not on "the list." I was given a new visa form to fill out. At some point, the clerk took pity and invited me to peruse her book myself. I had already seen two visa-hopefuls come unglued in the three hours I had been there and I did not want to be next. I was abruptly taken behind the inner door to view the hallowed approved list, and reading upside down immediately spotted "Carol Wilder" handwritten in the Dickensian ledger. I have never been so happy to see my name.

At last, the final leg of the interminable journey. The first descent into Vietnam took my breath away when the green squares of land and clusters of red-tile roofs came into view. On that first visit to Hanoi, I thought I had fallen in a rabbit hole or was dreaming or both. I don't know what I had expected to see. Maybe a city full of bomb craters, in any case a bleak landscape. But Hanoi was lush, steamy, with narrow twisting streets in the old town and wide boulevards in the French quarter south of Hoan Kiem Lake, the most special lake of many that dot the romantic city. I walked around the lake every chance I got, and years later for a long period after my father died in November 2007, I visited the Ngoc Son Temple daily with an offering and remembrance. He was not Buddhist but he temperamentally could have been and likely would have been if he had been presented with the choice. We were often not sure if he was Zen or just checked out, but in either case he was easy to be around and we loved him for it.

On the 1993 visit to Vietnam, I began to discern the broadest outlines of the country and culture and people that had only been defined for me through war. One lesson came from a trip to the Ho Chi Minh Museum, built in 1990 in the shape of a giant lotus blossom. I recall walking up the winding ramp past historical dioramas and displays contributed by mostly Soviet bloc countries, and going up and up and wondering: Where is the American War? Finally, we arrived at the display, but if you blinked you would miss it. The war that had been 100 percent of my consciousness of Vietnam was little more than a blip on the vast panorama of Vietnamese history. It was a concrete lesson with lasting visceral effect.

Vietnam in 1993 was slowly emerging from its long subjugation. Iyer wrote in that year "its pleasures feel unrehearsed, and surprise is still a growth industry" (116). Nothing surprised Sue and me more than our journey from Hanoi to Hue. We insisted on traveling by train, against all advice and a good deal of active resistance on the part of our hosts. We both loved trains. What could go wrong? We were bemused that plenty of folks back home had asked us if we would be "safe" in Vietnam, but I am sure they were not thinking about train travel. We secured the most expensive "soft sleeper" compartment, and settled in for a long rackety night. We finished our sole bottle of wine. We came to regret that economy. I calmed my nerves listening to a tape made from San Francisco's "Light Rock Less Talk" radio on my walkman. We were finally sound asleep when we were nearly thrown out of our bunks by the impact of the train crashing into a fuel tanker stalled on the tracks. Lurched awake in a haze of diesel fuel and cigarette smoke, Sue ran up and down the car "No Smoking No Smoking," hoping the urgency of her voice would compensate for the fact that no one understood a word she was saying. I knew for sure we were soon going to explode in a fireball. I never thanked the nice radio programmers for saving my sanity that night with their soothing elevator music. We made it until morning and we were ravenous. During a brief stop, I bought a baguette and what I thought was a boiled egg from a woman reaching in the train window. The warmth of the egg turned out to be a freshly laid chick. I screamed and everyone else on the train giggled. I get wild with manic exhaustion even writing about this. Eventually, I adapted to expecting the daily unexpected, and by the time of my fifth and longest visit in 2007 I finally understood I was not in Ohio anymore.

On the plane to Hanoi for the 2007–2008 academic year I thought about the path that brought me to this unlikely place, a country I once could not find on a bet let alone on a map. Vietnam is as far from home as an American can get on this planet. If you stick a pin through the earth at Hanoi, you will come out the other side about a thousand miles due south of Ohio, more or less in Havana, Cuba. Getting to Vietnam is uncomfortable if only because of the jet lag that awaits you after more than a day in transit. Being there is often no picnic either, with choking smog and sweltering heat or torrential rain much of the year. Yet I have been repeatedly drawn back, and fallen more deeply each time for the country and its people. I hope that this book conveys some of the richness of that experience in language that a reader who has never been and perhaps never intends to go to Vietnam can appreciate. For those who live in Vietnam or are fellow Vietnam lovers, I hope I have done right by your own passion and that you find some new ways to frame your experience. For those of you from my generation—especially veterans who are skeptical or fearful or angry about the war for one of many legitimate reasons—I hope these stories put a human face on what was an inhuman experience.

When I began preparing media and popular culture lectures for the Vietnam class, I had never been there, but somehow youthful enthusiasm covered for my inexperience. I did know that Vietnam is a complex, obscure, and faraway subject and I believed—and still do—that if you start on common ground with your audience you can lead them many places. Movies are good for this. Everyone likes them and they can be used to back into history and culture. Rambo is an example of a well-known popular culture subject that can be used to open the door to a wide range of topics like Post Traumatic Stress Disorder or corporate media or culture wars and Agent Orange. I became fascinated with each of the topics in this book as they found me one by one. The *Life* story began with a box of memories rescued from a dumpster in Buffalo. Hoa Lo Prison Museum was within sight of my balcony during a year in Hanoi. *The Quiet American* first appeared as a street vendor staple. Combat vets in film were a favorite of students and the subject of an earlier article (1990). May 4th, 1970, at Kent State was where the Vietnam war came home and where the heart of the book lies for this Ohio girl. When I would get discouraged, remembering May 4th would always remind me of the obligations of witnessing. And I could not write a Vietnam book without some homage to Ho Chi Minh. In addition, each chapter tells the story of someone who embodies the subject at hand. One of the gifts of an abiding interest in Vietnam has been meeting many Americans and Vietnamese whose fates have been shaped by the Vietnam/American War but whose lives have evolved far beyond it. I tell their stories here as a way of personalizing and investing immediacy in the war and its remembrance.

The trail of memory is strewn with shadows and dreams. Writing about how "the past is not dead," Tessa Morris-Suzuki tells us that the crisis of history is not simply a matter of amnesia, "rather it reflects a profound dilemma: in an age of global mobility and multiple, rapidly changing media, how do we pass on our knowledge of the past from one generation to the next? How do we relate our lives in the present to the events of the past? What bits of the past do we claim as our own, and in what sense do they become our property?" (2005: 6). The stories in this book are told with these questions in mind.

The War That Won't Die

In Vietnam the American War is gone but not forgotten, reflected upon but resolved, remembered with sadness for the loss and sacrifice it exacted, acknowledged with a quiet pride. Seventy million out of Vietnam's 93 million people were not born when the war officially ended in 1975. It also helps to be the victor. It is instructive to recall that the United States was but one of a long line of invaders—China for centuries, Japan, France—who tested their will on this country not much bigger than California and failed. America to Vietnam is just an uncouth cowboy country that passed through. Vietnam in America is still seen almost entirely through the lens of war. President Bill Clinton's sound bite during his November 2000 visit—"Vietnam is a country not a war"—did not change that. Clinton's enthusiastic welcome by the Vietnamese people was tempered by more guarded official speeches, but the net effect was open arms. The Vietnamese are understandably wary about their former enemy turned friend, but the American War is history in Vietnam.

The Vietnam War in America is the undead war. Just when you think the corpse has been laid to rest, it bolts upright in the coffin in the middle of the funeral in the form of Nick Turse's detailed account of war crimes in *Kill Anything That Moves* (2013) or a war hero like Bob Kerrey whose dark secret is revealed decades later or a non-soldier like Bill Clinton criticized for avoiding the draft or a weekend warrior like George W. Bush accused of pulling strings for soft duty or a veteran-candidate like John Kerry being "Swiftboated" with challenges to his Vietnam service. It exists in the ongoing suffering of Agent Orange victims and their children and in the families who live with the life-long effects of losing a loved one to PTSD or suicide. It lives in the echoes from Iraq and Afghanistan for a whole new generation.

The Vietnam War in America is a zombie/vampire hybrid whose psycho-signature movie is closer to George Romero's 1968 *Night of the Living Dead* than to *Platoon* (Stone 1986) or *Apocalypse Now* (Coppola 1979); whose television show was not *M.A.S.H.* but *Dark Shadows,* aired from 1966–1971 at 4 p.m. daily just between school and the evening news. Vietnam lives in America as part of a national embarrassment and shame at what was lost; it lives in anger for those who believe the United States cut and run and could have won. America's fascination with Vietnam is never far from the surface, though sometimes years might pass between hauntings. Martin Luther King said in 1967 "If America's soul becomes totally poisoned, part of the autopsy must read 'Vietnam.'" Has that day come?

The undead war cannot make its peace in the United States because it runs counter to the national narrative of the United States as good guys and winners. The American misadventure

Figure 1.2: Vietnafghanistam, Fogelson-Lubliner, *The New York Times.*

in Vietnam is treated as an anomaly instead of the quintessential expression of U.S. foreign policy that it more closely resembled. In the nineteenth century the U.S. marines invaded Mexico, Cuba, Dominican Republic, Puerto Rico, Panama, Nicaragua, Uruguay, Brazil, Haiti, Argentina, and Chile, so foreign interventions were hardly a novelty even prior to the twentieth century. Many disagreements continue to exist on how and why the Vietnam War was lost and on the morality and need for it in the first place. Was it the result of Cold War propaganda? Was the domino theory really just a theory of dominos? Did the United States become involved to help "our friends the French" so De Gaulle would not withdraw support from NATO? Did the geographical isolation of the United States contribute to its acting like a big dumb teenager? Is hubris an incurable condition?

Hot buttons like Jane Fonda and MIA soldiers continue to inflame in some quarters. Vietnam is full of secrets and lies, not the least of which was perpetrated by the U.S. government. *The Pentagon Papers* (1972) confirmed that decades before Robert McNamara's belated *mea culpa*. The legacy of Vietnam is carried by the baby boomer generation who are not going to let anything having to do with them die ever if they can help it. Vietnam is sexy, sweaty. It is associated with a time—the 60s, much of which took place in the 70s—of sex and drugs and rock 'n' roll and freedom in a prosperous country that young people today can barely comprehend. Vietnam references an intensity of direct living and feeling that eludes today's mediated second-hand lives. Vietnam is seductive. Faraway, fragrant, colorful, a mysterious land reminiscent of ceiling fans, French baguettes, straw hats, bicycles laden with goods, the *mission civilisatrice*, Graham Greene, beautiful girls in silken *ao dais*. It has even been asserted by Calvin Trillin, presumably tongue in cheek, that the *banh mi* sandwich is the best argument for colonialism (2011).

Vietnam is a great commodity with thousands of books written, dozens of films, millions of dollars on Ramboiana alone. The subject of the Vietnam War is mediagenic. It works for books, plays, video games, movies, talk radio, and endless Internet chat and self-expression. Three million people a year visit the Vietnam Veterans Memorial in Washington and there is now even a "Virtual Vietnam Wall." Vietnam itself has become a popular tourist destination, visited by 4.5 million tourists in 2010, nearly 10 percent of them from North America. Tourism accounts for nearly 5 percent of Vietnam's gross domestic product. Vietnam has become a major trading partner of the United States exporting more than $15 billion in goods in 2011, though a significant deficit exists given the five billion exported by the United States. I recall being startled the first time I saw "Made in Vietnam" on an item of clothing in the United States not too many years ago. Now a lot of Americans are walking around in entire ensembles of jeans, T-shirts and sneakers made in Vietnam. Whether this is a good thing for Vietnam is debatable, and there is some concern—not nearly enough—about worker exploitation. Is grandma better off being bussed to work in a remote Nike factory than she was selling oranges on her front stoop? Surely, the Vietnam economy has improved, but the mighty magnetism of capitalism could be winning a war that could not be won with bullets and Vietnam, despite its communist ideals, has its own version of income inequality.

One thing that keeps Vietnam alive for Americans is the lack of catharsis that Aristotle prescribed as a necessary condition for the resolution of tragedy. Cinematic revisionism can only do so much. Many Americans, especially veterans, travel to Vietnam to see reminders of the war and they are not disappointed, though the Vietnamese do not go out of their way to rub it in. Closer to home there are war memorial sites in cities and towns across the United States—lesser known ones like at Kent State and iconic ones like the Vietnam Veterans Memorial in D.C.—that exist precisely in order to keep the memory of the war and those who fought it alive. Vietnam remains almost as vivid after 40 years as Iraq and Afghanistan have ever been through the fog of watching war as multiply mediated by the tightly managed military propaganda machine. The genius of "embedding" correspondents in Iraq and Afghanistan made them identify closely with the troops and become part of the story that as a consequence no one was actually reporting. Our "twilight sleep" continues.

It took the May 4th shootings at Kent to jolt me out of my new mother reverie and get my attention about politics and media. I was home that Monday in 1970 with my toddler when my girlfriend called: "What the hell is going on at that school of yours? They're killing people." They were killing my generation 10,000 miles away and now they were killing us at home. Accurate news reports took a day to get out. First reports were that the guard had been killed, then that there had been a sniper. Anything but what really happened. Kent Dean Mike Lunine had to go through Senator Edward Kennedy's office to get out accurate information to the press. I was completely blindsided by this turn of events, probably more so than people who had been paying closer attention to the undercurrent of civil war between the government and the draft-age generation. The more I learned and the more disbelieving I became, the more I wanted to understand what I had not known and why I had not known it. It is no excuse that I was raised in a bubble of middle-American insularity. Girls married young and did not worry their pretty little heads about foreign policy or finance. My father urged me to get a teaching credential so I would have something to "fall back on." This turned out to be the best advice he ever gave, although I doubt he had in mind that one day I would be crossing the street in Hanoi to get to class.

Chapter 2

Hoa Lo Prison Museum: "The Fury Burning Within"

Figure 2.1: Hoa Lo Prison Museum Exhibit.

For nearly a year, I lived at #5 Da Tuong "Wild Elephant" Street, a few minutes from Hanoi's soul center Hoan Kiem Lake and a stone's throw from Hoa Lo Prison Museum. It took me nearly the whole year to learn to pronounce the name of my street so a taxi driver could get me home. To my tin ear, "Da Tuong" when said properly sounds something like "Dzahuh Duockh" if you clear your throat while saying it. I could not get it. I felt marginally better when my Vietnamese tutor told me that it is one of the most difficult sounds even for Vietnamese children. It helps to remember that the language was Romanized by a French monk, because if you look at the letters when Vietnamese is pronounced it sounds nothing like English and vaguely Francais. While I have not made great progress speaking the language I learned to passably pronounce most sounds, although Da Tuong was never among them.

My flat was on the 4th floor of a nondescript gated building set back from the street. The small rooms seemed bigger than they were because of wide windows overlooking an enchanted terrace garden lush with palms, ferns, and bougainvillea.

The elaborate family altar off to one side felt like it was in the middle of the jungle, not the middle of the city. With vivid hues and delicate fragrances the terrace was part of the sensory overload to be had everywhere in Vietnam, yet the garden was free from the industrial

Figure 2.2: The Terrace Garden at #5 Da Tuong.

rot-tinged scents and bedlam of the street. The terrace was open to the whole building but I was the only person I ever saw there except for the maid who used it to air the daily washing.

Late on a summer afternoon the air quality was at headache level and my hair had sprung into corkscrews. All was fresh and peaceful on the terrace with its thick mix of flora that cleaned the noxious air. There was not much to look at on the other side of the balcony facing the street except for two looming skyscrapers capped by what appeared to be pyramid domes. They were probably a quarter mile away, but it looked as if you could reach out and touch them. I soon learned that this was the Hanoi Towers complex built in the mid-1990s on most of what had been the site of Hoa Lo Prison.

The Towers complex is home to a high-end shopping mall including the grocery store catering to foreigners I visited almost daily, dozens of executive apartments, an Olympic size pool, tennis courts, Jaspa's sports bar and restaurant serving some of the best Western food in Hanoi, and, I envisioned, a legion of spirits rising from the razed prison below. Every one

Figure 2.3: Hanoi Towers from the Terrace of #5 Da Tuong.

of the visitors I had that year in Hanoi got a tour of the prison and the towers complex, partly because it was endlessly bewitching to me and mostly because it was across the street.

The posh Hanoi Towers erected in Hoa Lo's place—or in most of its place—is in every way imaginable antithetical to its predecessor prison. The upper floors of the 24-story tower consist of "serviced apartments" starting at about $3000 a month, three times the country's annual per capita income. One end of the ground floor complex is anchored by a spacious Highlands Coffee, Vietnam's answer to Starbucks. Cutting across the ground floor is an indoor mall with furniture shops, a fancy candy store, a travel agent, a jeweler, and an eatery called "Papa Joes" serving Western fast food. Citimart grocery is at the other end from Highlands and passes pretty well for a Western supermarket. Prices are triple what they are in the neighborhood market, but the shopping experience is lower stress for foreigners already assaulted by the culture shock of Hanoi. Of the shops in the mall, an eclectic home furnishings boutique fittingly called "Morbido" always offered surprises to the browser, but never more so than the day I found a tiger cub skin for sale for $295 amid the silk cushions and comforters. Still, the pelt was not nearly as unsettling as the glistening roasted dogs piled high every morning at the nearby market.

Figure 2.4: Dog Market, Thuong Kiet Street.

During dozens of visits to the prison museum and hundreds of visits to the Towers, the ghosts of Hoa Lo became a daily presence in my experience of Hanoi. It was during such a visit a guide singled out the photograph of a woman in the prison from 1940 to 1942 and told me she had been the first wife of the celebrated General Giap. It was on another visit that a guide pointed to the image of Nguyen Thi Phuc Hang and said in hushed tones, "That lady is alive." I knew at once I had to find her.

The guide said I would need "a letter" to contact Mme. Hang, but she did not say what kind of letter. I asked my friend at the Ministry of Education about the proper protocol, and he said the university should issue the "letter." One thing led to another and within a few weeks Mai Lien and I found ourselves waiting outside of St. Joseph Cathedral for Mr. Huy to

Figure 2.5: Prison Museum Entrance and Hanoi Tower.

pick us up for the drive to a scheduled meeting at Mme. Hang's apartment. We were giddy with anticipation, a feeling soon dampened when Huy rang us from his cell phone to let us know that at the last minute he had been told we were not permitted to see Mme. Hang despite confirmed arrangements. Having conscientiously gone through high levels at both the university and the ministry to gain access, I could not understand why we were denied at the last minute, but Vietnam was filled with mystery and surprise. It was not until later I learned that the problem was that Mme. Hang was the widow of one of Vietnam's most famous pro-democracy dissidents General Tran Do, and despite his death in 2002 she and her family were under continued observation. No one called it house arrest, but it was a delicate situation.

Before leaving Hanoi as we were driving to the airport I gave Mr. Huy a list of questions, some expense money and a secure email connection in case he could contact Mme. Hang. Six months later a mutual friend took me aside in New York to relay a personal message from Mr. Huy (no email for him) that he had tried three times to visit "The Lady," as we called her, and been threatened by the police to stay away or be arrested. Another year passed and after exploring various discreet channels, Mme. Hang was finally able to join Mai Lien, videographer John Coogan and me for a private conversation in the moody cabaret room of Hanoi's *Cinematheque*.

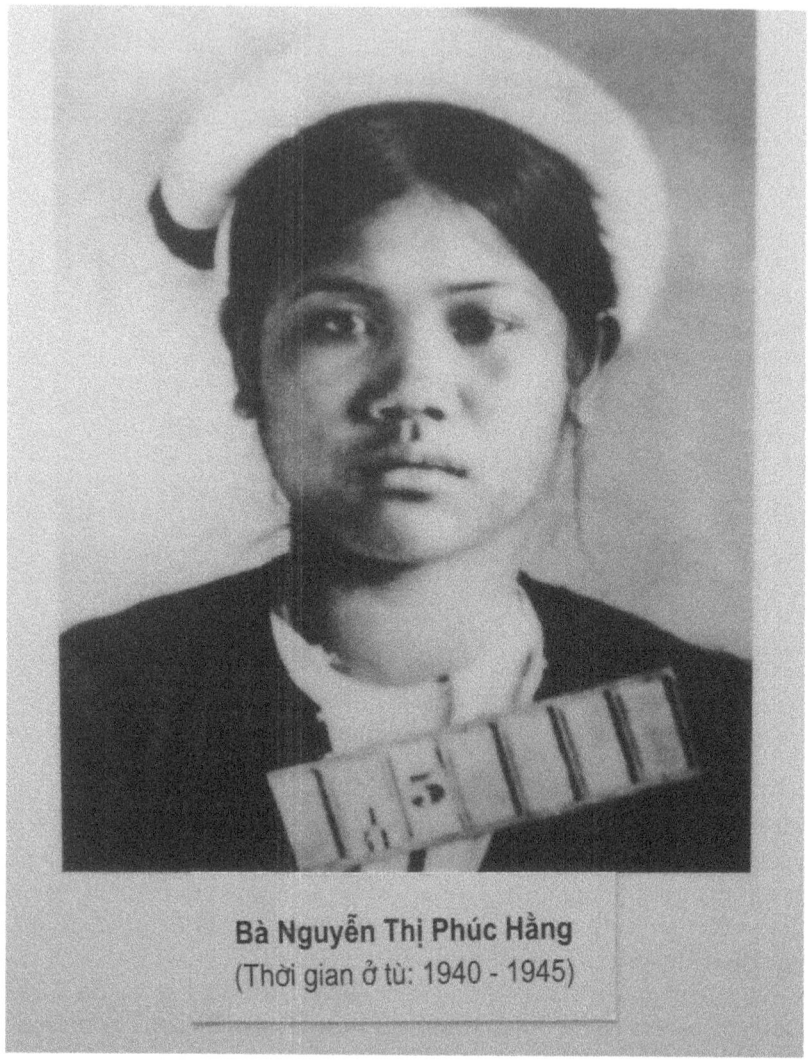

Figure 2.6: Mme. Nguyen Thi Phuc Hang, 1940.

"The Lady"

At 91, Mme. Nguyen Thi Phuc Hang has lost none of her passion for life or for the revolution she joined without hesitation as a teenager. When asked in 1938 if anyone from her village wanted to go to the front, she volunteered immediately. She was challenged: "Life at the front can be very tough with a lot of difficulties. Are you sure you can handle all those hardships?" Her life to that time had known nothing but hardships. "Yes, I can handle them. I can go to the front." She was led to Hanoi by Mr. Mai Vi, later Vice Minister of Culture in the Northern Vietnam Government, leaving her home in Thanh District for the first time "while my parents stayed in the countryside worried, tracing and searching for me constantly" (Hang 2011).

Bac Ninh Province where Hang was raised is 30 well-traveled kilometers east of Hanoi. It is Vietnam's smallest province and one of the most densely populated. There is evidence that the ancient Viets, ancestors of the country's Kinh ethnic majority, inhabited the area at least 5,000 years ago. Bac Ninh is one of the wellsprings of Vietnamese civilization, known for its traditional love of culture, religion, and learning. At one time, the province produced one-third of the doctoral laureates in the country, but schooling of any kind was not an option for a Bac Ninh girl born to a peasant family in 1920.

Nguyen Thi Phuc Hang was raised working the fields dawn to dusk and at the age of 15 she was sent by her parents to live with an aunt as a housemaid. Eight decades later she recalled:

> My daily chores were herding buffalo, cutting grass, feeding the pigs. I used to wake up at four in the early morning to pick and to slice the water fern and cook it for the pigs. My hands started itching each time I touched the fern. Five to six a.m. was the time for cutting grass. Hard work day by day made my figure stay tiny. As a teenager, I looked so much smaller than I was supposed to. We often had nothing to eat. My family was too poor. My father was just a peasant and my mother worked in the fields all year long.

Formal education was out of the question, at least until 1936 when an illiteracy eradication campaign initiated by the Communist Party reached the village. Hang and her girlfriends established a Mutual Friendship Association "to support one another, to encourage people to go to school, and to find tutors and teachers for the school." These humble beginnings of learning led to a political enlightenment that within two years secured Hang a place among a thousand other inmates in fearsome Hoa Lo, where she would remain for five years of camaraderie and torture. She was one of 93 women in a prison population of 928 (Zinoman 2001: 106).

Mme. Hang began her political journey as a liaison officer for the Central Committee, delivering letters, newspapers, and messages along the Bac Giang, Bac Ninh, and Lac Dao routes. Soon the party appointed her to open a tavern at the gate of Van Dien Station that was a place for comrades to eat and rest. The tavern was under constant surveillance and after a few near misses with the authorities Hang returned to her job as a liaison officer publishing newspapers, reports, and fliers from a house at 2 Hang Non Street. It was on Hang Non where she was finally arrested in a raid where she had stayed behind to guard the valuable printing machinery. The day she was sentenced to Hoa Lo

> the foreign soldiers with weapons in their hands stood in three lines surrounding me. Seven judges sat behind the jury desk with seven silver blades in front of them. After sentencing me, they all held up their blades. I remember that it looked quite scary but I found it funny. I wasn't afraid at all.

Hell's Hole

All that remains of Hoa Lo Prison today is a fragment of the original structure housing a museum that includes a display in remembrance of Mme. Hang and 13 other women held by the French. Making for strange bedfellows is a nearby exhibit featuring the hundreds of U.S. pilots incarcerated in the same prison a generation later. The women's display case and the pilot rooms are in different areas of the museum and reflect the radically divergent ways these populations are memorialized. Considered together, the exhibits deliver a complex message about how Vietnam has chosen to curate its past. While the women's exhibit is a candid display of consummate horror set in the shadow of a vintage guillotine, the pilot installations suggest that prison might actually be something like, well, fun. The women's exhibit is as stark and straightforward as the subject allows, while the pilot exhibit is a lesson in the use of strategic ambiguity to communicate mixed messages to serve multiple rhetorical objectives. In addition, while there have been enough memoirs, literature, and film to establish the "Hanoi Hilton" pilots as their own genre, little has been written about the women of Hoa Lo.

The section of the original prison that has been preserved is overshadowed by the massive 1993 Towers and nearly smothered by its bounty of luxury goods and services. Hanoi Towers is superimposed on most of what was the prison site, which had itself been built on the destruction of Phu Khanh ceramics village. This layering of skyscrapers over prison grounds over craft village tells multiple histories that inform each other in a unified ecology of the site. The story of Phu Khanh is a narrative of Vietnam's traditional

Figure 2.7: Hoa Lo Prison c. 1950.

heritage, the Hoa Lo site reflects the colonial tensions and ambitions of France and later the U.S. Hanoi Towers exemplify the struggle between progress and preservation that has been the cultural price of Vietnam's rapid pace of development from the 1980s onward. Taking a step back from the prison museum itself, the broader Hoa Lo site is a microcosm of Hanoi's history. William Logan (2000) writes in his wonderful biography of Hanoi that Vietnam's cities are multilayered, with strata of Chinese, French, and Soviet histories. The Hoa Lo site includes even more complexity. Covering over five acres, a large city block, Hoa Lo can be deconstructed both vertically through time and horizontally through space.

The first known historical occupants of the site were the 48 families of Phu Khanh village, relocated prior to the prison's construction beginning in 1886. There may be no intentional connection between the "Hell's Hole" of round-the-clock fiery kilns used in pot making and the hell hole of Hoa Lo, but the resonance is palpable. The first exhibition room in

Figure 2.8: Hoa Lo Prison Museum and Hanoi Towers, 2009.

the museum contains artifacts and illustrations remembering the pottery village that was leveled to make room for the activist Vietnamese who did not find the imposition of French culture and values agreeable, and that included almost everyone.

No doubt some of the apparitions lingering in the vast Hanoi Towers complex had been eager students in what could be called the Hoa Lo Prison School for Revolutionaries. Peter Zinoman writes about how "by subjecting hundreds of thousands of colonial subjects with diverse regional backgrounds, social identities, and political commitments to the same terrifying ordeal, the prison system encouraged fraternal affinities and a sense of shared predicament that contributed to a national community" (2001: 238). The brutal confines of Hoa Lo—*Maison Centrale* (Hanoi Central Prison)—served inadvertently to incubate many of the leading Vietnamese nationalists of the early twentieth century, including patriot-scholar Phan Boi Chau, Yen Bay Mutiny leader Hguyen Thai Hoc, and future president of the Democratic Republic of Vietnam Le Duan. "The revolutionists made the prison a school, where they trained themselves to the communist ideology, the iron will in their fighting, and to literacy" (Hoa Lo Brochure, n.d.). In the 1880s, the French were in a hurry to build enough space to contain the growing ranks of Vietnamese dissidents. Prisons were typically built in rural areas, and the plan to build a prison in central Hanoi was unique. "Incarceration was not the usual way of dealing with offenders in Confucian societies, where punishment was a responsibility of the family and the community" (Zinoman 2000: 27). Because the villagers of Phu Khanh fired their kilns around the clock, the village was known by the other name of Hoa Lo—"fired pottery kilns" or "furnace with coal" or, figuratively, "Hell's Hole." The French named their new prison *Maison Centrale*, but it was always known as Hoa Lo until the American pilots dubbed it the "Hanoi Hilton." Today

Figure 2.9: Phu Khanh Ceramics Village c. 1870, razed to build Hoa Lo Prison.

there actually is a Hanoi Hilton Hotel across town, whose opulence is a far cry from its namesake.

Despite the fact that some foreign developers were understandably spooked by the idea of building on the Hoa Lo site and local preservationists put up a fight, in 1993 a Vietnamese-Singaporean venture raised U.S.$60 million to build the Hanoi Towers complex. In the end, the People's Committee was able to save less than one-third of the original compound for a museum run by the Ministry of Culture and Information in remembrance of the nationalist and communist struggle that played out within the prison walls as well as without. Only one side of the massive prison compound remains, running the length of Hoa Lo Street between Tho Nhuom and Hai Ba Trung. The 10,000 VND (50-cent) price of admission permits a visitor to the prison museum to walk a carefully choreographed circuit, wherein Logan observes "almost all of the horror of the place has disappeared" (2005: 157).

Some who have walked somberly through the dungeons and guillotine room might beg to differ, but it is true that the clean, quiet and antiseptic-washed corridors make the barbarity of the place once teeming with squalid life hard to imagine. Signage is limited, and it would be impossible to learn much about the context from a single visit. The prison museum offers a brochure and a small 31-page booklet. There are no guest books to record visitor reactions that might produce the sort of documents Scott Laderman (2009) used ingeniously in his study of the War Remnant's Museum. The Hoa Lo museum conveys an atmosphere but does not tell a story in the sense of a narrative arc. The visitor is left to put the pieces together in a slow montage.

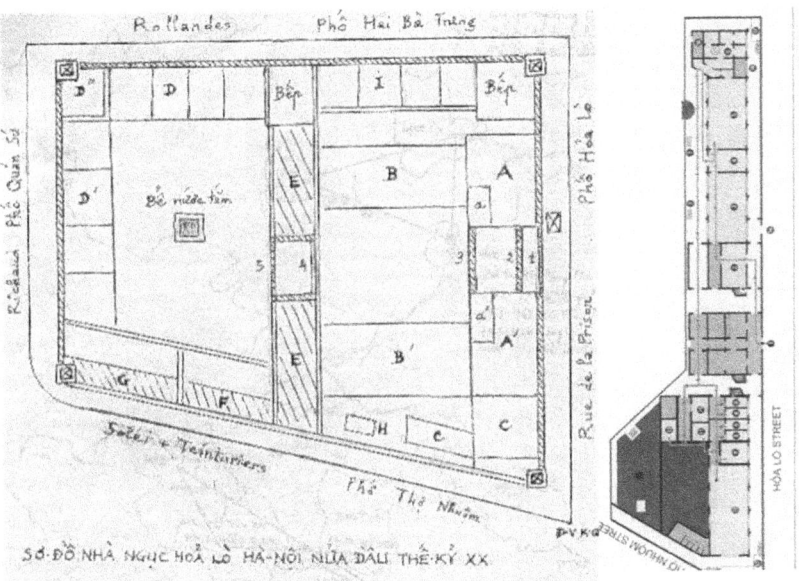

Figure 2.10: Hoa Lo Prison Original Floor Plan and Remaining Museum Space.

The prison walls are built of stone on an iron frame, 12 feet high and 18 inches thick, and are calculated to inspire fear both from within and without. Menacing multicolored shards of broken glass cover the top of the wall, which was further fortified by electrified barbed wire. Individual cells are dank and narrow with only a high sliver of light to remind the occupants of their miserable lot. Some cells retain the original chains and leg irons. Observed journalist Tom Mintier, "So many ghosts, so much torture embedded into the concrete walls" (Logan 2005: 158). One of the larger "detention camps" or group cells is inhabited today by Disneyfied prisoner replicas that are far less wretched looking than those in a nearby 1908 photograph of an authentic inmate population.

The largest space in the museum is dominated by the "mobile" guillotine that in one execution adventure was taken by train to Yen Bai in January 1930 to behead eleven members of the Vietnamese Nationalist Party. Next to the guillotine and its bucket receptacle is a photograph of three severed heads in baskets from a 1908 execution in Ha Thanh. Like all of the museum exhibits, this one is accompanied by minimal signage and commentary, and I will spare the reader the images.

Figure 2.11: Hoa Lo Prisoners 1908.

Figure 2.12: Hoa Lo Replica Prisoners c. 1993.

Hell's Hole University

Prisons often breed revolutionary thinking, and Hoa Lo was no exception, becoming in the 1930s a virtual academy for nationalist activity. Communist party leaders wrote books and pamphlets and led training courses for other prisoners. Publications such as *The Red Prison, The Prison Review,* and *The Prisoner's Life* appeared and at least for a time escaped detection. Theater was used as a vehicle for political education. "In the early 1930s, communist prisoners in Hanoi Central Prison put on a production of *The Bombs of Pham Hong Thai,* a biographical drama about the famous Vietnamese patriot who died trying to assassinate Governor-General Merlin in 1924" (Zinoman 2000: 224). Many future leaders of Vietnam were among the party faithful cultivated in prison. Education was highly valued.

> To earn literacy the prisoners used pieces of coal and bricks as pen and cigarette pack and cement floor as notebook. They invented special kinds of ink to write their secret documents. The ink was two types of medicine namely mercurochrome which had red color, and methylene blue; both were taken from the healthcare center. The diluted mercurochrome used as ink made the writing invisible. To read it, the prisoners would soak it in the liquid of cooked rice. The jailers were surprised and scared when they once discovered kilograms of documents and books and newspapers written with tiny letters and hidden skillfully in the four bare walls of the cells.
>
> (Hoa Lo Brochure)

Inmates were highly disciplined along the party's Leninist orientation that promoted hierarchy, secrecy, and organization. Mme. Hang explained that the female prisoners:

> Set up functional committees for our community in Hoa Lo such as the Nutritional Care Committee took care of our meals and nutritional issues in prison. They would receive food from the guards and distribute to everyone in order to make sure that we all have food to eat. Prisoners were counted twice a day, standing in two queues. The guards used a long stick to point at us or tapped it on our heads and counted. There was one woman who got so frustrated she pushed the stick away. Immediately, the guard lashed her repeatedly, then got her fettered. We protested the guard's action and all got fettered for a whole week. We had to fast and struggle whenever we wanted to have our requests met. For example, we fasted for better meals. Day in and day out we had to eat moldy rice with nothing but boiled carp. We would rather be starved than swallow such crap. People who were sick wouldn't be taken to hospital, either. Sometimes we had to fast for three days. Starved. That was so miserable. It wasn't easy at all when we asked for something. Whenever we struggled for something we would immediately get fettered.

Despite the fortress-like confines, Hoa Lo inmates engineered a series of spectacular jailbreaks, organized like military battles and featuring "flying" over walls and "vanishing underground" into the sewer system. The most spectacular of these escapes involved 17 death row prisoners on 24 December 1951, who were armed by imprisoned party leaders with saws, files, and a detailed map of the sewer system. Only five successfully escaped, and a section of sewer is fashioned into a monument at Hoa Lo commemorating their bravery. Hoa Lo was a prison built to hold 450 inmates and by 1954 was packed with 2,000. As many as 13 percent of the prisoners at Hoa Lo were women, some incarcerated with their children. The conditions were wretched. Zinoman quotes a 1932 report by de Gery:

> From a hygienic and moral point of view, and from the standpoint of simple humanity the women's quarter presents a truly revolting spectacle. 225 of these miserable creatures are locked up in a space meant for a hundred. They form an incredible mob, neither classed nor categorized composed of political prisoners, common-law convicts incarcerated for various crimes, defendants and minors, not to mention twelve women with infants (2000: 107).

Mme. Hang remembers that in Hoa Lo:

> We couldn't talk loudly nor make any noise. I was locked in a very small room. Day after day there were more and more prisoners coming to Hoa Lo, and the room just got smaller and smaller. Each of us was provided with two sets of uniforms, one blanket, and one mat. There were dozens of prisoners staying in one room. We were locked inside most of the time and the guards would bring food to us. We were divided into political prisoners

Figure 2.13: Hoa Lo Prison Sewer Fragment.

and economic prisoners and were locked up separately. There was only one bathroom for hundreds of prisoners to share. It was awful.

The building of Hoa Lo took three years, with most of the materials imported from France. It was located near the French Quarter, the architectural center of France's *la mission civilisatrice* aimed at bringing the unruly natives under control. Designed by chief Hanoi architect Auguste-Henri Vildieu, it represented the grislier end of the *beaux arts* style then in fashion. Not long after a Vildieu-designed *Palais de Justice* was erected nearby to complete the law enforcement complex and announce France's domination for all to see. Hoa Lo stood intact for nearly 100 years before succumbing to the imperatives of *doi moi* ("renovation"), Vietnam's 1986 adoption of economic reforms that greatly expanded the possibilities for free enterprise, of which the Hanoi Towers project is a highly visible result.

The richness and texture of Hoa Lo's history is exemplified by the extraordinary parade of residents over its century of existence. First, and for the longest stretch, were the Vietnamese political dissidents for whom the prison was erected in the first place, and whose struggle made Hoa Lo an international symbol of the evils of colonialism. During a little-known period of Japanese control from 1940 to 1945, some nationalists were released to be replaced by hundreds of French civilians suspected of sympathizing with the Allies. In 1954, after the Vietnamese routed the French at Dien Bien Phu, Hoa Lo was run by the communist regime of North Vietnam. In 1964, it again became a symbol of anti-colonialism, this time with the Vietnamese having the upper hand when the first of hundreds of American pilots was shot down. Built by the Colonial French to suppress Vietnamese nationalism, subsequently overseen for a time by the Japanese in part to suppress French sympathy with the Allies, and finally run by the Vietnamese in an attempt to hold out against American imperialism and to quell anti-communist dissidents at home—Hoa Lo reflects Vietnam's turbulent history during its lifetime, well earning its official status as a "building of national significance" as well as its unofficial status as a "symbol of transcendence" (Logan 2005: 156).

Falling from the Sky

Scott Laderman observes that Hoa Lo "has come to exemplify a fascinating reality of contemporary Vietnamese tourism: Many Americans travel to Vietnam to learn not about Vietnam but about the United States" (2009: 3). The main draw of Hoa Lo for many tourists, indeed the reason for its widespread recognition, is the "Pilot Exhibit," two galleries tucked in the back corner of the museum designed to depict the prison lives of the U.S. pilots who passed through during the period from 1964 to 1973. There is a striking contrast with the nearby display of imprisoned Vietnamese women as well as significant differences in the pilot exhibit itself pre-2008 and afterward following a major renovation by museum officials.

A large measure of the Hanoi Hilton's contemporary notoriety is due to the political prominence of John McCain, who spent several stretches of his five and one half years in captivity in Hoa Lo. On 26 October 1967 McCain was piloting a A-4E Skyhawk fighter jet on his 23rd mission over Vietnam with the objective of taking out the Hanoi municipal power plant when a Russian anti-aircraft missile blew off his right wing and McCain ejected down 4,500 feet ending up at the bottom of Ho Truc Bach next to Hanoi's largest lake. When he surfaced with multiple injuries he was both saved and further roughed up by Vietnamese bystanders.

McCain was a prize prisoner, a third generation Annapolis graduate and the son of the Navy commander of the Pacific Fleet. He was told by his friends that the Vietnamese said "We have the crown prince" (1973: 5), so from the start he was the rock star of POWs. This put McCain in a highly visible position, but did not earn him any favors as he reports numerous types and instances of mistreatment by his captors. The Vietnamese deny any torture was inflicted on U.S. fliers, but it is worth noting that at the same time they claimed the Americans were "pirates" and "criminals" to whom the Geneva Conventions did not apply because war had not been formally declared, much in the same way that the United States later denied those rights to "enemy combatants" who were sent to Guantanamo and darker sites. As befits McCain's celebrity status, he has his own display in the Hoa Lo Museum and he has visited on several occasions to great fanfare.

McCain remained in solitary confinement for more than two years after his capture, learning that "the most important thing for survival is communication with someone, even if it's only a wave or a wink, a tap on the wall, or to have a guy put his thumb up. It makes all the difference" (1973: 8). The primary function of communication was to boost morale, and "we would risk getting beat up just to tell a man that one of his friends had gotten a letter from home." In time, the pilots developed an extensive communication system of hand signals and, more commonly, of taps on the wall. McCain "learned a lot about acoustics. You can tap—if you get the right spot on the wall—and hear a guy four or five rooms away" (1973: 9).

By the time McCain was moved to Hoa Lo, the American prisoners had already reinvented the geography of the place with familiar names: the punishment complex was "Las Vegas," including "Stardust," "Riviera," "Thunderbird," and "Desert Inn." "Camp Unity" was a communal environment where human contact was a welcome feature. "New Guy Village" and "Heartbreak Area," including "Heartbreak Hotel" was where prisoners were usually taken for their initial interrogation. Naming is a powerful way of asserting some measure of control over an environment, and just as the Communist Party inmates of the 1930s, the American fliers had a strict internal hierarchy based upon rank and time served. Because of McCain's family status he was given the opportunity to leave on several occasions, which he rejected because he would have been out of order given the Code of Conduct that bound him to his mates. McCain was so highly prized as a prisoner that he was seen by General Giap himself, then Minister of Defense, who visited his cell briefly and left without saying a word.

His prisoner status offered little protection, and McCain has written about frequent mistreatment. In one reported incident,

> They bound me from pillar to post, kicking and laughing and scratching. After a few hours of that, ropes were put on me and I sat that night bound with ropes. Then I was taken to a small room. For punishment they would almost always take you to another room where you didn't have a mosquito net or a bed or any clothes. For the next four days I was beaten every two or three hours by different guards. My left arm was broken again and my ribs were cracked.

McCain reached his breaking point, and wrote a "confession" (1973: 13).

Numerous U.S. prisoners testified to the use of rope punishment. In the PBS documentary *Return with Honor*, Mike McGrath recounts

> We called it the Vietnamese rope trick, and that was to take the arms behind your back, tie your hands together, tie them up real tight and then rotate your arms beyond and over your shoulder until your shoulders dislocate ... I finally said I can't live. I can't live another day. And no food, no water, no sleep, twenty-four hours of this and I started talking.
>
> (Mock and Sanders 2000)

In 1969 with the war beginning to wind down the punishment abated, and in 1973 the remaining pilots were released.

War Crimes and Misdemeanors

Twenty years later the U.S. pilot exhibit became the main attraction at the Hoa Lo Museum. The modest detailed installation comprises two adjacent galleries, or "exhibition halls," in the southeast corner of the museum. Each space is about 15' × 30', and the narratives they weave through pictures and artifacts are strikingly different. In the hallway outside that joins the rooms a large poster announces in English and Vietnamese:

Some Pictures and Objects
Of United States Pilots in Hoa Lo Prison

United States government carried out a sabotage warfare by air force and naval force against the North of Vietnam from 25 August 1964 to 15 January 1973.

Thousands of planes were shot down. Hundreds of United States pilots were arrested by the North army and people. Some of them were imprisoned here.

During the war the national economy was difficult but Vietnamese Government had created the best living conditions to US pilots for they had a stable life during the temporary detention period.

Upon the agreement on war termination concluded in March 1973 in Paris, all the arrested US pilots were released to US government by Vietnamese government.

Some of pictures and objects on these two exhibition hall show some details of US pilots' life when they were temporarily imprisoned at Hoa Lo prison.

At the far end of the room to the left of the poster, John McCain's flight suit, parachute, and boots are displayed as prized possessions in a tall vitrine. This room by virtue of its contents could be called the *war is hell* or even the *war crimes room*. The gallery is filled with photographs of devastation, many from the Christmas 1972 Bombing, and blowups of statistical charts that show a scorecard of U.S. planes shot down and other Vietnamese victories. A B-52 fragment is encased as a trophy. There is a cot on display along with prisoner clothing.

The pilot exhibit closed for renovation at the end of 2007, and when it reopened four months later the war crimes room featured a dramatic new installation, with a vivid mural of burning and bombed out buildings behind a faux bomb-damaged wall, with a gel covered flashing light behind the brick illuminating the mural to audio of a B-52 raid.

The message of this installation is at least in theory hard-hitting—war is hell, the Americans did many very bad things, and the people won. But the vivid whimsical style of illustration and the rubble chic construction of the wall mitigate if not contradict the war is hell message. The Vietnamese creators of this exhibit work it both ways: putting it in front of your face, but not in your face. Informing without offending; telling the logical

Figure 2.14: Hoa Lo Pilot Exhibit, 2008 Renovation, McCain display far right.

tale and suppressing the emotional component; reprimanding, but at a comfortable distance; not forgetting and not forgiving, either. The colorful illustrations soften the impact of the adjacent black and white photographs of bombed out Bach Mai hospital in a typical display of juxtapositions that complement each other to suggest multiple interpretations for mixed audiences. Less nuanced are two five-minute video loops added in 2009 in both galleries. *Road to Hoa Lo* in the war crimes room begins: "Having trampled the Geneva agreement, American Imperialist and Sai Gon administration headed by Ngo Dinh Diem ruthlessly suppressed and terrorized the Southern people ..." (Hoa Lo Video 2009).

Hoa Lo Holiday Camp

More reassuring to visiting Americans is the gallery across the hall that could be called by virtue of its artifacts "Hoa Lo Holiday Camp." Somewhere between 600 and 700 U.S. pilots were captured by the North Vietnamese beginning with Lt. Everett Alvarez, Jr., who was shot down during the Gulf of Tonkin incident on 5 August, 1964, and imprisoned for eight and a half years. Many of the prisoners spent part of their incarceration in Hoa Lo, although the precise numbers are unclear. In addition to McCain, numerous U.S. prisoners have offered accounts of their experience (Alvarez, William Stockdale, Pete Peterson, who became the first U.S. Ambassador to Vietnam) and it can be said that not one of them thought prison was a holiday. Even in the absence of mistreatment, the conditions in Vietnam during the pilot period were economically desperate and many Vietnamese were starving, reflected by the introductory sign to the pilot exhibit acknowledging that *"during the war the national economy was difficult but Vietnamese Government had created the best living conditions to US pilots ..."* This acknowledgment of poor living conditions suggests an attempt to preempt criticism of the treatment of the pilots, but given the upbeat exhibits in the Hoa Lo Holiday room, this is hardly necessary.

The 30 photographs of pilots on Hoa Lo Holiday are grouped into themes: pilots practicing religious beliefs; pilots receiving medical care; pilots receiving packages; pilots playing sports and games (basketball, volleyball, checkers, chess, cards, billiards); pilots raising chickens and trees; pilots being released in 1973).

Nearly half of the photographs pertain to events surrounding the release process. Some panels, like the six photographs of pilots exercising religious beliefs, are presented with framing that reinforces their content, in this case the message of religious freedom, represented by the outline of a chapel with a cross, a new installation introduced in the 2008 renovation.

Figure 2.15: Pilots at Play in Hoa Lo Prison.

Hoa Lo Prison Museum

In a 2009 visit to the prison, upon viewing a photograph of pilots opening letters from home, John McCain remarked "This always entertains me. A wonderful life." Nonetheless, McCain has been among the strongest anti-torture voices in the U.S. Senate.

Several display cases hold artifacts from the prisoners' stay. One case holds an empty medicine box, a card from the American Red Cross, and an empty carton of L&M cigarettes, also from the Red Cross. The largest display case holds checkers, playing cards, Frances Fitzgerald's *Fire in the Lake* (1972), billiard balls, sport shoes, volleyball net, and a guitar. Another case holds shaving and eating instruments.

What is not on view is any evidence of prisoner capture, interrogation, confinement, discomfort in the least (except for injured prisoners being tended to by medical personnel), let alone mistreatment or torture. There is no artifact, such as a map, of the prison culture actually created by the Americans. There is no representation of the infamous 1966 Hanoi March, where prisoners were paraded through the city to jeering crowds. There are no copies of "confessions" such as McCain's extracted under extreme duress. "I was a U.S. airman in the crimes against the Vietnamese country and people... I received very good medical treatment" (1969). Experiences widely reported by former Hoa Lo inmates such as solitary confinement, beatings, withholding medical care, and rope torture are nowhere to be seen. A museum official told me that the question she gets most frequently from visitors is about the absence of any suggestions of prisoner punishment. I tried without apparent success to explain the concept of propaganda to her, suggesting that the

Figure 2.16: Faux chapel added in 2008 renovation.

exhibit might have more credibility if it showed a more comprehensive view of the Hoa Lo experience, even interrogations or actual living conditions. Her reply "Oh, we would not do that."

The holiday camp room, like the war crimes room, also has a length of faux bombed out brick wall running along one side that was added in 2008. Ho Chi Minh's 1969 *New Years Greeting*, his last, is framed nearby:

> *Last year was full of glorious victories*
> *This year the forefront's sure to bring still bigger ones*
> *For independence, for freedom*
> *Let's fight so the Yanks quit and the puppets topple*
> *Forward! Fighters, countrymen!*
> *North and South reunited*
> *Could there be a happier spring?*

John McCain is the only pilot pictured in both galleries. In the holiday camp gallery, he is shown in a hospital bed receiving medical attention at the time of his capture, and also in his 1995 visit during the normalization of relations between Vietnam and the United States. In the adjacent war crimes room in addition to McCain's flight paraphernalia is now the famous image of him being fished out of the lake after being shot down. During the renovation, this photograph replaced an almost as famous McCain photo that resembles a celebrity headshot, where he is wearing a Cal football jersey looking determined and roughly handsome in a semi-shaven way. The difference in these two photographs is the difference between dominance and utter submission, and it hardly seemed possible that they were switched without thought of this. Yet prison officials told me that they are both part of a collection that is circulated, the implication being randomly.

Quintilian (96) said of rhetoric that "the perfection of art is to conceal art," an objective the prison museum realizes most completely in the pilot exhibits. The separation of the two galleries allows full depiction of the pilots "crimes," and across the hall a representation of their lives in prison that is entirely divorced from both the consequences of their actions and in fact from the reality of life in prison. Still, it is evident that the exhibit has been curated with utmost thought and care to achieve maximum message value with minimum provocation. The switch of the McCain pictures and introduction of features like the faux chapel frame and especially the Fauvist-like new mural and wall installation are the expressions of a meticulous sensibility, both aesthetic and political. If the upbeat portrayal of prison life is an accident, then one must explain why down the hall the women martyrs of Hoa Lo are pictured in the same display case with their instruments of torture. This would suggest that there is no cultural prohibition on such displays, except when there is, and that the striking contrast between the women and pilot exhibits was a rhetorical choice and not an accident.

Figure 2.17: John McCain.

"The Fury Burning Within"

The pilot exhibit fills two galleries, yet more arresting to many a museum visitor is a compact 8' × 10' display set inconspicuously along one wall of the cavernous guillotine room. Mug shots of 14 young women hover hauntingly above the instruments of their torture: electrical equipment, beating cane, and glass bottle. There is no irony. The exhibit is what Umberto Eco (1984) would call a closed text leading the reader to a single interpretation. When American POW Ron Bliss (2000) said of Hoa Lo "you can look at this place and just hear the screams of about fifty years," these women would be among the voices.

The mug shots are dated with years from 1929 to 1945. Many died in Hoa Lo, including Nguyen Thi Quang Thai, the first wife of General Vo Nguyen Giap, hero of Vietnam's 1954 victory over the French at Dien Bien Phu.

Giap and Quang Thai married in 1939, and friends observed that it was the happiest time of his life. World War II was breaking out when they gave birth on 4 January 1940 to a baby girl Giap named Hong Anh, or "red queen of flowers," who became a prominent physicist. A few short months later, the communist party's central committee decided to send Giap

Figure 2.18: Hoa Lo female prisoners with torture implements. (*Mme. Hang is second from right in middle row.*)

to China so he could plan the revolutionary movement in Vietnam in safety. When he departed in May 1940, it was the last time Giap and Quang Thai would see one another.

Quang Thai was arrested in 1942, leaving Hong Anh in the care of Giap's mother. She was sentenced to life in prison for conspiring against the security of France and sent to Hoa Lo. Within two years she was dead, a suicide by hanging according to the account of her jailers, but hung by her thumbs and beaten to death according to later U.S. intelligence reports. Mme. Hang knew her well and had a different recollection:

> I stayed with Mme. Thai—the first wife of General Giap. She was a very noble woman. Her French was so fluent that she was elected to be head of the External Affairs Committee. There was a French interpreter who used to insist on seeing Mme. Thai whenever he visited Hoa Lo. He treated her very respectfully. Although she was the leader in almost every struggle in Hoa Lo, she was still highly respected by all the guards and French officers. They used to say behind her back "She is very outstanding! She speaks French fluently and her thinking is absolutely critical!"

Contrary to reports that Mme. Thai had been tortured to death in Hoa Lo, Mme. Hang remembered that

> At the time she got ill in prison, they didn't take her to hospital nor send in any doctor so we had to fast one more time. Then all the male prisoners followed our struggle and that finally made them take her to hospital. However, she was too ill to recover by then, and she died after a week. Mme. Thai's death was a real loss to all of us. Mme. Thai was like such a kind sister to us. Although she was very tall, which was unlike the traditional Vietnamese woman and almost like a young man, her beauty was still outstanding and her kindness was memorable.

Mme. Hang, pictured in the row above Mme. Thai on the wall, survived her years at Hoa Lo to marry another war hero General Tran Do, who was instrumental in both the defeat of the French at Dien Bien Phu and the 1968 Tet Offensive.

Vietnam was under Japanese occupation during the years from 1940 to 1945 that Mme. Hang spent in Hoa Lo, but administration of the prison system was left to the French. Upon her arrest they tried to extract a confession

> I got forcibly stripped and beaten. It was terribly painful. My whole body seemed to be torn into pieces. Punch. Hit. Kick. Too much of the worst violence. They even hung me up and beat me. They pricked my nipples with needles. The torture used to last for three to four hours until my face, legs and arms were swollen. It was too painful for me to move. After every torture they grabbed my hair and pulled me back to the prison room and locked me up. All the other prisoners just sneaked through the window to see how I was. Mr. Tran Quoc Hoan was also imprisoned there and knew about my case. I got beaten for four to five hours every day. The torture might start in the morning, afternoon or evening. I was beaten incessantly until I got faint and unconscious. It was unimaginably vicious: kick, punch, slap, rope spanking. Then they put an electric stick into my vagina and to the most sensitive areas of my body. I was awfully terrified, yet I still could keep my mouth shut.

They never broke her. "I remember telling myself I would rather die than betray my Union. I had nothing to lose but the fury burning within."

A lucky break freed Mme. Hang from Hoa Lo when the short-lived provisional government of Tran Trong Kim, prime minister of a puppet state created by Japan, came into power in 1945.

> It was so unexpected and spontaneous that they released all political prisoners from Con Dao to Son La. There were many other prisons in the South applying the new policy as well. This gave new strength and created larger human resources for the Central Committee, who were working so hard in preparation for the Revolution coming up. It was like a flow of strength to us.

Figure 2.19: Mme. Nguyen Thi Phuc Hang, 2011.

Mme. Hang resumed her political activities with even greater zeal, burning down a factory with Japanese workers inside because they had refused to accept return to Japan in exchange for their release.

Though the story of Hoa Lo's residents is little told and the museum displays require a lot of guesswork or a guide, few in Vietnam escaped tragedies associated with the prison, from the families of revolutionaries to the communities that felt the destructive power of American bombs to the nationalist heroes themselves who won Vietnam's independence after millennia of foreign domination. One of those who suffered was General Giap himself, who did not learn the fate of his wife Quang Thai until three years after her death. On 15 April 1945, Giap looked forward to a meeting where he believed he would hear news of his family for the first time since he had left the country. Instead, he was told that "Thai was caught because she didn't have time to find someone to care for the baby. She died in prison before we could do anything." Love and revolution are too often condemned companions, and Giap is credited with these lines in a poem called "Kiss"

Even if I die, my love,
I love you, though I am unable
To kiss you with the lips
Of a slave

Even the survivors suffered long term consequences. Unlike the tragedy of Giap and Thai, Mme. Hang and General Tran Do had a long and happy marriage that ended only with his death in 2002. Tran Do emerged as a war hero in unified Vietnam, appointed head of ideology and culture for the Communist Party, but in the 1990s he began to express his doubts about what he believed to be the repressive political system that had evolved and after 58 years he was expelled from the party, his memoirs confiscated, and his family placed under surveillance. He died in 2002, but the family is on the government radar. Despite the ongoing challenge, Mme. Hang carries on with the strength that led her to survive far worse.

Mme. Hang and her comrades in the women's exhibit are heroines today in Vietnam; venerated for their vision and sacrifice. The U.S. pilots met a more mixed reception upon their return home, and their stories embody the continuing ambivalence as well as a lot of revisionist history about the war. "Honor the warrior, not the war" is a good sound bite but a paradoxical piece of logic. An open text, if you will, subject to multiple and contradictory interpretations.

William Logan argues that history has been rewritten by the altered architecture of Hoa Lo, its sanitization, and the "bland version of prison life" depicted therein. "History is being turned into heritage, serving current day's needs rather than attempting to reflect the past in a more scholarly and objective way" (2003). Thousands died at Hoa Lo, and many thousands more suffered unspeakable torment. The walls hold secrets of misery, determination, and passion. Vietnam's independence was not ignited at Hoa Lo, but the flames were fanned by generations of nationalists and communists using its stark environment to promote their education in the art of revolution. Hoa Lo played a heroic part in Vietnam's multiple struggles for independence, and today serves as an enduring monument to the resilience of the human spirit and the uncommon strength that sustains freedom fighters wherever they may be. This self-story is complicated by the imprisonment in Hoa Lo's final years of anti-communist dissidents like poet Nguyen Chi Thien, who was detained at Hoa Lo from 1979 to 1985, and subsequently patriated by the United States after poems he managed to deliver to the British Embassy were translated and distributed.

Nguyen Chi Thien writes that as teenagers in the 1950s he and his friends used to ride their bicycles near the prison, wondering to each other what it would become with the French gone. Some imagined a university in its place, others a youth center. "As for me," wrote Chi Thien, "I dreamed the dreary prison would turn into a public park, shaded by leafy trees and adorned with fragrant flowers where the people come to relax on the green lawn" (Nguyen 2007: 12). Such youthful yearnings were not to be realized at Hoa Lo, unless one counts the lavish tennis courts and private pool open only to current residents of Hanoi Towers.

Dancing on the Grave

The cultural ecology of the Hoa Lo site inflects the present with the past in surprising ways. Highlands Coffee is situated in the location previously occupied by "Camp Unity." The "Las Vegas" area, feared and loathed, is a space that has been retained and includes the current

Figure 2.20: To Mai Lien, Mme. Hang, the author, 21 January 2011, Hanoi. (Photo: John Coogan.)

pilot exhibit. Hoa Lo Prison has the best gift shop in Hanoi. It actually has three shops. You can buy Buddhas and tortoises and key rings and pith helmets and Graham Greene's *The Quiet American* as well as many other books and souvenirs, but you cannot buy anything that hints of the dark past. The grand driveway to Hanoi Towers, perpendicular to Hoa Lo Street, is on Hai Ba Trung Street. Every town in Vietnam has a Hai Ba Trung Street, after the two Trung sisters, whose first century A.D. death resisting the Chinese set the bar for Vietnamese martyrdom.

The Hoa Lo site taken as a whole encompasses the tensions between Vietnam's past and future, between conservation and development, between remembering and forgetting, between poverty and prosperity. Just as Hoa Lo inmates learned to write in disappearing ink, its palimpsest elicits ghostly content. Vietnamese children learn about Hoa Lo and its role in their history in school, but a foreign visitor to Highlands Coffee or to Papa Joe's or to the guillotine room in the prison would have no context for grasping the totality of the environment, making up probably five of the most historically and culturally complex acres on earth.

Patterns of paradox move in many directions: the prim hat-wearing prison women with the tools of their torture; U.S. pilots enthusiastically playing basketball and planting trees in the shadow of evidence of the destruction of their bombing; an exhibit featuring a few hundred American fliers trumping the thousands of other Hoa Lo ghosts, most of whom were lost in the fight for freedom; a truncated museum imbued with nationalist pride dominated by a sky-high monument to capitalism. Hoa Lo is a microcosm of both the history of political struggle and the present tensions between preservation and progress. The uneasy compromise that resulted in a luxury development being erected on the hallowed ground of martyrs suggests an agnostic attitude toward history that may sacrifice meaning in the service of the moment.

If visitors to the Hoa Lo Museum or even Hanoi Towers were provided adequate context for the history and intricacy of the site it could be one of Vietnam's greatest educational and political memorials. As it stands, dining at Jaspas or shopping at Citimart or even casually touring the museum itself feels more like dancing on a grave.

Chapter 3

Bac Ho: "Casting Pearls before Swine"

Mme. Nguyen Thi Phuc Hang remembers Ho Chi Minh's speech at Ba Dinh Square on 2 September 1945 as if it were yesterday, although it was an eventful 70 years ago. She had just been released from Hoa Lo Prison along with thousands of other patriots when the five-year Japanese occupation of Vietnam ended with the Allied victory in World War II.

> Yes, of course I remember being at Ba Dinh Square! I was with Mr. Tran Duy Hung, who was then Chairman of the Hanoi People's Committee. I was in the delegation from Dong Anh District. It was after our victory over the Japanese army in Hanoi. In 1945, I was released from Hoa Lo while the workers' movement against the Japanese army was at the peak. People got so frustrated after the famine [of 1944–45]. Mr. Tran Do, who later became my husband, and I were appointed to work with three hundred other workers to destroy the Japanese food stock warehouse. Our success led to the victory of the revolutionary forces over the Japanese army. I was then promoted to be Madam Chairman of Dong Anh People's Committee for my success and devotion.

At one and the same time in 1945 Vietnam was subjected to a Vietnamese emperor, Vichy French rule, Japanese occupation and 200,000 Chinese soldiers arriving in Hanoi. Nothing was simple during this period. Still, with the end of World War II and the August 1945 abdication of Emperor Bao Dai, the Democratic Republic of Vietnam was declared, celebrated most famously by Ho Chi Minh's Declaration of Independence speech.

Who is the man that rose to the occasion of this historic moment that DeCaro called one of the most important events in history? What do we know about him that would place him in this grave and pivotal role, especially given that three decades of his life had been lived on the move outside of Vietnam listening, learning, planning, waiting?

Who Was Ho Chi Minh?

Bac ("Uncle") Ho, as he is universally known in Vietnam, did not attract half a million rapt listeners to Ba Dinh Square without reason. Ho is one of the most unique and compelling figures in history. Not just Vietnamese history, or modern history, but all of history and myth as we know it. Odysseus is the only comparison from Western lore who comes readily to mind. One thinks also of Joyce's Stephen Dedalus: silence, exile, cunning. Ireland has more in common with Vietnam than meets the eye with its colonial struggles, tenacious people, and endless vistas of green.

You may know that Ho Chi Minh had many names, or "aliases" as they are usually called: Nguyen Sinh Cung at birth, Nguyen Tat Thanh, Nguyen Ai Quoc, ("Nguyen the Patriot") finally Ho ("he who enlightens") Chi ("will" or "spirit") Minh ("light"). This fact of many names may be well known in the United States primarily because it casts a light of suspicion upon him and was a convenient propaganda morsel. You may know that Ho was a communist first and then a nationalist. Or is it the other way around? Or are communism and nationalism not so different in a Confucian context? The answer may be all of the above. The answer one believes makes, or made, a huge difference. You may know Ho from the U.S. anti-war slogan: "Ho Ho Ho Chi Minh!" (Admittedly not as catchy as "Heh! Heh! LBJ! How many kids did you kill today?") Or you might know that his body is on view in a Hanoi mausoleum, another fragment of information with the propaganda value of sinister overtones. Ho Chi Minh as portrayed in the United States is a caricature of the deep and variegated man he was, in truth an odd candidate for demonization and dismissal.

You may not know that Ho's father was a Confucian scholar and he was sent to a Franco-Vietnamese school "with the admonition of the 15th-century scholar Nguyen Trai that one must understand the enemy in order to defeat him" (Fitzgerald 2000). Or that he earned his living as a cook's helper on a ship on his way to the United States, as a laborer in Brooklyn and Harlem where he attended meetings of Marcus Garvey's Universal Negro Improvement Trust, as a waiter and a pastry cook under Auguste Escoffier at the Carlton Hotel in London, as a photo retoucher in Paris and a waiter in Milan. It was while in France that he became attracted to the idea of communism as a path to Vietnamese independence, and in his first invocation of the U.S. Declaration of Independence in 1919 (the second would be at Ba Dinh Square) he unsuccessfully appealed to President Woodrow Wilson, who was attending the Versailles Conference, to help Vietnam achieve its liberation. Wilson would not be the last U.S. President Ho turned to for help. Decades later he repeatedly petitioned President Harry S. Truman for support of Vietnam's independence in the belief that a country that accomplished its own independence would support that of others. Truman, like Wilson, never responded, leaving one to wonder how many similar overtures have gone unheard or unheeded.

It was only then that Ho turned toward the Soviet Union and China, leaving Paris for Moscow in 1923 and shortly thereafter for China. Before he was done, he would add Thailand, India, Germany, Belgium, Switzerland, Africa, Hong Kong, and many other ports to his itinerary. In 1932, the British imprisoned him for a year in Hong Kong where he wrote his affecting prison diaries (1971). William Druicker reports that Ho married a Chinese woman and later had a son by an ethnic Tay woman in Vietnam who became a prominent political figure (2000: 198). This research got Druicker's exhaustive biography censored in Vietnam.

By the time Ho returned to Vietnam in 1941 he was both a "Confucian humanist and Communist revolutionary" (Fitzgerald 2000). "Half Lenin and half Ghandi," in Druicker's words. Druicker emphasizes that Ho's "own brand of revolutionary ethics: thrift, prudence, respect for learning, modesty, generosity ... had far more to do with Confucian morality than with Leninism." Flexible, pragmatic, patient, worldly, and averse to military conflict, Ho would seem the perfect ally, negotiating partner, and diplomat. Unfortunately, "neither the French nor the American leadership had the sense to respond in kind" (Fitzgerald 2000).

Ho was naïve enough to believe the emerging power of the United States would sympathize with his nationalist dream. Mme. Hang recalls the elation of 2 September 1945:

> It was so exciting! The eagerness was on every street of Hanoi. Everyone was excited. I walked seven kilometers from Dong Anh to Ba Dinh Square in only one hour. I used to be very active and energetic, you know. Although I have a tiny figure, I could walk very fast for a long distance. There were many thousands of people at the stage with Uncle Ho: Mr. Pham Van Dong, Mr. Tran Quoc Hoan, Mr. Le Duan, Mr. Tran Dang Ninh, Mr. Le Duc Tho. They have all passed away.

It was at that event Ho himself started the Independence Day holiday while speaking to the reverent throngs near the site of what was eventually to become his final resting place. American planes flew overhead in support. It was a moment of ultimate hope and folly for Ho Chi Minh and the Vietnamese people, when they had reason to believe that America would be on their side in the struggle for independence and unification. Duicker describes the scene:

> Shortly after 2:00 p.m. on September 2 he mounted the rostrum of a makeshift platform hastily erected in a spacious park soon to be known as Ba Dinh Square on the western edge of the city. He was dressed in a faded khaki suit that amply encased his spare emaciated body and he wore a pair of rubber thongs... In a high-pitched voice that clearly reflected his regional origins, he announced the independence of his country and read the text of its new constitution (2000: 8).

Believing that the American revolution represented a model of liberation, Ho began his speech by quoting from the Declaration of Independence, "All men are created equal. They are endowed by their Creator with certain unalienable Rights; among these are Life, Liberty, and the pursuit of Happiness." He thought America would be Vietnam's friend in establishing an independent Vietnam, he thought that America would understand.

It is important to note how Ho adopted an entirely Western approach in this speech, stating his thesis in reference to independence declarations of both the United States and France—"all the peoples on the earth are equal from birth"—then enumerating the bill of particulars in support:

> For more than eighty years, the French imperialists, abusing the standard of Liberty, Equality, and Fraternity, have violated our Fatherland and oppressed our fellow-citizens.

Figure 3.1: Ho Chi Minh c. 1945.

They have acted contrary to the ideals of humanity and justice. In the field of politics, they have deprived our people of every democratic liberty. They have enforced inhuman laws; they have set up three distinct political regimes in the North, the Center and the South of Vietnam in order to wreck our national unity and prevent our people from being united. They have built more prisons than schools. They have mercilessly slain our patriots; they have drowned our uprisings in rivers of blood. They have fettered public opinion; they have practiced obscurantism against our people. To weaken our race they have forced us to use opium and alcohol. In the field of economics, they have fleeced us to the backbone, impoverished our people, and devastated our land. They have robbed us of our rice fields, our mines, our forests, and our raw materials. They have monopolized the issuing of bank-notes and the export trade. They have invented numerous unjustifiable taxes and reduced our people, especially our peasantry, to a state of extreme poverty ... (1977: 53).

Ho continued to indict "the double yoke of the French and the Japanese," resulting in the starvation of two million people. Not only were the French not capable of "protecting" Vietnam, "in the span of five years, they had twice sold our country to the Japanese." And then a bow from Ho's Confucian character: "notwithstanding all this, our fellow-citizens have always manifested toward the French a tolerant and humane attitude." He is "convinced that the Allied nations which at Tehran and San Francisco have acknowledged the principles of self-determination and equality of nations, will not refuse to acknowledge the independence of Vietnam." Therefore, the argument concludes, "the Democratic Republic of Vietnam solemnly declares to the world that Vietnam has the right to be a free and independent country—and in fact is so already."

Foremost among the many remarkable features of this brief 942 word speech is its classical Aristotelian rhetorical structure. This organizational pattern is familiar in courts of law and legislative assemblies. It is linear and syllogistic, sometimes aphorized as "state your case and prove it." Hank McGuckin calls Ho's application of Western epistemology "a valiant move to try to use rhetorical artistry rather than guns to achieve Vietnam's freedom. Casting pearls before swine, alas" (2012). This is clearly Ho's attempt to speak in the language of the oppressor, since this form of argumentation is not at all typical of Vietnamese rhetorical style, which favors a much more poetic quality of expression. Scholar Tran Dan Vinh, writing one of few academic treatments of Ho as a communicator in *Journal of Communication*, argues that it was "the very poetic quality of expression which endeared Ho to the Vietnamese audiences" (1976: 143). Himself an esteemed poet, Ho made generous use of wordplay, popular sayings, songs, and metaphor. Typical of his mode of address are these lines from a 1951 political report:

Today the locusts fight the elephant.
But tomorrow the elephant will be disemboweled (1976: 144)

Similarly, in his handwritten testament four months before he died in 1969, Ho wrote:

Mountains, rivers, people will be here forever
The enemy defeated, we will build up our country ten times more beautiful (1976: 146)

Rachel Leow deconstructs Ho's "fiendishly clever" wordplay to show how he manipulates the multiple tones of Chinese language with the idea that you can break up phrases and words and turn them into different words in order to "conduct divination or tell fortunes from the results" (2009). This is not a man whose natural mode of thought was the syllogism that he displayed so brilliantly in the Ba Dinh speech. DeCaro argues that Ho's approach is closer to Kenneth Burke's emphasis on "identification" (over persuasion) between the speaker and audience as a key term in the rhetorical process (2003: 64). Wrote Burke: "You persuade a man only insofar as you talk his language by speech, gesture, tonality, order, image, attitude, idea, identifying your way with his" (1969: 20). The sad irony may be that Ho, the skilled metaphor-maker, did not recognize that "all men are created equal" is itself metaphorical—an abstraction not originally intended to apply to women, blacks, or surely not to polite and diminutive Asians.

Over Mango, Cakes and Tea

Ba Dinh Square is near the current site of the Ho Chi Minh Museum and the mausoleum that is his place of rest, or at least repose. It is hard to imagine anything restful about being on display as a venerated relic and tourist attraction. Westerners generally cannot understand at all the appeal of this tiny man with the shaggy goatee, but according to Tran Thanh, former director of the Institute of Ho Chi Minh Studies, Uncle Ho was a strategic and deliberate communicator. When I spoke with Professor Thanh at the Institute over refreshments of mango, cakes and tea, he told me that in preparing a presentation, Ho Chi Minh simplified concepts by having his staff such as his cook or driver give him feedback on speech drafts until they were clear to "the people." In addition, he used native idioms in his speeches, such as proverbs and poems, addressing love and mutual support among the people and appealing to sentiments and aspirations held by all. Also, his style included interactive call and response. He would ask "Do you understand me?" and "Can you hear me clearly?"—as he did in his Independence speech. As an example of Ho's perceptiveness, Professor Thanh related the story of when the Indian Ambassador from the Geneva Accord Observation Team compared the more distant style of Indian officials with Ho Chi Minh to illustrate how he was clearly understood. Ho Chi Minh was "like a father talking to his children." He attempted to "clear out the gap between himself and the audience." Most important to him was how to transfer thoughts to the common people, and he was masterful in gaining and keeping their allegiance (Tran Thanh 1993).

Ho was a born teacher, who in 1925 taught a several month "Special Political Course for Vietnamese Revolution" in Canton, China. One of Ho's students recalled:

> He used to stop at difficult words and to give long explanations until everybody could understand. He urged his students to engage in free discussions, to ask questions, and then answered all the problems raised. He took part in the debates organized by the study groups and asked the brighter students to help the weaker ones. He checked the notes taken by each one and gave them advice (2003: 68).

In true Confucian spirit, Ho valued education above all as a means to the revolution he spent his life trying to realize. When asked "What is the aim of study?" he replied

> One must study in order to remould one's thinking ... to foster one's revolutionary virtues... Study is aimed at action: the two must go hand in hand. The former without the latter is useless. The latter without the former is hard to carry through (Truong Chinh in Fitzgerald 1972: 23).

Ho Chi Minh died in 1969, 24 years to the day after his Declaration of Independence speech and six years short of Vietnam's victory over the United States. The Vietnamese public was not informed about his death until 48 hours after it occurred so as not to dampen their 2 September Independence Day celebration.

Uncle Ho and Henry

Vietnam achieved its independence 30 years after Ho's optimistic Ba Dinh declaration, and despite the many blessings the revolution has brought, a law akin to the U.S. Constitution's First Amendment is not among them. To understand just how seriously the Vietnamese regard their Ho Chi Minh, consider the incident faced by a friend I will call Henry, an expat history professor and colleague in the Hanoi Media Lab. One day during my teaching year in Hanoi, my minder Mr. Huy took me aside to whisper that Henry was in big trouble because of something that happened in his Vietnam History class. Henry is a voluble guy who often has Vietnamese and Viet Kieu students in the same class. While the students look alike, their cultural upbringings are often diametrically opposite. Viet Kieu—literally "Overseas Vietnamese"—can be from California or Australia and have names like Britney and Tammy. Most of their parents were born in Vietnam but the children were not. Vietnamese are baffled by Viet Kieu because while they look like native Vietnamese they act like the foreigners they are. If someone who looks like an American acts like a "foreigner," it is expected. All foreigners are strange and crazy to the Vietnamese. But when someone who looks just like your sister acts like a valley girl, it is confusing. Mr. Huy was never comfortable with the Viet Kieu who were his charges in the International Cooperation Office. He recoiled at their directness and animated style in addressing him, so different from the reserved and deferential Vietnamese students.

Henry knew he was in for trouble with a class split between Vietnamese and Viet Kieu, who bring to the class often contradictory understandings about Vietnamese history. Disaster struck one day when Henry was least expecting it during a mild-mannered lecture on the revered Ho Chi Minh. A Viet Kieu student raised her hand. "Isn't is true that Ho Chi Minh was married three times and had a child and one of his wives was killed by the party?" Silence. Henry replied in measured tones "Well, some scholars say one thing and some say another." At least that is what he reported he replied. Knowing Henry and his diplomatic eagerness to please everyone, he may well have talked himself into a corner. Whatever was actually said, one of the Vietnamese students reported the incident to her parents, who in an unlucky coincidence were professors at the university. The parents reported it to the dean who reported it to the rector and Henry was in very hot water. He came to me distraught.

"Henry, why didn't you just say 'interesting subject but it's not on the syllabus?'"
"I guess I should have, but the story about Ho is no secret. It has been reported by credible scholars in the West. You can find it on the Internet even here in Vietnam."
"Then why didn't you just tell them that you were trying to counter the rumors that Bac Ho was gay?"

I thought this was wildly funny, but Henry was not in the mood to make light of the situation. In fact, he was worried sick. He was newly married to a Vietnamese girl and was trying to be an upstanding husband. The university gave him a big title but paid him little, as with most professors. What would Phuong think if she learned of his seditiousness? Henry's university title conferred upon him great status and credibility, but the salary barely covered food money, and like most of his colleagues, he made the bulk of his modest living from teaching and consulting for private institutions that were springing up like mushrooms in Vietnam.

Mr. Huy took me outside away from the walls with ears to tell me that Henry was in such big trouble that they were not going to let him teach history any more, a threat that never materialized. Then Huy proceeded to tell me a story commonly shared among the Vietnamese about Ho Chi Minh, a twisting tale brimming with political treachery, torture, rape and murder. It was quite a hair-raising yarn. There may be no First Amendment in Vietnam, but the grapevine and a tabloid mentality are alive and thriving. But lesson learned—proceed at your own risk when coloring outside the lines on Bac Ho. The furor died down quickly but left us a little shaken and perhaps none the wiser, as my retelling of the incident here may suggest.

No Tank Tops, No Hats, No Cameras

Although the rules do not explicitly say so,
It is suggested that you don't ask the guards
"Is he dead?"

—Vietnam Travel Guide c. 1991

Ho Chi Minh's monumental tomb shimmers in the surreal heat. Uncle Ho did not want to end up this way, on display in a glass box in a concrete shrine. He requested cremation and the spreading of his ashes in north, central, and south Vietnam. The Third Politboro overruled, deciding in secret that Ho's 1969 death, with the American War raging, was awkwardly timed for such an inauspicious farewell. So his lifeless body was moved via air-conditioned transport to a bombproof cave for a year of artistry by chief Soviet embalmer Dr. Sergei Debrov.

It was not until 1975 that Ho Chi Minh was ready for his post-mortem close up and the mausoleum was complete, its design often compared to the tomb of Lenin. It also bears some resemblance to the facade of New York Stock Exchange headquarters. There is no mistaking that the edifice holds something important. I have visited the mausoleum five or six times which sounds creepy on the face of it, but the first time in 1993 as a guest of the Ministry of Labor was obligatory and during subsequent visits I was escorting friends passing through Hanoi. The last time, a little bored with the macabre ritual by now, a friend shot a few seconds of video inside the hallowed halls with a tiny iPod, but visions of incarceration in Vietnam led quickly to its erasure. Each visit I try to absorb a little more of the ineffability of Ho's spirit, but the documentary will have to wait.

This time I am prepared for the drill: no cameras, no bags, no tank tops, no hands in pockets, no hats. Today I learn that anything sleeveless is a tank top, and am loaned a polo shirt the way private clubs lend neckties to gentlemen who overlook the dress code. The line for admission is long, never visit on a Sunday. The weekday crowd consists primarily of restless schoolchildren from the countryside in their neat uniforms waiting for this once-in-a-lifetime experience. Weekends are full of foreign tourists clutching guidebooks and water

Figure 3.2: The author at Ho Chi Minh Mausoleum, 1993.

bottles. The wait is worth it. Anticipation builds during the slow ascent of the steps and the walk down the cool interior marble hallway.

The tomb room is dark except for pinkish orange spots turned toward Ho's paper pale face and hands. He is dressed in a blue mandarin jacket and covered by a waist high blanket. We are marched briskly around the bier, attended at each corner by a crisp armed guard in full dress white uniform and gloves. Ho seems larger than expected, wispy beard wispier, composed, definitely dead but only in a clinical sense and very much alive in the heart of Vietnam. I have heard many people complain about Vietnam's one party government, but rarely is a critical word uttered about the cult of Bac Ho.

Walking out of the stone mausoleum into the dazzling day, I try to catch my breath. You can smell, taste, feel, weigh, bathe in the Hanoi air even when it is not the height of summer. Ho Chi Minh's extraordinary life warranted his exalted final resting place notwithstanding the fact that as Logan notes "the attempt to present him as a legend and a gift to the ages remains a growth industry supported by the regime" (2005).

I left Ho's resting place thinking that if Robert McNamara had studied Nguyen Trai as did Ho, he would have understood before and not after the Vietnam war that you must know your enemy. In both McNamara's book *In Retrospect* (1997) and in the Errol Morris film about him *The Fog of War* (2003), he makes a point of this precept, observing that "our misjudgments of friend and foe alike reflected our profound ignorance of the history, culture, and politics of the people in the area, and the personalities and habits of their leaders." For those who deemed McNamara's insight as too little too late, it was not too late for Iraq or Afghanistan. It was simply ignored.

To know thine enemy may be to not have one. Both civilian propaganda and military training are focused on dehumanizing the "other" so that our general aversion to killing is overridden. When the enemy is not a seen as a person, how is it possible to understand his history, culture and politics? Nonbeings do not have history, culture, politics, families, memories, hopes, and dreams. Or they don't when war is finished with them. The tragedy is that the warriors are as wounded as the victims. As Mike, the poet, says in a later chapter, "the ones who died were the lucky ones."

As to the "personalities and habits of their leaders," Ho Chi Minh was a mysterious and avuncular hero who ruled with cunning and affection. The decades of his political travels on behalf of Vietnam independence took him around the world. What U.S. or French leader ever covered so much territory in pursuit of knowing the enemy? Ho Chi Minh is the most underestimated revolutionary leader of modern times, and the ethnocentric blindness toward his strengths defeated the technologically superior French and Americans. The lesson I have taken away from this is the astonishing lengths to which people will go to gain control of their own lives. Examples of this determination abound in Vietnam, perhaps none more dramatic than the hundred-plus kilometers of three-level tunnels dug out in Cu Chi with little more than sticks.

Or the old Austin car that has become a shrine in Hue's Thien Mu Pagoda because it drove Quang Duc to Saigon to burn himself to death in 1963 to protest the repression of Buddhists.

Figure 3.3: Diorama of Cu Chi Tunnels at Cu Chi Site.

Figure 3.4: Enshrined Austin at Thien Mu Pagoda, Hue. Photo: Michael McDonell.

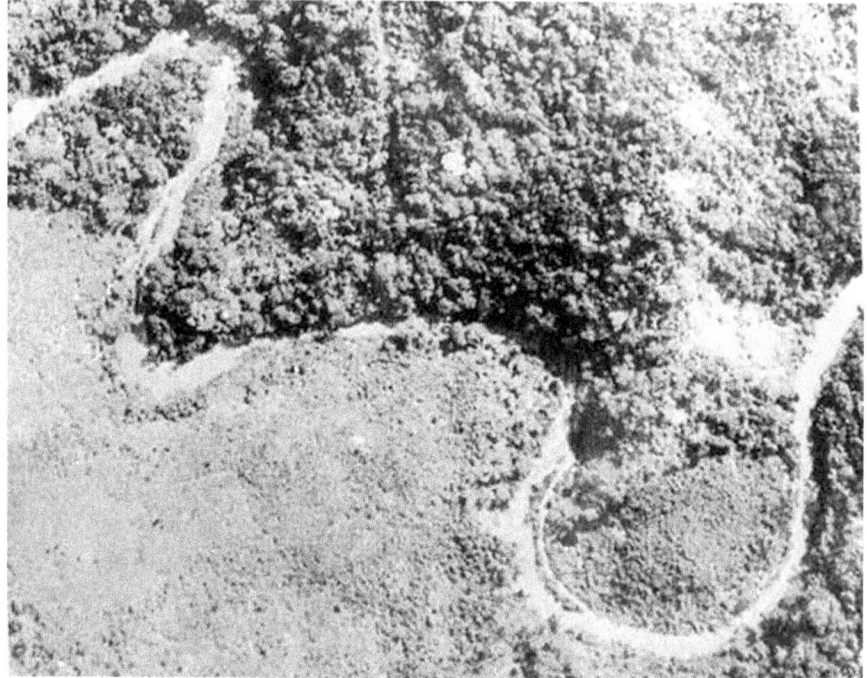

Figure 3.5: Along the Ho Chi Minh Trail.

Or the spectacular supply network of the Ho Chi Minh Trail that the U.S. National Security Agency history of the war called "one of the great achievements of military engineering of the twentieth century" (Hanyok 2002: 94).

Ho Chi Minh "never carried a rifle with him. His only weapons were his tongue, his pen, his native wit, his strong moral fiber, his passionate devotion to the cause of his people, and his determination to achieve his set purpose against all odds." (DeCaro 2003: 69). Never underestimate the will of the people for self-determination, much less underestimate Ho Chi Minh as a luminous example of leadership in the service of liberty.

Chapter 4

Life on Vietnam: "A Glory Preserved in a Wilderness Valley"

This has got to be the best life on earth.
— Lt. Stephen A. Tace, Quantico, Virginia, 7 July 1966

One cold January morning an ad in the local paper caught my eye.
This might be unremarkable in a city newspaper, but on the remote Northern California coast where I lived, 50 miles from the nearest stoplight, it was an odd message among the classifieds for log splitters, well digging and satellite TV.

It was a lazy Superbowl Sunday, so I picked up the phone and called. A woman answered, inviting me to drive the ten miles down Highway 1 to take a look. My snug house just off Main Street in town was filling fast with football fans, so her offer was especially attractive. I drove south on the winding road, turning up a long gravel drive to her house, new construction perched on a seaward ridge with a bluewater view. Only a few thousand people lived along this spectacular 30-mile stretch of Mendocino coast and we all knew each other. This woman was new in town.

We stood in the garage of her half-finished house making small talk and surveying the contents of a beaten up box that held a thick stack of *Life* magazines and dozens of

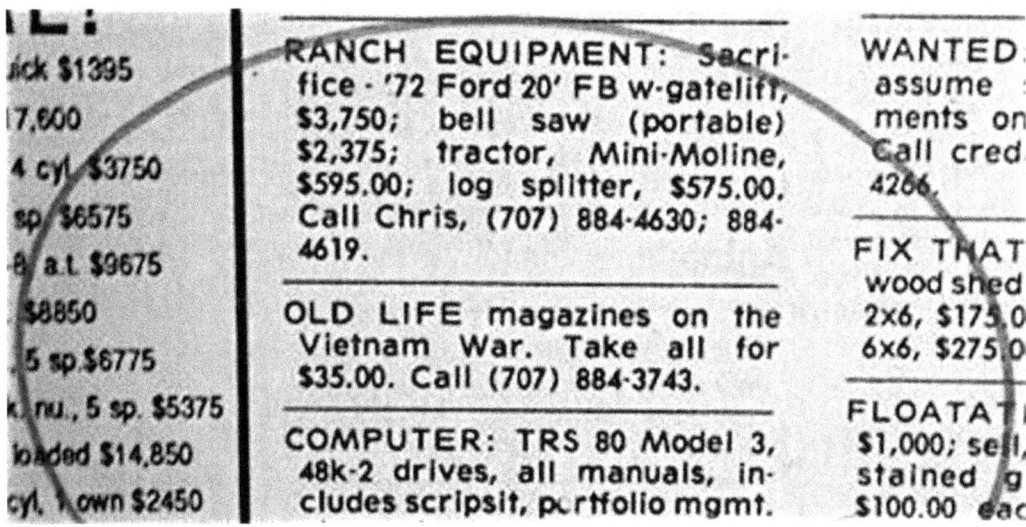

Figure 4.1: Old *Life* magazines on Vietnam War. Take all for $35.00.

assorted clippings. The woman looked to be in her late twenties, too young for the "Vietnam Generation" and probably too old to be the daughter of a vet. Maybe a sister. I told her about my interest in Vietnam and asked about hers.

> Oh, I don't really have any special interest. I found them. I was clearing out my house in Buffalo getting ready to move out here, and I took some junk to the dumpster behind the local shopping center. And there they were, the magazines and other stuff. In the box, next to the trash but not dumped out. Something told me they would mean a lot to somebody, and I didn't know anything about Vietnam and I guess I thought I should. So I took them and moved them all the way out here with me. Kind of crazy, no? But I'm glad you can use them (1985).

I told her about the class on the Vietnam War I was teaching at San Francisco State, and that my part of the course focused on how the war was represented in American popular culture, especially journalism, film and literature. *Life* magazine would be perfect for the students. I thanked her profusely and turned to leave. "Wait. I want you to have these, too. They were with the magazines." She held out a packet of letters. They were letters from a young marine to his parents beginning when he was in Quantico boot camp and ending when he was shot on 4 May 1967. "I don't know what happened to him. I didn't want to sell them with the magazines, being so personal, but I want you to have them. I don't know why they were thrown away."

"It Is a Nice Little Weapon."

Quantico, Virginia 20 July 1966

Dear Mom & Dad,

Well I guess we are right into the schedule now. I lost ten pounds and gained it all back in different places. We are starting to spend more time in the field. Today we fired about 100 rounds from our M14s and the .45. I like the .45, it is a nice little weapon. This is the third time we've fired in the past two weeks and I've really enjoyed it. . . .Take care and when you write please write in <u>full</u> sentences. It is really hard to figure out what you mean sometimes. Take care now, and write soon.

Love, Steve

Back home with the Superbowl crowd I installed myself in the middle of the living room floor to take inventory with archeological care. Twenty-eight *Life* magazines were soon being eagerly passed around the guests, a few of them vets. One fan did not watch a minute of the game over the next two hours as he pored over issue after issue. It was a weighty collection by any measure, concentrated from between 1966 and 1968 and including some of the finest combat photography of Henry Huet, Tim Page, David Douglas Duncan, and Larry Burrows. The box also held a copy of *Newsweek* with a fiery Khe Sanh cover, a *New York Times* "Week in Review" from 21 February 1965 with extensive coverage of the political issues of the war, a miscellaneous gung ho magazine called *Vietnam in Pictures* that was the print equivalent of *The Green Berets* film (John Wayne, 1968), a newspaper clipping of the first boy of their town of Niagara Falls to die in Vietnam, and more.

Then there were the letters. Twenty-three from the young marine to his parents, half a dozen from his wife to his parents, several letters from the mother of the marine that she had sent to him in Vietnam and had been stamped "Return to Sender," and even one letter from the mother and her third grade class to President Lyndon Johnson. It was clear that the contents of this box had belonged to the mother. They had been carefully chosen and saved. Why did she throw them away? Or maybe she died and someone else had tossed them. But who? Why would anyone throw away letters from a war?

Quantico, Virginia. 29 July 1966

Dear Mom & Dad,

Well, it is Thursday night and we are still going like mad. This week we've run night marches, night compass marches, and many other little things. I'm enclosing our schedule for this week so you can see what we do... This coming week should be a real fun one. Monday we have classes in the morning, and then go to the range at noon. We then spend 12 hours firing the machine gun. It should be fun, but it will be late. Then we have these tests and a hike next week. I'll tell you, the Marine Corps earns their money... Right after Christmas we should be shipping out. For most of us it will mean overseas—Viet Nam. Everything here is aimed at combat. It's amazing how you grow used to it. They even set ambushes for us on our hikes. Today was funny. We were marching along a trail to one of our demonstrations. Well, they set a beautiful ambush. We really weren't expecting it—in fact we didn't even have our rifles. Well, about four men opened up with automatic weapons. At the same time they had planted about 500 feet of demo card in the trail. The card blows up on an electrical impulse. We were walking along and all of a sudden the autos opened up and the whole road blew up. This stuff won't hurt you, but it makes a lot of noise and one heck of a lot of dust. I'll tell you, it scared hell out of me to have the ground under me blow up. But it's good, it prepares you... So take care and write soon. I've got to hit the rack now. Tomorrow is another day.

Love, Steve

Having read my way through the contents of the box, a mother's memories of her son's Vietnam combat, I got to know her in a strange way, this middle class devout Catholic

Figure 4.2: Mother's notes on envelope: *This letter arrived N.F. Saturday 27 April 1967. April 23 Hill 881–861 started 12 day fighting. Operation 1. Bighorn 22 April 1967, 2. Shawnee.*

woman with a penchant for military strategy. It was as if I burrowed inside her information space and for a time from the corner of a room I could enter part of the world as she had seen and felt it. I read the notes she made on her boy's letters home, marking the number of days each took to arrive and his locations during that time. She was obviously struggling with the geography, trying to pinpoint where he was and track his movements on the back of the envelopes of his letters: "April 1, Rockpile to Dong Ha. Phu Bai to Da Nang to remain 3 days then to Chu Lai April 3. 2 letters arrived April 6."

I read him begging her not to send any more packages—eight had arrived at once—and trying not to hurt her feelings while asking her to stop "generaling" him. It seems that Mother, the military strategist, offered her tactical suggestions not only to President Johnson. On 11 April 1967, he pleaded:

> *When you write, I really don't care to hear about Viet Nam because it is constantly upon me. When you are away you like to hear about the place you have left. It is really nice to hear about home, and all the little things that happen there. I don't mean to be angry, but please look at it from my point of view.*

Sharing in the personal documents of a mother with a son at war offers insight into some of life's most private moments. Taken as a text, this collection allowed me to reconstruct the way she fought her own battle to understand a country that had sent her only son in harm's way for murky objectives. It was not by accident that *Life* magazine figured so heavily in her worldview.

The Coffee Table War

Michael Arlen (1969) called Vietnam the living room war because it was the first war to be televised into people's homes, but it was a coffee table war, too. No television network matched the viewer numbers of *Life* magazine, which in its heyday reached 36 percent of all U.S. families. With a pass-along rate of four to five people per copy, *Life* achieved an estimated weekly readership of up to 40 million, a greater market penetration than any network now or then. *Life* was ubiquitous, a staple of American culture. It was transparent, part of the wallpaper. At the doctor's or dentist's office, on your neighbor's breakfast table, *Life* magazine was as much a part of American values as motherhood and apple pie, and it played a special role in bringing the Vietnam War home. Hank McGuckin recalls being six years old in 1936 sitting on his mother's lap as she opened the first issue of *Life* and explained how everything would change now that we could see the images of world history as it happened. He was one of five children in a depression-era Central California home and eagerly awaited his place in line each week as the treasured magazine was passed down through the family to him, the youngest devoted reader (2012).

William Prochnau in his study of Vietnam War correspondents *Once Upon a Distant War* called *Life* "the premiere publication of Middle America," "flossy, glossy" and "an unabashed propaganda organ for The American Way or, at least, the view of it as seen by its messianic founder and publisher Henry Luce" (1996: 30). *The New York Times* served the elite readership; *Life* was there for everyone else, unwittingly preparing audiences for the transition to a visual age. In the 1960s *Life* was not just an example of a magazine, but virtually a medium itself. In those years before the domination of television became complete and when the Internet was barely imagined, *Life* represented a transitional medium between print and visual worlds, making it a unique vehicle for popular culture. *Life* was as visual as television, but with the added dimension of written text and the presence of a physical reality that—unlike TV—could be touched, turned and read over and over again. As an artifact of the vanishing material media world, those who come in contact with copies of the vintage magazine handle it like the old world treasure it is, turning pages slowly and carefully in full engagement with its lavish physical beauty of vivid inks and lustrous paper.

Unlike linear print media, "we tend to flip through popular general magazines, looking at them in bits and pieces, backward and forward, alternately grabbed and interrupted by their contents" (Doss, 2001: 7). Print media deal largely with issues; television with symbols. *Life* dealt in both. Still, Doss argues "for all its iconicity and influence, *Life* has been surprisingly unstudied" (4). Because of *Life's* omnipresence and unique graphics plus text formula, there is no question it had considerably greater influence on American public opinion about the Vietnam War than is generally acknowledged. This suited publisher Luce just fine, who had always thought of *Time/Life* as an unofficial arm of the government. Loudon Wainwright (1988) called *Life* a "virtual house organ" in its coverage of World War II over more than two hundred issues. Luce was famously chauvinistic and anti-communist during the Cold War, turning his magazine editorials into open letters to the presidents of the United States, and he knew them all.

Luce's prospectus for *Life* magazine stands as what Alan Brinkley calls "a minor classic of journalistic writing":

> To see life; to see the world; to eyewitness great events; to watch the faces of the poor and the gestures of the proud; to see strange things—machines, armies, multitudes, shadows in the jungle and on the moon; to see man's work—his paintings, towers and discoveries; to see things thousands of miles away, things hidden behind walls and within rooms; things dangerous to come to, the women that men love and many children; to see and take pleasure in the seeing; to see and be amazed; to see and be instructed… Thus to see, and to be shown, is now the will and new expectancy of half mankind. To see, and to show, is the mission now undertaken by a new kind of publication the *Show Book of the World* (2010: 214).

Show Book of the World was rejected as too clumsy and *Life* prevailed over many other suggested names including *Frame, Sight, Picture, Earth, Eye Witness, Canorama, Snaps,* and *Eyes of Time*. *Life* was a smashing success from its 1936 debut, ironically bleeding money the first few years because circulation soared despite early locks on low advertising rates. By the end of 1937 weekly sales had reached 1.5 million—"more than triple the first year circulation of any magazine in American (and likely world) history—while the losses continued to grow" (Brinkley 2010: 221). *Life* overcame the perils of early success and became an American institution, something that can said rarely of media products or platforms.

Into the New Blue Yonder

Studying the mother's magazine collection, made up exclusively of Vietnam-related issues, one can readily see that *Life* went through several very different moods in coverage of the war. Until 1965, the theme could be called "Heroes and Hello Dolly." This is the period when the mother of the young marine wrote to the president:

January 17, 1965

President of the United States Mr. Lyndon B. Johnson
White House, Washington, D.C.
Mr. President:

Last fall one of my pupil's brothers was the first Western New York casualty in Viet Nam. In a letter that he had written to his mother, he stated that the Viet Cong came out of nowhere. My son will soon enter the Marine Corps upon graduation from college and we discussed the element of surprise. Then research started about how Asiatics would fight. We read about the Tartars and their invasion of Europe... To conceal their footsteps or horse markings they use caves... Further research divulged that many times pits were covered with young trees... Their tunnel openings or cave openings may be along these watersheds... The most faithful and policing dog is the Irish Wolfhound... I approached my grade if they would like to write our President a letter on the subject of caves. Enclosed letters are repetitive but one surprised me with his research on chipmunks... 'Chippy' may be worth studying... I wish I were an expert to help more, but please accept our sincere interest in our united nation.

Most respectfully yours,
Mrs. Andrew Tace

At almost the same time that Mrs. Tace was sending LBJ military strategy advice from her class, in the *Life* issue of 8 January 1965, Editor-in-Chief Hedley Donovan asked "L.B.J.: What IS Our Aim in Vietnam?" "Only the president, by insulating our policy and boldly implementing it, can stop the process of Vietnamese disintegration and a growing U.S. mood of to-hell-with-it." This was still early in 1965, with only 23,500 American "advisors" in Vietnam. Donovan was a formidable presence at *Life* and more hawkish than nearly all of his colleagues.

Also in the mother's collection was *The New York Times* "Week in Review" section of 21 February 1965 featuring "The Debate over our Vietnam Policy" that stands even today as a remarkably thorough analysis of the issues, confirming Daniel Hallin's (1986) observation that a careful reader could know what was going on in Vietnam. This was the week Lyndon Johnson said "we seek no wider war," words that would return to haunt him. In February 1965 *The New York Times* broke with the Johnson administration and editorialized "a great debate on the Vietnamese war is now raging all over the United States," concluding that "the course of sanity is to explore the initiatives opened up by Secretary General Thant and General de Gaulle for negotiations to seek a neutralization of Vietnam and all Southeast Asia." A map of U.S. demonstrations in 19 different cities and around the world as well as pointed editorial cartoons look in hindsight like writing on the wall so blindingly clear that the consequences of escalation were inevitable. This "Week in Review" section was the only *New York Times* clipping in the mother's collection.

In the same month, on 26 February 1965, *Life* featured a group photograph of 16 proud and dashing pilots posed in front of a fighter plane next to a dramatic shot of a soaring MIG jet with the caption "Into a New Blue Yonder—Objective Red Sanctuary." This heroic image was not unlike an article from August 1964 on "Heroes of the Gulf of Tonkin." During this time, the war was still portrayed as a "clean" war with vigorous young troops posing proudly. The more clinical air war is featured over the messy military actions on the ground and there was less emphasis on combat coverage with the notable exception of Larry Burrows' 16 April 1965 searing photo essay of a helicopter crew under attack and Horst Faas' 2 July 1965 pictures of war dead and wounded.

1965 was a critical year in the course of the Vietnam War. While in a broader sense there might have been the force of some historical momentum by then, it was still a conflict with fewer than 50,000 U.S. troops committed, a president who stated he sought no wider war, and world opinion strongly opposed to expanded American military involvement. The first 3,500 combat ground troops were committed to provide "security" for Da Nang air base in March 1965, and the critical threshold had been crossed. Most Americans had given little thought to Vietnam before this time, and Hallin points out that the facts about Vietnam policy "emerged in the news in such fragmentary form it is hard to see how the average member of the public … could have had more than a hazy awareness of the momentous decision the administration was making" (1986: 77). The government spin that downplayed troop escalations and bombings further managed the message to the point where daily life inside the consciousness cocoon was comfortable indeed. The invasion of Da Nang took place the day before my 21st birthday. It will come as no surprise which one of those events I remember.

"A Glory Preserved"

1965 was also the year I worked, if you can call it that, for *Time-Life* Books, selling door to door during a college summer. My Dad was skeptical of the ad in the paper, figuring it was a crummy sales job, but I interviewed anyway with an energetic New Yorker who had apparently been exiled to the Cleveland office. During the interview, he took me up in his tiny airplane for a 360′ spin over Cleveland. First impressions notwithstanding, he was a gentleman and I took the job, though I did not think it necessary to tell my Dad about the airplane part.

Here was the sales pitch: for five dollars a month, you would receive five years of *Life* magazine (which barely lasted that long), the *Life Picture Cookbook*, the impressive *Life Atlas of the World*, and a huge but functionally worthless *Webster's Dictionary*. It was when trying to look up obvious words that were somehow missing I learned that any book can call itself a dictionary or even "Webster's."

We spent a week in sales training, a crass variant of the persuasive speaking class I had taken in college. One of the gambits we were taught was to open the massive atlas to a double-page spread of Yosemite with the caption "A Glory Preserved in a Wilderness Valley." We then closed the book and asked with all the smarmy sincerity we could muster:

"Can you describe the picture?"
"Yes, of course. A beautiful waterfall."
"Great. Now, can you recall the words across the top of the page?"
No one remembered, ever.
"A Glory Preserved in a Wilderness Valley!"
"Aha!"

"Now doesn't that just prove the point of *Life* magazine that one picture is worth a thousand words and that you owe it to your family to provide them with this educational and entertaining resource?"

In spite of this compelling logic, during my first week in the field I sold one subscription to my mother and one to her best friend. I felt sick to my stomach going up to people's front doors, and if I got in the living room I agreed with every excuse they gave despite all of the comebacks we had memorized in training. When things were hopeless, our sales manager Johnny would step in and sell ice to an Eskimo. How did he do it? I dreaded waking up in the morning until Friday afternoon of the field week when we were gathered in the small office and told that *Time-Life* was closing the Cleveland operation and we would all be getting a week's severance pay. I had just made my first real sale that afternoon. What luck, but it is a tangled memory. My three weeks working for Henry Luce selling his picture magazine occurred at a time when *Life* published some of its most graphic Vietnam coverage. I remember Yosemite's "glory preserved" to this day, but not a thing about Vietnam either as present in the magazine or in my life.

"We Are Ever Watchful."

Da Nang, Viet Nam 5 Feb 67

Dear Mom and Dad,

It's been about one hour since I put the date on this letter and started to write it. I was sitting here and had just put the date on the letter and I heard an explosion. I looked out and at my second squad position there was a column of smoke. I ran over and discovered that someone had thrown a grenade in the trash barrel ... thank God no one was injured. Very easily someone could have been killed. Other than that it has been a very quiet day. We went to services this morning: an all faith service. The chaplain was Protestant, but it really doesn't matter. We see one so infrequently I'm sure God doesn't mind ...

As I sit here looking out over the Esso Plant my platoon guards it is very peaceful. Every once in a while shots can be heard in the distance but we are not involved. But we are ever watchful. We guard over a million gallons of gasoline and an Esso storage plant. It is valuable and the VC would like to get it...

You should see my house, a hootch as we call them! The Platoon Sgt. and I live above a concrete bunker. Half way up we have wooden walls surrounded by sand bags. The rest of the walls are made from dark green ponchos and the roof is tin. We've got it made, though; we ran a line to the Esso plant and have a light bulb with one of these straw sampan hats as a shade. It's not very big, about 8 feet by 12 feet, but it's home...

Love, Steve

Figure 4.3: Tace map of his location near Esso Plant.

The New York Times may have broken with U.S. government policy early in 1965 with its call for negotiation, but the magazine of the people—*Life*—stood editorially steadfast with the Johnson administration. The very week that the first Marine battalion landed at Da Nang, Hedley Donovan editorialized that "in this latest phase of the Vietnam crisis President Johnson has shown admirable toughness and skill." Called "Shape of a Vietnam Policy," the piece relentlessly belittled opponents of a U.S. policy that "seemed almost entirely isolated by so-called world opinion. Peking was bellicose, Moscow minatory, DeGaulle avuncular,

U Thant inept and intrusive." These "meddlings," wrote Donovan were from the "noisy maw of world opinion" and Johnson had "properly refused to bow to the premature pressure to negotiate." What was at stake, in Donovan's view, was "the credibility in Asia of an American commitment" (12 March 1965). It is little wonder that even a conscientious reader would find the "facts" nearly impossible to sort out.

Still, there was early internal dissent at *Time-Life*, exemplified by reporter Charles Mohr, who was admired by Luce and had served in Washington, India, and beginning in 1962 in Vietnam. Mohr's skeptical reports questioning the optimism of the U.S. military and the strength of the Vietnamese army were routinely reframed by *Time's* managing editor, and Mohr resigned in 1963 and moved to *The New York Times* (Brinkley 2010: 447). Mohr represented the leading edge of changes of heart by Vietnam War reporters. Ralph Graves remembers that "Hedley was no fun to work for–but you could always trust him":

> Hedley's most damaging obstinacy was the Vietnam War. Like the rest of the country in the late sixties, the *Time Inc.* staff was deeply split. But as the months and the casualties and the terrible cost went on and on, more and more of us turned against it. Not Hedley. He had made up his mind. He urged his magazines to do pro-war stories. He challenged our anti-war reporting from Vietnam and Washington. He wrote long signed editorials in *Life* insisting that we must stay the course and that we would triumph in the end (2010: 180).

Donovan stuck with the war almost as long as the generals, and in his memoir credited Graves as one of three editors who had finally changed his mind.

Broadway Goes Into Battle

By October 1965, more than 100,000 U.S. combat troops were in Vietnam and even the editorial writers for the *Times* had for the most part closed ranks behind the president. The window for early resolution had shut. "This is Really War" editorialized *The New York Times*. Still, it is clear that this escalation had not entirely sunk into U.S. public consciousness, nor had the meaning that this was "really war." One document that should be placed in a time capsule to memorialize the mixed messages being received by the American people about the Vietnam War at this crucial time is the 22 October 1965 issue of *Life* magazine. The cover reads "Mary Martin in Vietnam" with a subhead "Vietcong Ambush." The cover photograph by Charles Moore (shot from above and behind) is of Mary Martin wearing a flowing flowered gown, outstretched arms rising as she poses Madonna-like over hundreds of G.I.s seated on the tarmac of Nha Trang air base. In the background is a mammoth B52 bomber that spans the width of the page. Beneath the plane's landing gear in small point type: "Hello Dolly at Nha Trang." Inside the issue are back to back stories "Hello Dolly" and "Hellish Ambush" that juxtapose photo essays

Figure 4.4: Mary Martin in Vietnam. 1965.

of Mary Martin taking her bows at a production of "Hello Dolly" in Nha Trang followed by a four page spread including some of the most horrifying gore from an ambush taking place at about the same time in Bien Hoa, where the "Dolly" troupe had performed several days earlier.

The "Hello Dolly" part of this gruesome synchronicity was the brainchild of producer David Merrick. Shana Alexander (who was along) reported that when the Russians canceled out of a State Department-sponsored "Dolly" tour with the company already in Tokyo, Merrick called the White House to see if the fan-in-chief might want to book the show into Vietnam. "Oh yes, that's the show that has my song in it," replied the president. And thus the arrangements were made. This bizarre theatrical event might not add up to a Machiavellian scheme to make the war look like fun, but it does suggest a certain naivete and denial that "this is really war." At the very least, it was not an inspired decision to put one of America's best loved entertainers in the middle of a combat zone, but somehow it seems the war was not yet taken very seriously. Shana Alexander (1965) wrote "it was difficult for me to view the whole tour as anything but an episode in a musical comedy." Of course, she also wrote of being there during the "very height of the war," and as we now know 1965 was the very beginning of U.S. involvement, which reached half a million troops in a little over two years, about the time the young marine's letters home take a darker turn.

"It's a Lousy War But What Can We Do?"

10 Feb 67

Dear Mom & Dad,

The last couple of days have been hectic. I had a man wounded, more sick, burned down parts of a vill and promoted people.

First of all we are supposed to be in the New Years truce. But that doesn't mean anything, they still shoot at us. Yesterday we had a patrol out and one man hit a booby trap. He took shrapnel in the face and legs, but he'll be alright. He'll have a few nice scars but nothing real serious. It really burns you up when you lose people and you have no way of shooting back. Last nite we were firing illumination from our mortars which is routine. But about 2:00 a.m. I was awakened to find that they had started a fire down in the vill. So I took 12 men and two corpsmen and went down to investigate. We had completely burned down two homes so this morning the civil affairs officer came out and we had to go over the whole thing so a claim can be filed. And I have my usual paper work. I'm willing to bet that the U.S. uses more paper than bullets to fight a war. You would be amazed.

So such is my happy routine. It's good though and I really love having my own platoon. They are a good group of men and work hard. Some are only 18 or 19, but they age fast here. It is simply a case of grow fast or perish... Well that's about it for now so take care and write soon. Mail does mean a lot to the men here.

Love, Steve

In March 1965, the first modest numbers of ground troops were deployed to Da Nang, but the end of that year there were 184,000 combat troops in Vietnam. By the end of 1966 the number had risen to 385,000, peaking in 1968 with more than 536,000. This rapid and massive escalation under the command of a president who sought no wider war was

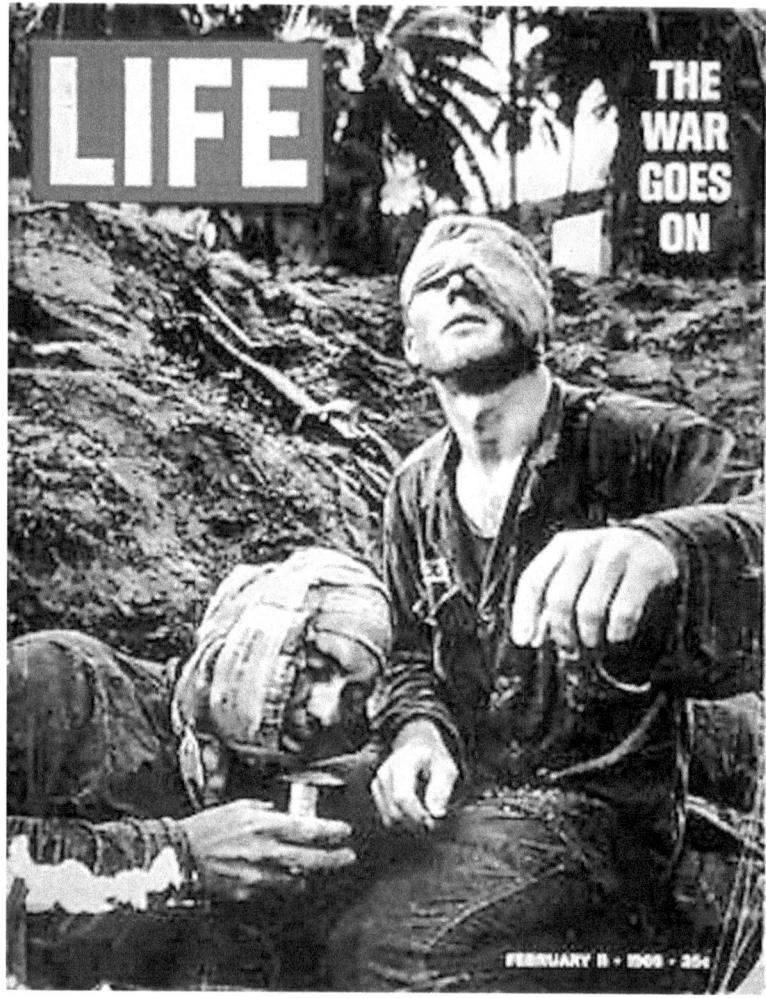

Figure 4.5: "The War Goes On" February 1966.

accompanied by growing anti-war sentiment. The administration's public opinion management strategy during this period, largely successful, was to avoid any appearance of crisis by making all policy decisions appear routine, incremental and automatic (Hallin 1986). *Life* published 28 covers on Vietnam between 1964 and 1969, half of those in the years 1966 and 1967, the period of most rapid troop build-up. The mood of "heroes and Hello Dolly" was clearly changing, shown starkly in the 11 February 1966 black and white cover by Henry Huet of two wounded and heavily bandaged G.I.s with the caption "The War Goes On."

A weariness was creeping into the text. The long and gritty photo essay inside was the most sobering coverage to date. Sometimes you really have to wonder if Henry Luce read his own magazine during this period. John MacArthur observes:

Such was the self-confidence of the United States during Luce's American Century. Horrifying pictures of war could be published, but the Johnson administration kept sending more troop ships. Uncensored reporting seemed to shock virtually no one's conscience, and certainly not the editors of *Time, Inc.* (2004: 126).

The most graphic *Life* cover and photo story ever published on Vietnam carried the date 26 October 1966. Shot by Larry Burrows, later to die in the war, and Co Rentmeester, the cover read "Invasion DMZ Runs into the Marines." The images suggest something else. On the cover is a head shot of a tattered Marine cradling the head of another marine so bandaged that only his nose can be seen. The story inside includes some of the most vivid war photography ever published in the mainstream media. This is the Vietnam that the young marine encountered in February 1967 shortly after he arrived in country stationed near Da Nang.

"Some Day Those Who Are the Cause of This Will Pay."

23 February 1967

Dear Mom and Dad,

The last few days have been very busy indeed. One of my men's father died and we were occupied with getting him off on emergency leave. We had just returned from an operation where we were used as a blocking force. It's like a deer drive, we sit while others drive towards us. We didn't catch anything, though.

Last nite we got hit. A lot of firing and all but we didn't get any bodies. No one here was hit so we were lucky there.

Today I went to the rear for a court martial. While back there I was talking with a friend from Quantico and he had some very bad news for me. Al stepped on a mine and has lost both legs. It really burns me that these gooks won't come out and fight but they ruin a man with a stinking booby trap. Another friend of mine was killed 36 hours after we got here. It's a lousy war but what can we do. They tell us to make friends when I'd rather go down to the village with a flame thrower. That really burned me up about Al, but there is nothing I can do now. I'm trying to get his address and will let you know when I do. But some day those who are the cause of this will pay. I'll do my best to see to that... It's 10:00 p.m. and time to check the post. I go around and make sure all positions are manned and all are awake. So take care now and write soon. I hope you are both well and keeping busy. I do.

Love, Steve

This personal disillusionment of one Marine was a microcosm of growing dissent both private and public with the course of the war, but there was a long way to go before it was over. By the end of 1966, 5,008 Americans had died, by the end of 1967 16,000. By the end of 1969, the figure was over 40,000, with more than 18,000 U.S. combat fatalities yet to come as well as millions of Vietnamese, most of them civilians. *Life* communicated a steady stream of mixed messages through these years. The official editorial stance of the magazine was supportive of the administration nearly until the end. *Life* published 36 Vietnam editorials. Stubborn Editor-in-Chief Hedley Donovan was something of an expert on Vietnam and had been there several times. While deferring of necessity to his expertise, most of his editorial staff were opposed to the war long before *Life* made its own anti-war statement of sorts in 1969. When Donovan endorsed a second term for Richard Nixon in 1972, 100 of 145 *Life* staffers signed a petition in support of McGovern (Doss 2001: 17). So in an official editorial way, *Life* was a conservative if not hawkish publication. The inside articles conveyed a more balanced message, but the pictures told a very different story.

Picture Magic

In the early 1930s, Henry Luce became preoccupied with what he called "picture magic" and with the idea of the "candid camera." He intuitively understood the power of photojournalism, though the idea for a picture magazine is actually credited to his wife Clare Booth Luce. The creation of such a magazine depended on several technological innovations: the introduction of small cameras (specifically the Leica), the ability of paper companies to make coated paper in rolls, and a process for quick drying inks. These technologies came together in the 23 November 1936 inaugural issue of *Life*. Interestingly, the format owed much to the movies. Luce had introduced a monthly filmed newsreel *The March of Time* as a promotion for *Time* magazine, and he had his staff work backward from the film format in designing *Life*. Luce wanted *Life* to be "all the newsreels on your knee." Picture stories were called "acts" in a peculiar theatrical reference. Luce wanted *Life* to embody "charm" and "relaxation." Above all, "*Life* is here to inform," he wrote, "indeed, it exists to harness a whole new art of communication to the business of informing." Doss claims that "*Life's* structuring of visual experience was understood by Luce and others at the magazine to be a new language, difficult, as yet unmastered, but incredibily powerful" (2001: 11). Luce's goal was to be nothing less than the Master of American Media, a goal that he did indeed for a time attain.

But how did *Life* convey the message of the Vietnam War? Did the pictures tell the story? The text? The editorials? How did it function as a medium to bring the coffee table war home? Much attention has been given to the differences between print and television as communication mediums. Print is more linear, more complex, capable of sustained information and argumentation. Of course, it can also exploit the tabloid style, but tabloid headlines that can be inhaled in one breath are closer to images than words. Television as a medium—and screens in general—privileges symbols, images, and dramatic narrative, and it appeals to a much wider and "down-market" audience than print. Television blurs news and entertainment with greater ease than print. Television is the medium of the sound bite, and they have been getting shorter for years. Screen images are fleeting, ephemeral. Our collective consciousness of memorable television moments is a rather short list, indeed. Television news was far more consistently supportive of administration Vietnam policy than the major newspapers. On television, the war was presented as a morality play, "while the coverage of a paper like the *Times* had a dry and detached tone, television coverage presented a dramatic contrast between good and evil" (Hallin 1986: 109). Today's screen convergence complicates the media landscape, but media platforms still embody their own messages.

Where does this leave *Life* as a medium? With text and photography, it had elements of both television and print with several additional features, creating a visual/verbal montage. Image persistence is one distinctive feature of *Life* Vietnam photography. Unlike fleeting television footage, the combat pictures of a *Life* cover or story could be on view for weeks. Images could be glanced in passing or studied and reread, with details emerging over time. *Life*'s combat photography was sending a message quite different from its editorial position in the sense that combat photography is almost by definition anti-war. At the same time, the very persistence and ubiquity of *Life* might function as a message frame that in fact neutralizes—even legitimizes—extreme images and renders them more routine and less dramatic. Combat photography within the context of a middle-brow magazine that featured all manner of other subjects from fashion to football becomes just another set of pictures. The process of desensitization to images has become so pervasive over the years that attention itself has become media's most highly prized commodity.

All media seem to work in mysterious ways because there is rarely a one-to-one correspondence between a message in any medium and its observable effect. It is the exception for any one message to register a significant impact on the viewer or listener. Typically, any single message is but one piece of the vast environment of information bits where our larger message on any given topic is an aggregate of data from a variety of sources, all subject to the machinations of our own perceptual and political filters. With this in mind, we cannot know precisely what effect the *Life* magazine collection had on the thinking of the mother of the young marine, but we do know that they were important enough for her to keep over many years.

One Week's Dead

It took *Life* until 1969 to publicly turn the anti-war corner with its classic issue "The Faces of the American Dead in Vietnam." The editorial staff had always been "dismayed" (Loudon Wainwright's word) at the way the magazine had covered the war and "many on the staff felt that much more should be said, that *Life* should speak up for withdrawal" (1988: 407). The conservative tilt of the magazine persisted despite Luce's somewhat unexpected death in 1967. Wainwright had the idea of doing a story on all of the Americans killed in one week, an idea he knew would be difficult to get past Hedley Donovan. They chose the week of 28 May to 3 June 1969, and dispatched stringers and correspondents to get in touch with all 242 families and do a photo roundup. Donovan was not to know of the project until the basic layout was completed. Collecting the photographs was filled with "heartbreaking ironies," but only about 20 families wanted nothing to do with the idea. When new Managing Editor Ralph Graves finally called Donovan in to see the preliminary pages and copy, he took a long time reviewing the material, finally saying to Graves "All right. Run it" (2010: 110). And with those words Donovan both changed *Life*'s editorial policy toward the war and sanctioned an unforgettable issue of the magazine, with page after page of yearbook size pictures—12 pages in all—of boys from across the United States who had died in a single week in Vietnam. It was to become an often-repeated design format for commemoration of multiple fatalities of victims of drunk drivers, HIV/AIDS, and both civilian and military dead in subsequent wars in Iraq and Afghanistan. *Life* received more than 1,300 letters about "One Week's Dead," reflecting the diversity of its readership from accusations that it was "supporting the anti-war demonstrators who are traitors to this country" to exhortations that "it should be plastered all over this country, on every billboard, telephone pole, storefront, and even American flagpoles. Wherever people go, particularly congressmen, they should be engulfed in this sea of faces."

On 29 December 1972, *Life* magazine published its final issue after 1,862 consecutive weeks. "We persevered as long as we could see any realistic prospects," said Donovan. With its former advertising dollars diverted to television and printing and postage costs soaring, the magazine had been losing money for years, and there was no saving it. Luce had seen early on that *Life* might not have the endurance of *Time* or *Fortune*: "*Life* might only last

Figure 4.6: One Week's Dead, 27 June 1969.

20 years… Every issues of *Life* is like bringing out a new show on Broadway" (Brinkley 2010: 455). Several attempts at resurrection have been short-lived. We cannot know precisely what role *Life* played in the formation of public opinion during the Vietnam War, but there is no question its vivid and compelling coverage made a difference. Reflecting back to the mother of the young marine, it struck me as I was writing this chapter nearly four decades later in Hanoi that my own son was visiting Hue, Da Nang, and Marble Mountain as a tourist, not a soldier. Vietnam won the peace at a great price. The searing images of *Life* have not been equaled in American media coverage of the wars that have followed, and we are left to wonder what difference similarly graphic depictions in mainstream media might have made on subsequent U.S. military interventions.

"Don't Worry"

5 Apr '67

Dear Mom & Dad,

Since I wrote last we've been out again. I went out on a short two day operation here at Da Nang. We got back last nite and are moving out again tomorrow for Chu Lai and Operation Canyon. We will probably be out about four or five days, so don't worry again if you don't hear from me for a while. Don't worry though because I'm fine …

Enclosed is a money order for $30.00. It's all I can afford this month but I'll try to send more later.

Well, that's about all for now. I am tired and tomorrow will be a long day. So take care and keep writing. All is well here and happy. I am healthy and well so don't worry. I won't be able to write for a while so don't worry. Take care and don't work too hard.

Love, Steve

Lt. Stephen Tace saw some of the heaviest combat of the Vietnam war and was in the area at the time of the heaviest spraying of deadly Agent Orange, which they were told was mosquito spray to keep malaria down. In the six weeks between 15th March and 4th May 1967 from the evidence of his letters Tace was constantly on the move, covering an area that included the Rockpile, Da Nang, Hue, Dong Ha, Cam Lo, Razorback, Phu Bai, Chu Lai, Hill 881–861, and the O Lau River. He fought in combat operations Canyon, Bighorn, and Shawnee. The last letter from Vietnam in the mother's collection is dated 21 April 1967.

Dear Mom & Dad,

Well here we are again on the move. I got back from the last little operation only to pack up and move again. Now we are northwest of Hue and due to go out on an operation tomorrow.

We've been on Operation Big Horn and I think this new one is called Shawnee, but I'm not sure. It doesn't really matter. Little is known from a name. Apparently this will be quite a big operation, though… That's about all I have for now so once again I must say don't worry if you don't hear from me for a while. I don't know how long this next operation will be. The word is anywhere from 3 to 30 days, so take care and don't worry. All is fine and I am healthy and fine. Take care now and write soon.

Love, Steve

Then the letters stop. The next letter in the collection was written 4 May 1967, from the mother. It reads "Steve, we hope all is well with you and your platoon. News is not good for Marines." The letter was returned in an envelope stamped "Returned to Sender—Moved Left No Address." The collection ends with a yellowed newspaper clipping with the headline "Falls Residents Visit Son Wounded in War."

Mr. and Mrs. Andrew Tace have returned from St. Albans, L.I. where they visit their son, 2nd Lt. Stephen Tace, USMC, who is a patient in the Naval Hospital there.

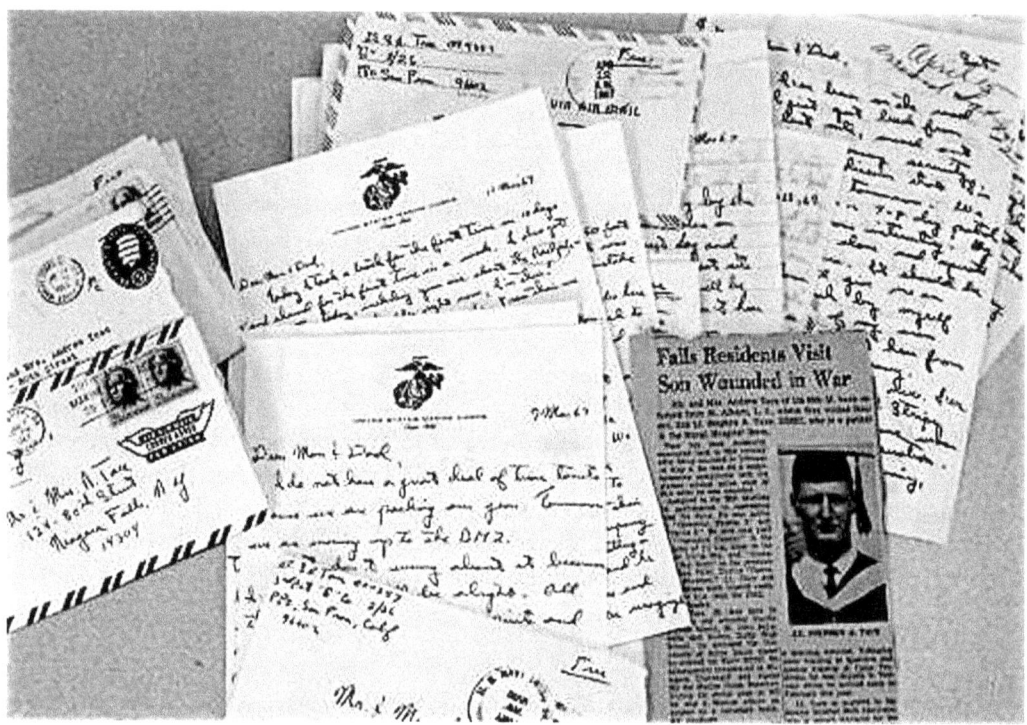

Figure 4.7: Stephen Tace letters and clipping.

Tace was medically evacuated to the United States after being wounded in Vietnam on 4th May on a reconnaissance assignment with his platoon several miles west of Hue.

This abrupt end to the collection prompted me to go to some lengths to learn what had happened to the young marine and his mother. Was he an alienated Vietnam vet living in the woods? Was he a businessman? Or maybe he was dead or in prison? Through a fortuitous series of pre-Google telephone inquiries, including mistaken identities and distant relatives, I located him and his family and made the call. They were surprised but gracious hearing from a woman on the other side of the country who had come into possession of a box that had been left for trash in Buffalo. His wife Heather was especially curious and appreciative and we have maintained a friendship over the years. And Stephen Tace? The once young marine was a career officer, a colonel assigned to NATO. And the box? The collection? "Yes it belonged to my mother and when she died I threw it out. Do whatever you want with the letters and then burn it. It doesn't mean anything to me." When I was able to return the letters to Heather and their daughter Noelle during a memorable 2010 meeting in New York, I was glad I had resisted his request.

Stephen and Heather settled in the military community of Virginia Beach where they raised three children while Steve pursued his career with the Marine Corps. In 1995, seven years after our conversation about the letters, he was on assignment in Istanbul where he suffered a massive heart attack and died at the age of 51. On 30 October 2010, the Veteran's Administration formally recognized an association between Agent Orange and ischemic heart disease. Heather and Stephen Tace's son Marc died of muscular dystrophy at the age of 19. While Agent Orange is implicated in many neurological and neuromuscular conditions, the link with muscular dystrophy in children has not been officially established.

Chapter 5

Reading Graham Greene: A Promise to the Dead

Sooner or later... One has to take sides. If one is to remain human.
Graham Greene, *The Quiet American* (174)

On a rainy April morning in 1993, Professor Nguyen Ngoc Hung and his driver picked me up for the half-hour ride to the Hanoi Foreign Language College on the outskirts of the city. It was the first time I had seen him since his U.S. visit in 1989 marking the broadcast of the *60 Minutes* profile. By 1993, Hung was director of the Vietnamese Language Center, where everyone from foreign students to diplomats and spies received first-rate language instruction. On this grey Hanoi day nearly two decades after the end of the war Professor Hung the war hero is a modest mandarin and an accommodating host. As director of Hanoi's premier language college Hung offers an oasis for Americans seeking a connection with Vietnam. After a dusty drive out Nguyen Trai Road where the horn-honking made me want to pull my ears off, we turn into the Institute's parking lot, one of only two cars among a thousand bicycles. The Institute was then housed in a crumbling former army barracks, softened by touches of open colonial architecture that allowed the occasional damp breeze to drift through the battered shutters.

The institute enrolls 4,000 students training to be teachers and translators. Hung suggests it takes about three months of study to get a foothold on the Vietnamese language, an estimate I have found to be far too conservative. Most of the institute's teaching faculty have just been intensively retrained from teaching Russian to teaching English. The dissolution of the Soviet Union in 1991 signaled the end of its outsize influence in Vietnam, and the need for Russian language training disappeared overnight. I told Hung that in the United States the teachers might just lose their jobs. "Oh, we would not do that."

Hung has asked me to speak to a class of second-year English students. Fifty beaming faces are crammed into four long rows. I say a few words of introduction and open the floor for questions. A hand slowly rises.

"Why did you come to Hanoi?"
"To see you, of course!"
Bursts of giggles and the mischievous reply.
"I was born in Hanoi to see you!" More giggles.

These students give frequent recitations in language classes and are poised at public speaking, more so than some of their American counterparts. More questions: "How old are you?" This is the question asked frequently of foreigners in Vietnam not because of impertinence but because knowing one's age is critical in selecting the proper form of address. The first two words of a Vietnamese greeting establish the relationship of the speakers in terms of age, kinship, gender, role and status. It is the ultimate in concise high context communication that determines the protocol for all subsequent conversation. Whether I am addressed as *em* (a younger person of the same generation, child, or woman in a romantic relationship) *chi* (older woman of the same generation), *ba* (middle-aged married woman) *co* (female teacher/older woman) or *di* (a woman as old as one's mother) signals immediately the speaker's assessment of my relative age and hence our relationship status. Over my years visiting Vietnam I have gone from *chi* to *ba* to *co*, which would be more unsettling if not for the fact that age confers respect in Vietnam, not the opposite.

"You Had Me at Hello."

There are specific terms of address for almost anyone you can imagine, including the younger brother of your father (*Chu*) or mother (*Cau*) or the wife of your mother's younger brother (*Mo*). To complicate matters further some of these forms differ in northern and southern dialects. Mr. Huy tells me the protocol gets especially awkward when a wife is older than her husband, which precludes the usual husband-wife terms of *chi* and *em*, because *chi* is assumed to be younger. As a result, couples in this situation call each other by their given names, and it reverberates through how the rest of the family addresses them. Frances Fitzgerald described the cultural importance of Vietnamese pronouns:

> In the Vietnamese language there is no word that corresponds directly to the Western personal pronoun I, *je, ich*. When a man speaks of himself he calls himself "your brother," "your nephew," "your teacher," depending upon his relationship to the person he addresses. The word he uses for the first person (*toi*) in the new impersonal world of the cities originally denoted "subject of the king." The traditional Vietnamese did not see himself as a totally independent being, for he did not distinguish himself as acutely as a Westerner from his society (and, by extension, the heavens). He did not see himself as a "character" formed of immutable traits, eternally loyal to certain principles, but rather as a system of relationships, a function of the society around him (1972: 30).

The importance of this linguistic detail can hardly be overstated in attempting to explain east-west differences. There are vast practical consequences between languages that enmesh the individual in a web of relationships and the I-centric structure of Indo-European grammars. Add to that the subject-verb-object syllogistic imperative of languages like English, and the expansionist individualism suggested by the grammar stands in stark relief against the holism characteristic of Eastern thinking. The Confucian values of kinship and hierarchy result in a way of being in the world that is antithetical to the rugged individualism that found its most perfect expression in the conquest of America's western frontier and native population.

Professor Hung's class had one more question: "Do you have any children?" I pass around a picture of my son and daughter and give each student a token sticker from my university, which they receive like great treasures. Interest in my children has always been foremost in questions from Vietnamese students, who have a wholehearted devotion to family. The class stood in unison to bid me farewell. I was no doubt one of the few foreigners and maybe the only American they had met and their curiosity about the world beyond Vietnam was boundless. I never forgot the warmth and radiance of that first class, although it was many years before I would return.

A Life Interrupted

One of Professor Hung's public recognitions is a profile Peter Jennings devoted to him in *The American Century*. Hung speaks:

> Life was pretty peaceful in Hanoi until 1964, when the American bombers came. I lived there with my family; my father worked and my mother stayed home and took care of us children. I knew that a war was underway in South Vietnam, but it seemed very far away and we children heard very little about it. When the bombing started, suddenly the war became something real, something very close to us that was threatening our lives. My brother and I had to evacuate to the countryside to study (1998: 400).

Figure 5.1: Nguyen Ngoc Hung, 1974.

Hung was soon drafted, leaving his studies at Hanoi Foreign Language College and serving for six years in the North Vietnamese Army.

> I didn't really want to go because I was very happy at school, but of course I went anyway. I went into training where I learned to handle an AK-47, antitank weapons, bayonets and hand grenades. Army life was very different from student life, and at first it was hard for me to catch up with the guys from the countryside who had been used to farm work and were very strong. But gradually I became a tougher person and a more responsible person as well. For us the army was like a family (1998: 400).

For the long journey south he stuffed his dictionaries, novels, diaries, and guitar on top of the survival gear in a 55-pound pack, soon abandoning these tokens of culture one by one along the arduous trail. "In the end, I threw away the dictionaries then the books and then the diaries, you know. And last of all the guitar went, too" (Safer 1990: 45). Hung saw five years of combat, most fiercely during the bloody 1972 battle of Quang Tri waged mostly between North and South Vietnamese troops—in other words, between brothers. When the war ended in 1975 Hung returned to college in Hanoi and then on to graduate work in England and Australia, earning an M.A. in language teaching and making him one of the most fluent speakers of English in Vietnam. His younger brother was not as lucky, becoming one of more than 300,000 Vietnamese soldiers missing in action. Hung lost 17 cousins in the war, and spent nearly 30 years searching for the remains of his brother.

> My father would like to go and find him, but I explained to him how difficult it is to find—you know, a missing body in the jungle. You know, in Vietnam we worship the ancestors and the dead. And the dead mean a lot to the living.
>
> *(60 Minutes* 1989)

As we walk through the Language Institute campus 20 years later, I wonder how it feels for Hung to be enveloped by the peaceful landscape that he has done so much to create, so far from the terrifying memories of B52 raids and long hungry days. He recalls that in the end it was not even victory to the victors.

> At first we thought we had won the war…but I look at this place and realize we did not. It was something like fighting with somebody in your own house with all the precious furniture around you. And after the stranger leaves, you look at the different things in your house. And they are all broken. The war actually took place in our house. It was a very sad thing.
>
> (Safer 1990: 112)

Hung's spirit still fills the air of this campus many years later, a school now all grown up from a language institute into Hanoi University with more than 10,000 students in languages, literature, tourism, business, international studies, and information technology. It was through Hung that I met another distinguished educator Nguyen Xuan Vang in 2001 at a memorable dinner at the Metropole Hotel, that elegant shrine to French colonialism. Vang, now a high official with the Ministry of Education and Training, was then the rector of Hanoi University, and his offer of a visiting professorship opened the door to the year I spent there 2007–2008 as a Fulbright Senior Scholar.

Through the Asian Looking Glass

I was raised in the rust-belt city of Cleveland and have split my career between universities on East and West U.S. coasts, one a large, humble union-shop public institution steeped in master plans and bureaucracy, the other a small quirky private college with a big ego where, as Heraclitus had it, nothing is permanent but change. Both have progressive political histories and oddly conservative organizational cultures. Headed for Hanoi, I thought that with this triangulation of geographic and academic experience under my belt I was well-equipped for university life in Vietnam. Nothing could have been farther from the truth upon entering the world of "unknown unknowns" that had certainly caught Donald Rumsfeld and many of his fellow interventionists—notably Robert McNamara—by surprise.

Take the simple matter of getting the answer to a yes or no question. One of my first lessons was that in Vietnam "yes"—even when accompanied by vigorous head nodding—does not mean "yes," but something more like "I heard and possibly understood what you just said." I never heard "no" from anyone, a word that does not seem to be an option in polite company. In the United States, this might be described as passive aggressive behavior; in Vietnam it is just behavior. In some weird way it is like being in England, where "I'm sorry" is as likely to mean "I'm sorry you are such a twit" as it is to stand for a sincere apology.

In preparation for my visiting Fulbright year, I peppered Vang with emailed questions and he patiently answered them all. As the time grew closer, I sensed that I was driving him crazy and I was wrapping up many years as a beleaguered college administrator, so I was preoccupied as well. I later learned that Hung and Vang are exceptional if not unique in their fluency in English and understanding of (especially United States and Australian) culture. Most scholars of their generation were sent to the former Soviet Union for graduate work. Hung and Vang somehow avoided that path in favor of the English-speaking world, a bet that paid off much better in the long run. Observing Hung's language skills, Morley Safer quipped "I get the feeling he is not fully trusted in Hanoi, his English is too good" (1989). On the contrary, both Hung and Vang achieved great distinction in both education and government careers.

Only after several consecutive months in Vietnam did I realize I had not even known the right questions to ask Vang. One of my faulty assumptions was that all universities run on a credit-based system that permits some latitude in course selection, typically including free-choice electives outside of the major field of study. While the Ministry of Education and Training (MOET) has legislated that Vietnamese universities convert to a credit-based system, few have done so. This means that students enter a field of study and spend 20 hours a week for three or four years memorizing a set curriculum. No electives permitted, exams mean everything. A student in this system cannot independently decide to take a media class or any other class as an elective. Any work aside from the prescribed course of study is extra, and any motivation to do such work disappears the moment exams in the required courses loom on the horizon. I was dumbfounded upon learning that students were not receiving actual "credit" for my media classes, although it did help to account for the spotty attendance and reluctance to write papers. My reaction was that they did not need to bring me 10,000 miles to teach noncredit courses to their students, but then again I guess they did. It was a first step. It took three more years for our media courses to be approved for full credit, but it did indeed come to pass.

I meticulously wrote my syllabi months in advance and I responded to and initiated emails about dates, contact hours, audiovisual needs, and anything else I could think of. Once I was on the actual campus, Vang delegated minding me to Mr. Huy, whose main responsibility seemed to be keeping foreign students and scholars out of trouble. Huy did his best and we became close friends, but on a regular basis some group or another of foreign students was out of control, most often the Russians or Mongolians who stayed in the euphemistically named "guest residence" on campus. I abandoned living in the guest residence after a 6 a.m. visit in my toilet by a scrawny mottled rat. Yes, it happens—rats come up through the plumbing. I was totally traumatized. The Vietnamese thought it was hilarious. Miss Binh's grin was so wide she could barely speak: "Oh we are very famous for our rats!!" Mr. Huy said it is interesting that people from the United Kingdom and Australia are bothered by the rats but not students from China and Mongolia. "Huy, do I look Mongolian to you?" When the guesthouse worker came up to help with the situation, he ceremoniously flushed the toilet without even lifting the lid and said: "He back on street now."

The day that class is scheduled to begin Huy delivers the news that I will not be starting class this Wednesday as expected but "in a week or two." And my one class will start at 12:30 instead of 12:00, because 12:00 is unlucky. At least that's what I think he said. The academic calendar here is clearly outside of my American experience. In every university I know the academic calendar is sacrosanct and planned years in advance. I call my friend Gerry to ventilate. Gerry is a fixture in Hanoi's small film community and with his right hand man Hung does amazing programming at his *Cinematheque*. He knows everyone in the diplomatic community and is filled with great stories of intrigue. We met through mutual friend Peter Davis, director of *Hearts and Minds*, who said "You two have got to meet each other." Gerry was heaven sent, introducing me to Hanoi, showing me how to grocery shop and find a pair of size nine shoes in a country of size five feet. When I explain my plight at the University Gerry does not exactly say "I told you so," although he had told me so about the baffling situations I would encounter. "Relax, Carol. Don't take it so seriously. Nobody else is." While everyone likes the cachet of hosting a visiting scholar, at the same time "you're just something else they have to do." One popular expat saying goes that if you stay in Vietnam a month, you will write a book; if you stay six months, you will write an article; and if you stay a year, you will write nothing at all.

I reflect on the epigraph that introduces this book: "God save us always from the innocent and the good" (1955: 20). I am not sure if I qualify as either or both at this point, and I have no idea what is going on around me most of the time. There is something relaxing about not understanding what people are saying; it removes any pressure to participate beyond nodding and smiling. I will do a lot of nodding and smiling over the next year.

A/V Around the World

I am scheduled to teach two classes, one on "The War Film" and the other an "Introduction to Media Studies: History, Theory, Practice." I reviewed virtually the entire media and film literature in preparation for these classes and found little that even had a chance of translating to Vietnamese culture. The short list of readings I eventually selected did not fare much better.

"The War Film" class meets today at 3 p.m. for the first time. There are 81 students on the roster. I go to Huy's office about 2:30 and he is nowhere to be found. By 2:45 I am edgy because I do not even know where the class is being held, let alone if the audiovisual support I requested ("Yes, yes") will materialize. (It did not.) The office assistant Binh seems to take great delight in tracking down Huy, and she comes back from her search smiling. "He was sleeping in his car because he was drinking beer." Huy drags in behind her, looking sheepish and unsteady. "I only had two beers with Mr. Bao and the finance officer who invited us to lunch." He adds later that he thinks there had been a few whiskeys as well, which helps account for the "only two beers" wobble as we head for the classroom. Huy and Bao have a few beers most days during the long civilized Vietnamese lunch break. As far as I can tell, everyone arrives about 8 a.m. and breaks shortly after 11 for lunch, returning about 2 p.m. and leaving for the day by 4. I am sure they think it peculiar that I came in at midday when the campus is deserted and stay into the evening, but no one says anything. So many years of teaching in a graduate program offered mainly at night has programmed my biological clock with a resistance to the early morning hours. It was several months before I even became aware that no one was around because I was on an opposite schedule. When I learned sitting at my desk via email that my father had died, it was lunchtime and the building was deserted and in a blind panic the only door I could find open was the president's assistant, who helped me phone the United States on their international line.

When we finally locate the classroom the heat is suffocating and the air is not moving despite several ceiling fans. Students drift in. Since I am my very own department, administrative communication is rocky and students had a hard time learning where the class was to be held. I begin setting up the computer and projector I have hauled over from the United States, muttering to myself that this just about figures when it comes to tech support. Huy repeatedly calls the IT head Dung, who was supposed to arrive half an hour ago. I am feeling very much at home and not in a good way, stranded by A/V. I consider it a miracle given my long experience with A/V services that any media classes that depend upon working equipment are successfully taught at all. Anywhere. I anticipate with dread the production lab part of the other class. I cannot believe what I have gotten myself into. Worse, I realize I do not even *know* what I have gotten myself into.

Dung from IT arrives and the projector immediately stops working. The speakers had not materialized so you cannot hear anything anyway. The image is 32' TV-size, not movie size. The 200 seat air-conditioned auditorium with state of the art projection I was promised is a distant dream. I learn months later that it actually existed but for some reason was not available as a classroom. Those who still imagine Vietnam as a peasant culture may think of A/V glitches as fancy problems to have, but Vietnam today is plenty fancy where it wants to be. Most of the universities I spoke at around the country had state-of-the-art facilities, often reserved for visiting scholars and public officials.

Huy is working hard to keep things from totally falling apart. Somehow we make it through the class, depending upon the kindness of strangers—in this case the patient students. While I show clips from upcoming films I mentally compose the polite memo I am going to write to everyone whose name I can spell detailing the technical specs for each of my classes. I feel like turning around and heading back to New York until I remember that the technical support situation is not much better there. By the time class ends, Huy has turned the corner to hangover mode, his eyes red and watery. It is a toss-up between Huy and me as to who is happier that class is over and we have dodged pedagogical disaster, at least for this week. It did not last.

Dear Huy,

Let me say at the outset that I do not want to be a troublemaker and I don't want to get on anyone's bad side, but I am obviously not getting through regarding the needs for the film class. I reread my last memo on this subject, and believe that I was not sufficiently clear about things like screen size and audio for a class of eighty.

Yesterday's class started forty-five minutes late because they brought the wrong equipment. When I was told that I would have a 'screen' for this class, I did not imagine that it would be a television screen, even a nice flat panel one such as was provided. The screen image was so small and the audio so weak that sitting in the back I could barely see or hear, and I am a native speaker of English. It is also challenging at this time of year to be in a room with no air con and few fans.

In the future we need to use the projector for an image 2-3 times the size of the television screen used yesterday and speakers that make the audio clear for the students. We cannot have a successful film class with eighty people watching a television set that they can barely hear while they are struggling with the language.

Thanks so much as always for your kind attention.
Let me know what I can do.
Carol

This email and a subsequent meeting resulted in a brilliant outcome for the next class: air conditioning, large crisp projection, and big brand new wall-mounted speakers. The luxurious appointments were thoroughly enjoyed by the small cluster of students who returned after last week's fiasco. Next week there will be either 40 or 80 or zero students. It is impossible to predict. I do not understand the registration system, the class schedules, or just about anything else I have been able to take for granted in the past. Everyone tries to be helpful, but there are only so many questions one can ask without knowing the important answers that hover just beyond my grasp. It should come as no surprise that a syllabus with assignments and papers due does not play well to an audience of students who are not getting any credit for the course, a detail I did not yet know, though those who stuck it out received an ornate certificate suitable for framing. Personally, I was delighted with the 15 steady students and a nice screening set-up. I realize that no matter what I have to change some of my film choices like *Paths of Glory* (Kubrick 1957) and *Triumph of the Will* (Reifenstahl 1934) because they will be utterly incomprehensible as was *All Quiet on the Western Front* (Milestone 1930) which would not have been enthusiastically received even if they could see or hear it. This is definitely more of a *Rambo* (Costmatos 1985) kind of audience, though *Indochine* (Wargnier 1992) also went quite nicely with my small band of devoted followers and the special screening of *Hearts and Minds* (Davis 1975) we held at the *Cinematheque* was unforgettable.

Question Authority

All things considered, the film class is going swimmingly compared to the "Media Studies" class, which came close to full meltdown. The syllabus clearly indicates that "practice" is only a small part of the class, but the students want only to get their hands on the equipment I brought over and make movies. My university has donated a small lab's worth of video and computer equipment which Fulbright was kind enough to ship via State Department diplomatic pouch. By some miracle the gear arrived squashed but otherwise intact.

A few weeks into the semester we attempted to put out the equipment so I could provide a demonstration: six camera kits and six computer stations including two new MacBooks, two older MacBook Pros, and two new MiniMacs. At least that was the plan. One new MacBook had already come down with an alien virus. The other MacBook had been appropriated at least temporarily by the IT manager presumably for his personal use. At the end of class, two camera kits walked off with girls who apparently just wanted to try them out at home and were unaware that might be a problem. We were down to four set-ups for 20 (25 or 5 or 15 depending on the week) students. I calculate that by week nine we will have no equipment at all, which will simplify matters if not improve them. I am beginning to feel like I fit Graham Greene's description of Aldon Pyle: "I never knew a man who had better motives for all the trouble he caused" (1955: 60).

Figure 5.2: Media lab equipment arrival.

The students want nothing to do with history, theory or other things that get in the way of their dream of making movies. They claim quite genuinely to not understand even the most elementary models like source-channel-message-receiver-feedback. I am not sure they have ever before encountered the abstract concept of a model, or anything that verges on what we might think of as social science theory. Coming from such an historic culture, my students are determinedly here-and-now oriented. They told me they want to learn only "new media" and "Internet." Several want to be talk show hosts "like Oprah." I am recalibrating my approach by installing the surviving equipment in my office for tutorials and shortening the theory part of the course:

Socrates: Question Authority
Plato: Be Good
Aristotle: Be Credible
Confucius: Be Compassionate
Marx: Be Fair
McLuhan: Bewilder

Prior to the 1970s, theories of human communication were seen as almost exclusively a project of the Greek rhetorical tradition, marked by the propositional and syllogistic form of argument; the law of non-contradiction precluding ambiguity, irony and paradox; the primacy of persuasion in law courts and legislative assemblies; the introduction of argument from probability; and the emphasis upon individual performance and success. Taken together these features construct a world that privileges argument over wisdom, the individual over the collective good, democracy over oligarchy, and winning over collaboration (Lu 1998: 29). In other words, Western civilization.

The corollary myth that Chinese rhetoric is characterized by harmony is equally simplistic, but nonetheless more true than not. The one world yin/yang of Daoism stands in contrast to the two-world notion of reality based in the distinction between essences and representations. By way of contrast to the Greek tradition, consider the pictographic nature of Chinese language, a high context culture where the most compelling arguments are from authority, a belief that truth is not propositional but humanly embodied, a preference for aphoristic and analogic communication and no practical concept of equality. Crosscultural mystification is almost inevitably the result as East and West try to fathom each other (Nisbett 2003).

These highly abstract cultural differences find their way into the practical world of the Vietnamese classroom as learning styles that excel at roteness and respect for authority to the discouragement of critical or creative thinking. The analysis of a text or a film presumes not only the vocabulary to do so, but also a belief in the very idea that a whole can be meaningfully deconstructed. It took a transformational thinker like Marshall McLuhan to give an Eastern cast to Western rhetoric.

"What if He's Right?"

In 1965, Tom Wolfe published what became a classic essay in *New York Magazine* on McLuhan posing the question: "What if He's Right?." McLuhan had recently made a spectacular landing on the cultural—especially Manhattan—scene with *Understanding Media*. A few years earlier he had made a lesser splash with *The Gutenberg Galaxy*. McLuhan's Delphic pronouncements—"The electric light is pure information.... The medium is the message.... Print gave tribal man an eye for an ear"—are well known if little understood. You can start a McLuhan argument anywhere two media academics gather. Overrated? Underrated? Borrowed too much from others? Intellectually irresponsible? Guru of the electronic age? Rubbish? Solid gold? And so on. McLuhan's aphoristic "probes," as he called them in an ingenious bid to deflect criticism ("If you don't like these ideas I have more") were hit and miss, aimed at a target no one else could yet see. If nothing else, McLuhan's insistence that media technologies change not just *some* things but everything—his insight that we exist in a mediated environment wherein "we shape our tools and therefore our tools shape us" (1964: xi) was pure genius. If he was not the only academic who thought that way—credit for many of McLuhan's ideas goes to Walter Ong—he was the only one who effectively used the media to his advantage to get the message out. McLuhan's mysterious, aphoristic, and fractured style led the way in postmodern media performance.

One phrase associated with McLuhan (though it can be found earlier) is "I don't know who discovered water, but I'm sure it wasn't a fish." Over the early months in Vietnam this became my mantra, as it slowly dawned on me that my entirely intellectual framework was invisible to my students. The very idea of studying and discussing and analyzing "media" and "film"—as opposed to just experiencing it—was alien. Movies were something to watch. Mediums themselves were transparent and it was my objective to make them opaque in order to introduce a mediated screen for analysis. To watch a movie and discuss whether it is good, bad or indifferent and whether or not you like the actors is one thing. To watch a movie and discuss it with a critical vocabulary that includes references to cultural and historical context, narrative, character development, cinematography, editing, acting, aesthetics, set and costume design, representations of race and gender, political implications and all of the other aspects American film students take for granted is something else again. Likewise, to give students a camera and send them off to point and shoot is one thing; to give them a camera and an editing station along with instruction in lighting, composition, storytelling, structure, sound, continuity, and all the rest of best media practices is a much more challenging proposition.

This is not to say that a thoroughgoing approach to understanding and making media is all that well taught or supported in most of the United States, but media and film studies as academic disciplines and industry practices have developed into mainstream fields over the past half-century in much of the Western world. In Vietnam, we are at square one, which was brought home to me during lengthy discussions with the Dean of International Studies on the merits of teaching documentary filmmaking to her students. "They all want to make movies. Why should we give them credit for what they want to do anyway?" I felt I was in a time machine, having this conversation in the United States 40 years ago. I answered something about the difference between random point and shoot filmmaking, and filmmaking practice done with an understanding of the technique and aesthetics of the craft and the role of the audience. "Would you give children their first pencils and expect them to write an editorial for *Le Monde*?" I am not sure I convinced her, but she didn't get in our way after that.

The force that drives me in Vietnam stems from a general belief that as an American I want to say I am sorry (and not in the British way) by doing something positive, however modest. "Reparations" is too big a word and too accusatory, but it is in the right spirit. To me human potential always starts, after basic needs are met, with nurturing freedom of thought and expression, and what better way to allow communication to grow than by providing the necessary tools and tactics. Through teaching beginning documentary filmmaking since 2007, we have provided students with the opportunity to find their voice and communicate persuasively about subjects important to them. It might not be democracy, but it is empowering in its own way.

Confucius Meets Karl Marx

The Vietnamese system of higher education is not by its nature especially hospitable to media studies. Try to imagine the result of combining aspects of Confucian, French, and Soviet pedagogies in a poor country that has been at war for most of the past 2000 years and currently supports a one-party political system. The first university in Vietnam, the Temple of Literature in Hanoi, was founded in the 11th century on Confucian principles that had been used in China for 1000 years. Confucius introduced the idea of meritocracy into education so that even one of lowly birth could rise above his station. Unlike Western education, which from the start encouraged debate and disputation, the Confucian system stressed rote learning, memorization of the classics, and a highly selective and rigorous exam system. Taken in combination with an emphasis on moral and ethical education and social and familial hierarchy, this is not a system designed to produce free or creative thinkers. It is very difficult for a Westerner to understand a culture that is not based on discussion and debate. The French colonial century in Vietnam left behind not only great baguettes and graceful architecture, but also a tight centralization of higher education in the Ministry of Education and Training. The decade of Soviet influence from the late 1970s to late 1980s reinforced regimentation, and many of Vietnam's leading educators today earned Ph.D.s in the the Soviet Union during that period.

There is great concern over the current state of higher education in Vietnam, and influential forces including the U.S. Embassy, the United Nations Development Program and many universities including Duke and Harvard are working to come up with a plan that will lift Vietnam's higher education above its current state as the weakest in the region. Economic development in an information age obviously requires an educated workforce. One story goes that Intel interviewed 10,000 Vietnamese college graduates before finding a handful they could hire. Despite the education-respecting and hardworking character of the Vietnamese, many believe the educational system is irreparably broken and would best be served by creating from scratch a top-tier "Apex University" rather than trying to institute widespread systemic change.

Most of the intractable problems can be traced back to the Confucian-Franco-Soviet legacy. Faculty appointments are often as much political as based on merit and faculty pay is so dismal at around $100 to $200 per month that most university professors are forced to hold down multiple positions. The curriculum and budgets are tightly controlled by the ministry with little local autonomy for individual universities. Faculty governance at the local level is almost unheard of. Not even a handful of universities meet global accreditation standards. Faculty produce few publications in peer-reviewed journals, few students are prepared to study abroad, and financial instability is a chronic problem. One outcome of this dysfunctional system is an almost complete lack of critical thinking skills, an outcome which should come as no surprise in a country with a Confucian past and a one-party political present where at all times harmony is valued over dissent.

"What's the First Amendment?"

Congress shall make no law respecting an establishment of religion, or prohibiting the free exercise thereof; or abridging the freedom of speech, or of the press; or of the people peaceably to assemble, and to petition the Government for a redress of grievances.

Huy walked into my office one morning while I was chuckling at a *New York Times* article online about New York City political performance artist "Reverend Billy," who had been arrested for refusing to stop repeating the 44 words of the First Amendment through a megaphone at Union Square. The offending amplification was either 3 or 15 feet away from the tender ears of the police, depending upon whose account you believe. Since it is not a crime to be annoying in a public place, which the faux-Reverend undoubtedly was, he was arrested under a statute—"second degree harassment"—originally intended for use against stalkers. Getting yourself arrested for speaking the First-Amendment-protected First Amendment in a public park, in addition to demonstrating Reverend Billy's genius for rankling the authorities, does manage to call attention to an idea Americans tend to take for granted: the First Amendment. This struck me as I tried to explain the Reverend Billy story to the U.S. educated Huy, who look puzzled at the whole thing, and said finally: "What's the First Amendment?"

Vietnam has no equivalent of the First Amendment, one of few facts about the country many Americans seem to know. There is a great deal of private opinion and discussion about the government, but speaking out or writing against the government or—especially—protesting in a group is simply not tolerated. Vietnam's motto "Independence—Freedom—Happiness"—is seen as frequently as "In God We Trust" in the U.S. Media in Vietnam are closely managed, including strict regulation of the Internet, especially of content deemed sexually explicit or politically sensitive. Facebook was blocked until recently, but I never met anyone who did not know the way around it. Sites in Vietnamese are blocked more frequently than sites in English. English language sites with politically sensitive content often pass through the filter, perhaps because there are not enough English-speaking inspectors available to do the censoring. The U.S. media are often justly criticized for being government-biased and state-influenced, but the influence is more complex and U.S. media are not state run in the same one-party sense as the media in Vietnam. Still, Vietnam does have elections and there are choices and things are changing generationally, though not fast enough for some of its very articulate and ambitious citizens.

Free speech was in the air the week of the Reverend Billy story when I received a call from an Al Jazeera producer who was doing a piece on Vietnam and wanted to interview a male student. This was intriguing because I did not know anyone who had actually seen Al Jazeera, banished as it is from U.S. cable and shut out of Vietnam as well. The faintly subversive activity of arranging the interview was enough to keep me unusually happy for a couple of days. My students jumped at the opportunity, but I had to clear the interview through the university where I was reminded that questions about the government are "sensitive." This put a little crimp in the Australian producer's list of questions submitted for approval that included:

"How do you feel about terms 'Marxist-Leninism' and 'market economy'?"
"How do you think these concepts fit into Vietnamese society now?"

The university also got nervous at the last minute wanting to make sure that Al Jazeera had the proper papers and credentials required of media. This did not turn out to be a problem because Al Jazeera arrived complete with their very own minder assigned by the Ministry of Culture. In the end, everyone left the student and the reporter alone, so there is a remote chance that something interesting was said. The piece was supposed to be available on YouTube, the primary distribution outlet for Al Jazeera to reach English-language audiences where it is otherwise blacked out. In Vietnam, YouTube is blocked as well, so we never saw the finished product. Internet filtering is a constant game of cat and mouse in Vietnam, with the mice usually finding their way onto Facebook and other social media sites one step ahead of the cats.

Reading Graham Greene

After the first month both of my classes are precarious and they are not going to fix themselves, so I hatch a scheme in an effort to make the transparent medium of film opaque for my war film students, to somehow *show* rather than *tell* how the medium is the message. I consider a variation on a comparative literature approach. What if we look at several versions of the same story, ideally in different mediums, and compare them to see if there are differences among modes of representation that make differences in the story? There is a growing literature on adaptation that I can refer to in the unlikely event I can get my Internet to work for a steady hour. I found a starting point right in the original syllabus, which included a screening of the 2002 film version of Graham Greene's *The Quiet American* directed by Phillip Noyce. I knew there was a 1958 version directed by Joseph Manckiwiez, and of course there was the 1955 book. Would looking at all three give some meaning to application of a media studies vocabulary and thus the idea of a medium itself? There was not much to lose.

Greene's quasi-autobiographical political thriller occupies a unique place in Vietnamese culture. As soon as the government introduced the economic reform policy of *doi moi* in 1986 effectively allowing everyone to start a small business, the boys who hawk postcards and chewing gum around Hoan Kiem Lake also began offering for sale badly Xeroxed copies of *The Quiet American* with a striking green and black jungle silhouette cover. It was the only English language book in their basket, and more than 20 years later the book is still part of their meager inventory, now joined by more familiar tourist-friendly tomes like *Lonely Planet*.

Michael Caine, who starred in the 2002 *Quiet American* film, reported that when they were filming in Hanoi he would be stopped every day by the gum-selling boys trying to peddle him a copy of the book. "I've read it. I've read," he would laugh while waving them off.

I proposed the three pronged book-movie-movie approach to my students, who readily agreed. I imagine they had no idea what I was talking about, but they were always eager to go along for the ride to find out what this unpredictable foreigner was up to. It then remained to secure a copy of the 1958 film, which as I expected was among the 5000 titles in Gerry's *Cinematheque* library, and to locate copies of the book. I did not look forward to the experience of buying a dozen copies one or two at a time from the Hoan Kiem sales force, repeatedly haggling from a likely starting price of ten dollars, and I did not feel like making even cheaper copies of the already blurry text. I wanted the students to have an actual book to hold. By coincidence that week I was taking a friend to see Hoa Lo, and in the prison museum's extensive souvenir and bookshop immediately found all the copies I needed for 50,000 VND—a little more than $3 each. It seemed right finding the books in the prison where the U.S. pilots did their hard time. *The Quiet American* is set 20 years prior to the pilots' capture and imprisonment but Graham Greene was among those few who saw the writing on the wall.

Greene's taut and prescient novel grew out of his experience as a journalist in Saigon in the early 1950s. These turned out to be the last years of the French presence in Vietnam, and the country was thick with intrigue. Greene's service as a British intelligence officer gave him insight into the nature of the rising political waters immersing the French colonialists, the communist Viet Minh, and what became in the novel the "third force" backed by the Americans. Greene tells the story in flashback and it has inspired a cottage industry of analysis and criticism over 50 years.

Harvard-educated young American Alden Pyle is murdered in Saigon, and the narrative is a ratiocination of that event. Pyle is widely believed to be modeled on American CIA operative Edward Lansdale. Greene protested to the contrary, but the similarities invite comparison. Pyle—the quiet American of the title (the French title is *Un Americain Bien Tranquille*)—had earlier met cynical aging British journalist Thomas Fowler. Pyle is a CIA agent under cover as an American aid worker. Greene tells us that "Pyle has taken a good degree in—well, one of those subjects Americans can take degrees in: perhaps public relations or theatercraft, perhaps even Far Eastern Studies..." (1955: 21). Among other transgressions, Pyle steals away Fowler's beautiful young Vietnamese girlfriend Phuong, although in Pico Iyer's remarkable homage to Greene he writes that the story "is much more about the difficult treacherous love between the two male rivals than about the love either feels for Phuong" (2012: 144). In any case, the act of winning Phuong combined with Pyle's covert political activity gets him murdered, set up by Fowler in an extreme act of passive aggression. It is a love story, a war story, a political thriller and all at under 200 pages. It is one of the great war stories in any genre.

I think my 15 students, 13 of them young women, and I began *The Quiet American* marathon with a reading of the book. I say I "think" we read the book, because it was not at all clear to me that anyone had actually read the book when we met to discuss it. Having anticipated that possibility, not an unknown occurrence even in the United States, where English is a first and not second language, I had selected a series of passages for them to read aloud to each other so we could at least experience the flavor and tone. This is an early scene when Fowler tells Phuong of Pyle's murder:

"Where is Pyle," Phuong asked. "What did they want?"
"Come home," I said.
"Will Pyle come?"
"He's as likely to come there as anywhere else."
　The old women were still gossiping on the landing, in the relative cool.
　When I opened my door I could tell my room had been searched: everything was tidier than I ever left it.
"Another pipe?" Phuong asked.
"Yes."
　I took off my tie and my shoes; the interlude was over; the night was nearly the same as it had been. Phuong crouched at the end of the bed and lit the lamp.
Mon enfant, ma soeur—skin of amber. *Sa douce langue natale.*
　"Phuong," I said. She was kneading the opium on the bowl. "*Il est mort,*
Phuong." She held the needles in her hand and looked up at me like a child trying to concentrate, frowning. "*Tu dis?*"
"*Pyle est mort. Assassiné.*"
　She put the needle down and sat back on her heels, looking at me. There was no scene, no tears, just thought—the long private thought of somebody who has to alter the whole course of her life (1955: 22).

The entire plot can be extrapolated from this exquisite scene and several others, but it did not take long in class discussions to discover that the heart of the matter having to do with political and cultural context was completely outside the frame of reference of my young Vietnamese students. They had never thought to ask why *The Quiet American,* and often only *The Quiet American*, was for sale on every street corner in Hanoi. They were unaware that this cautionary tale was well-received in Britain when published there in 1955 and widely denounced as anti-American when published in the United States in 1956 following the McCarthy era that ruthlessly hunted suspected communists at the height of the Cold War. A.J. Liebling writing in *The New Yorker* offered an especially scathing review, calling the book "Mr. Greene's nasty little plastic bomb" (Pratt 1996: 355). In *The New York Times* Robert Gorham Davis (11 March 1956) places Greene in heady company writing that his "caricatures of American types are often as crude and trite as Jean Paul Sartre." Other opinions were more enthusiastic. *The Saturday Review* (10 March 1956: 12*)* called it "a superb fiction" and the *Atlantic* "continuously intriguing." As expected, reviews were more favorable in Britain than in the United States. Not only was it Greene's home soil, but the United Kingdom was less seized by Cold War paranoia than its former colony.

The first *Quiet American* film was released in 1958, two years after the book's U.S. appearance. Director Joseph Mankiewicz, under pressure from the anti-communist fervor of the day and the very real Hollywood blacklist that destroyed the careers of those perceived as leaning too far left, changed some crucial plot elements of the book to defang its alleged anti-Americanism. The naïve but deadly Alden Pyle was played by real-life World War II hero Audie Murphy, in a wooden performance that nonetheless cast a halo over Greene's villain. A pivotal scene of bloody bombing of women and children in a public square is attributed in the movie to the communist Viet Minh, rather than to the Third Force (read Americans) as it is in the book. Phuong does not return to Fowler at the end of the film as she does in the novel. The film is even dedicated to United States backed Ngo Dinh Diem. Graham Greene was livid with this adaptation and called the film "a complete travesty" and "a real piece of political dishonesty." He also complained that "the casting was appalling." Greene observed bitterly that Phuong is played by an Italian actress (and her sister by an Algerian). To Greene, the Mankiewicz verson of *The Quiet American* was "a propaganda piece for American policy" (Pratt 1996: 312). With the passing of time, even Mankiewicz seemed to agree, saying "it was a very bad film I made during a very unhappy time in my life" (Dawson 2002).

I did not get much traction asking my students about the implications of the differences between the book and the 1958 movie, despite the fact that Mankiewicz had *changed the ending*. (A theme we encounter again in *First Blood* and *Forrest Gump*.) The students seemed to think it was just to be expected that an American would change the story to suit himself. The fact and fiction distinction still made in Western thinking, however fuzzily, does not seem to apply at all in Vietnam, at least not in any way I can discern.

I made marginally better progress pointing out to them that in August of 2007 U.S. President George W. Bush made a lengthy reference to *The Quiet American* in a speech to a Veterans of Foreign Wars convention, using Alden Pyle to stretch to the conclusion that the United States should not withdraw from Iraq as they had from Vietnam. Leaving aside the fact that Pyle's story was about starting the war and not ending it, the irony of Bush trying to bolster an argument citing a character whose naïveté and ethnocentrism had been compared to his own may have been lost on him and his speechwriters, but it was not lost on my students in Vietnam.

The final part of our *Quiet American* trilogy was the Phillip Noyce film version released in 2002. This was a big hit with the students, not because it is truer to Graham Greene's novel than the earlier (black and white) film (it is, but truth did not seem to matter) but because it is lushly shot and the female lead is the popular Vietnamese actress Do Thi Hai Yen. The standout feature of this film apart from Michael Caine's Academy Award-nominated performance as Fowler (he lost to Adrien Brody) and Brendan Fraser's spot-on Pyle, is the back story of how it nearly did not get released because of its proximity to 9/11 and the fears that it would be viewed as anti-American. "*The Quiet American* isn't anti-American," said Michael Caine, who led a one-man campaign aimed at Miramax' Harvey Weinstein for the film's release. "It's anti the Americans who got the country involved in Vietnam" (Lyman 2002). Appearing as it did on the eve of the Iraq War, the 2002 *Quiet American* failed to deter American intervention as surely as the book failed to deter the United States from Vietnam. America's giant blunder into Vietnam is sometimes attributed to the fact that red-baiting had decimated the ranks of U.S. intelligence personnel with expertise in Asia. Michael Caine has suggested that Graham Greene might have had something to do with the fact that the British did not go along with the Americans in Vietnam, speculating that Greene's contacts in the intelligence community would surely have consulted with him at some point, and his experience as both documented and imagined in *The Quiet American* leaves little doubt what he would have advised.

Brendan Fraser tells that he learned during the filming that Greene was rumored to write with a bottle, a glass, cigarettes and lighter, ashtray, lamp, and a loaded revolver arranged around the typewriter on his desk. Greene's distain for American Foreign policy was well-known. When asked why the title was *The Quiet American,* he replied "because he's fucking dead" (Fraser 2012). For Fraser, shooting the film "was a highlight I will be hard pressed to rival."

Conventional thinking about the symbolism in *The Quiet American* sets Fowler to stand for the crumbling colonial empires: decadent, cynical, impotent, failing; Pyle for the "innocent and good" new American dominance: naive, both wide-eyed and blind, a true believer; and Phuong as the tender vulnerable Vietnam—the prized exotic beauty brimming with natural resources.

Having made little progress with my class on the politics and the narrative of our trilogy, I asked:

"The girl. What did you think about the girl, Phuong. The one in the black and white movie."

Silence

"The name of the actress who played Phuong was Giorgia Moll. Giorgia Moll, is that a Vietnamese name?"

More silence, as they look in their laps and sideways at each other like they do when they don't know how to answer. Finally,

"I don't think the girl is Vietnamee" (The usual Vietnamese pronunciation of Vietnamese)

"No, she is not. What do you think of that?"

"Why do they do that?"

Gradually the ice broke and it became obvious that they were both confused and very disapproving of an Italian actress playing a Vietnamese woman, despite the lack of any framework for discussing race or gender. *The Quiet American* is a stark portrayal of the subjugation of women and the lengths to which they will go for protection and survival. In the book and the 1958 movie, Fowler and Phuong are more than 20 years apart. Smooth Michael Redgrave in 1958 looks like a plausible partner for his young Italian Phuong. In real life there was a 30-year age difference. The age difference between a poignantly dilapidated Michael Caine and glowing Hai Yen is nearly 50 years. A bit much, we all thought, although it serves to underscore the story. The discussion that followed about gender roles and patriarchy sparkled with fresh insights from the students who had always taken both for granted and had never before held the concepts up to the of light of analysis, let alone in a movie, not to mention in a classroom discussion.

The students were infinitely happier with Hai Yen in the 2002 version. I had met Hai Yen at a dinner Gerry hosted for visiting producer Albert Berger, and I told my students the truth—every one of them would have shined in that role. They were amazed that I had met her, but I found Hanoi to be a small town where everyone seemed to be passing through at one time or another and you could find yourself positively tripping over ambassadors at any given event.

Since both *The Quiet American* novel and film are from Fowler's first-person point of view, we see only his perspective of Phuong, who is described as a former "taxi dancer"—beautiful, needy, vacant, submissive. For entertainment she likes to look at picture books of the British Royal Family. When I asked the class why Phuong went with Fowler, the response was "It is obvious. She had to. He could give her things a bar hostess would never otherwise dream of."

Nonetheless, the film portrayals of Moll and Hai Yen differ in more than their class and ethnicity. Moll smiles and pouts and has an eerie resemblance to Natalie Wood, but it is all on the surface. Hai Yen inhabits the same subjugated role but with more attitude. Stephanie Zachurek wrote in *Salon* that "with a few barely perceptible shifts of her facial expression, she shows waves of feeling that are almost impossible to put into words" (2003). We do not hear much from Phuong in the course of Fowler's narration. What if we went a step farther and imagined the story from Phuong's point of view? We each devised a paragraph of *The Quiet American* in Phuong's voice, and delighted in the results. A sample of this approach, recreated by Rachel Morrissey, imagines Phuong's diary entry after she first meets Pyle:

> He walked toward me and Thomas like we were old friends. I only understood some of the broad syllables coming from his mouth, but his wide open face was unmistakable. He looked at me like a man in love, with just a hint of lust in his heart, but more sweetly and embarrassed about it than most Western men. I knew when I saw him that my sister would like him. He had to be rich. All Westerners in Vietnam were rich. He invited us to join him for dinner, and I turned to Thomas to decide. It was best to leave the decisions like that to Thomas and just enjoy the evenings.
>
> Thomas was good to me and I was happy to be with him. I was happy not to be a dance girl that had to compete with other girls for attention. I was happy to be in a home and a bit settled. I was happy that I was not a burden to my sister, although she worried about me so. Thomas couldn't marry me, and my sister knew that the longer I was his mistress, the dimmer other prospects became. But with war and poverty surrounding me, future prospects seemed like a silly reason to turn down a kind man and lovely house. Besides, he had asked his wife for a divorce. Surely, she would say yes soon (2012).

At last we had found a way to enter the world of criticism and analysis through the door of this character at once so much like the young women in the class and yet so different. Several students later came to me privately to talk about the conflicts they feel about being young educated women who, when they marry, will likely be expected to move in with their husband's family to cook and clean. Vietnam's family values look backward even as the culture rushes ahead. There is a whole generation of Vietnamese girls who are delaying marriage to maintain their independence despite their ultimate desire for family and children. Vietnamese women carry a very heavy load, yet they carry it with uncommon grace.

Did our triathalon of *The Quiet American* book and movies show that the medium is the message? That when we shape our tools, our tools shape us? Graham Greene said in writing about writing: "One is changed by one's own books. The writer plays God until his creatures escape from him and, in their turn, they mould him" (Pratt 1996: 493). I like to believe that in the end it did make a difference to the students whether Phuong was outsourced to a foreign actress or played by a Vietnamese one, that changing the end of a story can make a rhetorical point and should be attended to, that books and films play differently in our imaginations, and that the line between art and propaganda, fiction and nonfiction, is thin and permeable. Many interventions might influence us fish to notice that we are in water. With the support of my intrepid students we were able to bring a rich story to both life and mind, and in the doing make the process of critical analysis a little less strange in a strange land.

A Promise to the Dead

Back in 1989, when Hung attained the mother of all media achievements with his profile on *60 Minutes*, it was a measure of the complete U.S. lack of understanding of Vietnamese culture that 15 years after the war's end, the world's most esteemed newsmagazine was introducing the audience to "The Enemy." Hung is as unlikely a candidate for an enemy as you will ever find. Modest and soft-spoken (Safer describes him as "delicate"), Hung is never without a sweet and slightly bemused smile. Safer's crew took Hung to Quang Tri City, just south of the former DMZ, where he had fought the 1972 battle. Safer recalls that

> Hung is quite shaken as we pull into the southern suburbs of Quang Tri. That awful battle could have taken place a week ago, not 17 years ago. Both sides of the highway are littered with shot-up tanks and broken artillery pieces, and the buildings have had their faces shot off. After all these years of abandonment, one still feels slightly embarrassed, slightly nosy, peering this way into someone's privacy.
>
> (Safer 1990: 101)

Hung recalls waiting anxiously for the B52s one clear sunny day in southern Laos. They knew they were coming but they didn't know when.

> I was talking to a friend about what we would do after the war, and he was saying he would study civil engineering so he could build houses. I told him I wanted to become a teacher to share with the younger generation my experience of this war.

Then a few minutes later we saw three huge B52s coming in, and then we saw the bomb coming right down on top of us like a layer of golden cloth falling from the sky.

(Jennings 1998: 400)

Hung survived. His friend did not. Hung recalled that because he and his friend had talked about what they wanted to become just before his friend died and he had told him he was going to be a teacher, "It's a kind of promise to the dead. And when I returned to the university to study, all the time I thought about it and I would work very hard to be a good teacher" (*60 Minutes* 1989).

Hung became a very good teacher indeed, eventually appointed deputy minister in the International Relations Department at the Ministry of Education and Training. His promise to the dead has set an international example of reconciliation through his subsequent work with American veterans and provided an opportunity for thousands of students to build a bright future in a country of peace.

Hung's story continued with another promise to the dead fulfilled. For 30 years he searched for his brother's remains on the battlefield, through military records and by talking to top generals. Eventually, like so many other families of the hundreds of thousands of Vietnamese missing in action, he turned to psychic Pham Thi Hang, who sketched a map of a hilly region about 650 kilometers south of Hanoi and drew an "x" on an unmarked grave. "Before you dig," she said, "stick a chopstick in the earth. If an egg balances on it, your brother will be below" (Lamb 2001). If this seems odd, it should be noted that many

Figure 5.3: Nguyen Ngoc Hung, 2008.

Vietnamese would not consider making any big decision from buying a house to getting married without consulting the lunar calendar and a psychic or astrologer to interpret it. As Hung said, "Whether you're a communist or not, if you're Vietnamese you're a very superstitious person" (Lamb 2001). While the government officially frowns on superstitious practices, for the most part it looks the other way. This was of great help to Hung when his quest for his brother ended beneath a chopstick in Kontum province, and Nguyen Ngoc Cuong was exhumed and taken home for a proper Buddhist burial.

Chapter 6

Vietnam Love Songs: "Rode Hard and Put Away Wet"

Thou shalt not kill.
                                    – 6th Commandment, Exodus 20: 13

  Kill 'em all. Let God sort 'em out.
                                         —Infantry slogan, Vietnam War

Vietnam was a war of contradiction. Phillip Beidler called it "a Catch-22 world imitating art" (1972: 145). Jan Scuggs, moving spirit behind the national Vietnam Veterans Memorial, noted the irony of veterans building a memorial to themselves and to a war the country in truth wanted only to forget, commenting "What the hell. It had been that kind of war" (Beidler 1972: 19).

"That kind of war." A war of absurdities and contradictions, dilemmas and double binds, ambiguities and oppositions, disinformation and lies, lies, lies. A war that was never declared a war, a chain of escalations triggered by the 1964 Gulf of Tonkin resolution that was based upon incidents of North Vietnamese "aggression" that essentially did not happen at all. In any case, how could PT boats defending a harbor against war ships from half way around the globe be called "aggressors"? It was part of the twisted language that characterized the war: free-fire zones, destroying a village to save it, pacification, Vietnamization. The United States was always responding, retaliating, reacting, or "protectively reacting" to Vietnam the aggressor, a rhetorical sleight of hand that defied logic, common sense, and probably the laws of physics. Going 10,000 miles from home to call the other side the aggressor requires a willing suspension of disbelief usually seen only in front of the theatrical fourth wall. The fact that in any case "aggressor" referred to the North versus South Vietnamese, and not Vietnam versus the United States, was conveniently conflated to raise the specter of hordes of communists invading California, presumably on surfboards since they had no other means.

Vietnam was a war not really supported or understood by the people of the country that waged it against an elusive enemy whose identity changed night by day for objectives that were vague and self-defeating. A war that promised to bring "self-determination" to the Vietnamese whether they wanted it or not—a precursor to the Bush Doctrine of imposing democracy on other countries by whatever undemocratic means necessary. The reasons and hence the objectives of the war were never clear: Stop communism? Secure natural resources including the South China Sea? Keep DeGaulle in the U.S. camp? Flex the U.S. post-World War II muscle for the world to see? Spread democracy? Capitalism? Save face? Who knew? And thus to the devastating consequences of all wars, the bewildering paradoxes of the war in Vietnam added insult to injury for many of the three million American men and women who were sent, not infrequently against their will and the sentiments of their peers. In the words of one who served:

> *You and me, bro, we did what we were told*
> *They cut the deal and sold our souls*
> *And now we can't go home*
> *Now the warrior is deprived of his dignity and honor*
> *By chicken shit politicians and the corporate dollar*
> *They hate us, man, I'll tell you why*
> *They only sent us there to die*
> *And the ones who lived are cursed*
> *If it comes to death this is worse* (Collins 1985)

The "worse," is the tragic outcome that "fighting for one's country can render one unfit to be its citizen" (LeShan 2002). Post Traumatic Stress Disorder was only recognized by the American Psychiatric Association in 1980, but shell shock, battle fatigue, combat neurosis, or whatever it is called has existed as long as war. It is small comfort that young men (and it is still overwhelmingly men) do not rest easily in the wake of being either the subject or object of terror and violence, that such acts may not be hardwired to be part of the human experience after all. Herodotus wrote about a number of cases of battle trauma, including that of the Spartan Aristodemus "who was so shaken by battle he was nicknamed 'The Trembler' and later hanged himself in shame." Jonathan Shay's 1994 classic *Achilles in Vietnam: Combat Trauma and the Undoing of Character* parallels the stress of combat in Vietnam with the account of Achilles in Homer's *Iliad*, describing in a gripping way how the betrayal of "what's right" by a commander can lead to a "berserk state." Martin Luther King expressed concern in 1967 that troops faced in Vietnam more than the "brutalizing process that goes on in any war," because "we are adding cynicism to the process of death, for our troops must know after a short period there that none of the things we claim to be fighting for are really involved" (1967: 33). Life ever after becomes an ordeal of constant vigilance, as it did for one of Shay's patients:

> I haven't really slept for 20 years. I lie down, but I don't sleep. I'm always watching the door, the window, then the back of the door. I get up at least five times to walk my perimeter, sometimes it's 10 or 15. There's always something within reach, maybe a baseball bat or a knife, at every door. I used to sleep with a gun under my pillow, another under my mattress, and another next to the bed. You made me get rid of them when I came to the PTSD program here. They're over at my mother's so I know I can get them any time but I don't. Sometimes I think about them—I want to have a gun in my hands so bad at night it makes my arms ache. So it's like that until the sun begins to come up, then I can sleep for an hour or two. (1994: xiv)

PTSD can result from childhood abuse, assault, violent accidents or acts of nature, but it is most closely associated with the experience of military combat. According to the Veterans

Administration, more than half of all male Vietnam veterans and almost half of all female veterans—about 1,700,000—have experienced clinically serious stress reaction symptoms. To date, about one in five Iraq war veterans have reported signs of PTSD or major depression, but it is a condition that can have a long latency, not fully emerging until decades after the traumatic experience. Military suicides reached an all-time high in 2010 and 2011, despite the introduction of significant preventative measures, and there is no reason to believe the trend will reverse any time soon. *Time* reported an 18 percent increase in suicides among U.S. active duty troops in 2012 compared to 2011. "More U.S. soldiers have killed themselves than have died in the Afghan War. Why can't the Army win the war on suicide?" (July 2012: 31). President Obama's decision in July 2011 to send condolence letters to families of some military suicides spoke to the persistence and visibility of the issue, as did the campaign led by Michele Obama and Jill Biden in 2011 to support military families.

Prescription for PTSD

The ones who died were the lucky ones.
Mike

The most living relic of the Vietnam War—the most vivid and seductive and scary—has been the Vietnam combat veteran, whose place is being taken in turn by those who served in Iraq and Afghanistan. Of the 2.7 million Americans who went to Vietnam, (in addition to 61,000 Australians, 50,000 South Koreans, and a scattering of other allies), about one in five saw significant combat, and nearly all had a perilous experience in Vietnam, back home, or both. Consider the life of a young boy raised in a patriotic Christian culture to love God and country, to believe "thou shalt not kill." At the age of 18, not yet old enough to drink or even to vote until 1971, he is given a choice: fight in a mysterious war far away, openly resist and face imprisonment, or leave the country in exile. Unable by virtue of social class or education to defer service or join the National Guard, he enlists and begins a basic training calculated to override his lifetime of values and turn him into a killer.

He is sent halfway around the world alone on a one-year tour of duty in a situation so singularly merciless that he will never be able to share the experience with those who were not there. He is thrust into a war that is not even declared a war, a war in which he does not know who the enemy is, where the lines of battle are, or what the objectives may be, because the enemy is everywhere, the lines do not exist, and the objectives are both hopelessly confused and ultimately unattainable. He is issued a map only one kilometer square so he cannot see the context beyond his base. It is a guerrilla war of perpetual terror. He learns the thrill of battle that comes with the excruciating fear, the start of a combat adrenalin addiction. If he survives, he flies home (again alone) to Pittsburgh or Omaha or East L.A. He is barely 20. His peers call him "baby killer." Veterans of former wars call him "loser" or "coward." He hears a story making the rounds that a World War II vet will get his drinks bought for him, a Korean vet has to buy his own, and a Vietnam veteran has to buy for the bar to get out alive.

Everyone is now a little spooked by this brooding, strange and changed creature, and one thing for sure is that he does not want to talk about it. And so for years the movies do the talking for him, building an aggregate stock character from faces that may look different on the surface (Sylvester Stallone, Jon Voight, Gregory Hines, Charlie Sheen, Tom Cruise, Tom Berenger, Al Pacino, Gary Sinese, Samuel L. Jackson, Tommy Lee Jones) but add up to a driving cultural narrative of victimization and blame. As varied as these film portrayals of veterans may be, they almost always follow a narrative arc of patriotism, trauma, disillusionment, and blame along these lines:

> I was an Eagle Scout. I believed in America. Then they sent me over there and I ended up with my best buddy's guts all over me. And for what? For this lousy godforsaken hellhole of a country where they don't want us anyway? Fuck the generals. Fuck the gooks. Fuck the hippies. Fuck the government. Fuck the war. Fuck the world.

John Rambo is the most indelible of these characters, but many other actors in veteran roles have fused in the popular imagination to create a convenient shorthand to signify combat veterans and by extension to perpetuate the stereotype and to even shape the construction of their core identities.

More civilians and families have learned about Vietnam and its veterans from the movies than from direct engagement. As firsthand experience of the war recedes with time, mediated realities become the only realities of myth, cliché, or both; the only artifacts of remembrance. As John Gaddis notes, "with the passage of time our representations become our reality" (2002: 136). The myth of the wounded warrior combines the need to victimize, shame, and punish the veterans in order to distract us from the political causes of the war with the contradictory need for moral heroes in a culture that sanctifies greed and violence. The wounded warrior both carries out the cultural imperative and suffers for our sin of compelling him to do so. His atonement (and ours) can be realized only through his perpetual self-sacrifice. We can celebrate him only as long as he continues to suffer.

Irresistibly, the wounded warrior represents the secret, the dangerous, the forbidden. He has broken the rules. He has killed people, maybe worse. Violence echoes in his sensuality, making him at once impotent and omnipotent. Wild in a manageable way, he is more like young Brando or Steve McQueen than Rambo. He is emotionally if not physically disabled. We want to help. He is larger than life yet less than his youthful potential. He is at once heroic and fallen to earth. He is a living archive of the guilt and shame of a country that displaces blame from the architects of the war onto its victims. If the Vietnam veteran did not exist, we would have to invent him. The pantheon of American archetypes—hometown hero, lonesome cowboy, trophy wife, Wall Street fat cat, hooker with a heart of gold—would be incomplete without him. It remains to be seen if veterans of more recent wars will benefit from increased attention to their challenges or if the essence of the combat experience is simply a wound not capable of healing. It also remains to be seen if preventative measures taken with Iraq and Afghanistan veterans will mitigate the looming tragedy.

A Call from Central Casting

Any account of my own fascination with Vietnam would be incomplete without an acknowledgement of Motorhead Mike and the valuable lessons he taught me. In 1983, I moved deep into the redwoods to recover from being blindsided by a traumatic divorce that left me to cope alone with a teenager and a baby. One afternoon out of the redwood mist, Mike appeared at the squeaky screen door with his guitar, his '57 Harley Panhead and a backpack full of poetry. During the previous two-year period in addition to the divorce I was a passenger in a near-fatal car accident, I was being reviewed for tenure, and both my mother and my 16-year-old cat died, throwing me into a personal crisis I barely made it through. It was at this fragile moment that John Rambo escaped from Sheriff Will Teasle and came down off the movie screen into my life. Skinnier, more tattooed, but immediately recognizable as a combat vet out of central casting. Mike is how I came to know that Rambo can be both addictive and dangerously real on or off the screen. He was a charmer in the rough and I fell hard. Looking back, in my diminished state I might have missed a few signs of what was to come.

I was as surprised as anyone could be to find us shortly thereafter spending hours and hours driving around the hills of Mendocino County while Mike told me his war stories. It was the first time he had shared them with anyone. He loved to drive and something about being in motion made him feel comfortable talking. I was even more surprised during one road trip to find myself hanging far out the car window hurling Michael Jackson's *Thriller* tape over a sheer Jenner Grade cliff into the roiling Pacific, but Mike made risk taking seem cool. I would pay a price for experiencing Vietnam through the mind of a combat veteran who was decompensating before my eyes as he reported with full recall scene after scene of fear and carnage. I was so personally devastated at the time that his craziness made sense to my craziness and seemed like mindless fun until the fun part stopped. Mike had a genius for behaving himself when my kids were around and they adored his languid and accepting demeanor. Kids and animals all over town tagged along after him like he was a benevolent Pied Piper. Mike was walking wounded, but he had a lot of heart. He touched us all.

Mike was drafted out of Youngstown, Ohio in 1967 and spent a searing year in Vietnam's Central Highlands with the First Air Cavalry—"Custer's old unit"—as he liked to point out. Mike had a lot of stories to tell, but he put the heart of his experience into verse—he thought of them as lyrics—that we eventually collected in a small volume, *Vietnam Love Songs*.

There wasn't much of a choice back then
Everything was cut and dried
There was prison or marching

Figure 6.1: Combat vet from central casting, 1988.
Photo: Nicholas King

Tears well up inside
Bad experience turns into bad dreams
Guilt and anguish become pain
And pain is such a stressful thing
A concentration camp housed in the brain
I was nineteen the year I was there
Twenty years later the secrets I keep
Are the secrets the soul can't share
Most of the heroes weren't really brave
Fear is a screaming maniac
When you're running from your grave
At forty years old I can look back and see
What a child I was when I was nineteen
But time won't erase that Asian hell for me

Shortly after Mike returned from Vietnam to Ohio in 1969 he went to work for General Motors at their new state-of-the-art Lordstown facility where the subcompact Vega was being produced with a target of 400,000 cars a year, one every 36 seconds, twice the normal rate. Lordstown was the most sophisticated automated automobile manufacturing plant in the world and the most alienating for its labor force.

Within a minute on the line a worker in the trim department had to walk about twenty feet to a conveyor belt transporting parts to the line, pick up a front seat weighing thirty pounds, carry it back to his work station, place the seat on the chassis and put in four bolts to fasten it down by first hand-starting the bolts and then using an air gun to tighten them according to standards.

(Weller 1974)

It was maddening work at the pace of 100 cars an hour. Within a year the system was brought to a halt by a thousand acts of worker sabotage, and the United Auto Workers voted to strike. Mike said that the speed-up was not the only source of frustration. Workers had to park so far from the plant that the walk took longer than the drive from home. Many of the workers, average age 25, were fresh from tours in Vietnam. In Mike's words "GM picked the wrong guys to fuck with." The strike lasted only 22 days, but the conflict was nasty and was the icing on the trauma cake for Mike.

When Mike and I met in 1984, he was ready to talk about Vietnam and I was eager to listen. A hundred hours of those car rides followed. Mike knew every detail of every war story, something I later found common among combat vets whose memories have been etched in adrenalin and blood. While I cannot recall his words precisely, the affect and the anguish had much in common with Vietnam veteran portrayals on screen. Shay suggests that healing trauma depends upon safe and trusting communication where "before analyzing, before thinking, before trying to *do* anything—we should *listen*" (1994: 4). He warns against becoming a "museum-goer" whose listening experience is rubricized in convenient classification and analysis: "That's cubist ... That's El Greco ... That's Rambo…" The psyche of the combat veteran does not lend itself to neat categories, and Mike was not just out of central casting, but out of the PTSD book as well.

Rewriting Defeat

First Blood (Kotcheff 1982) was not the first Vietnam movie to depict a character with PTSD but the proximity of its release to my relationship with Mike made the Rambo connection especially strong. I am one of those learners who absorb lessons more readily from film and literature than from textbooks, and prior to Mike's appearance at the back door my knowledge of combat veterans had been defined by the movies. *Coming Home* (Ashby 1978), *The Deer Hunter* (Cimino 1978), and *Apocalypse Now* (Coppola 1979) had compelling veteran characters, and in those days before DVDs and even VCRs if you had not seen the movie in a theater you were out of luck. There was not the time-shifting culture of today where any film can be ordered up almost instantly and viewed again and again. As a result, the viewer's relationship to movies was more time-stamped than it is today and specific films were more closely linked to contemporaneous cultural and political contexts and events. The following chapter on "Reinventing Rambo" will look at the broader Rambo phenomenon from a number of angles over several decades. One slice of Rambo that pertains especially to Mike's story is the oddly moving speech John Rambo delivers near the end of *First Blood*. The speech is in the movie but not in the book, maybe because it is hard to deliver an impassioned peroration when you are bleeding to death as he does in the book's climax. In the *First Blood* movie, Rambo arises from the near dead to face the sequel of another day. The movie gives Rambo the opportunity to deliver a classic veteran monologue that moves through the stages of patriotism, trauma, disillusionment and blame. The speech could have been given by almost any Vietnam veteran character in film of the 1970s and 1980s. The occasion in *First Blood* is the arrival of Rambo's Green Beret commanding officer Colonel Samuel Trautman. Rambo has wreaked havoc and killed more than a dozen people, when Trautman approaches the beleaguered Sheriff Teasle: "I'm Colonel Samuel Trautman. I've come about my boy." Trautman finally catches up with Rambo, who is by this time cornered. "It's over Johnny. It's over."

> Nothing is over. Nothing. You just don't turn it off… It wasn't my war. You asked me, I didn't ask you. And I did what I had to do to win. But somebody wouldn't let us win… For me civilian life is nothin'. In the field we had a code of honor. Back here there's nothin'. Back there I could fly a gunship. I could drive a tank. I was in charge of million dollar equipment. Back here I can't even hold a job parking cars.
>
> (Kotcheff 1982)

It is a very un-Rambo scene, yet a moment closer to the hidden heart of the Rambo character than any other. The speech reveals the complex man behind Stallone's one-dimensional acting. Gaylyn Studlar and David Dresser, writing one of many scholarly analyses of Rambo, suggest that "in rewriting the Vietnam defeat, Rambo attempts to solve the contradiction posed by its portrayal of the Vietnam vet as a powerless victim and supremacist warrior by reviving the powerful American mythos of a 'regeneration through violence'" (1998: 9). The description suited Motorhead Mike to a tee.

Reel Life Shell Shock

Veteran portrayals on film are nearly as old as the medium itself. The first synchronized sound war film to receive an Academy Award for Best Picture and Best Director, in only the third year of the awards, was Lewis Milestone's *All Quiet on the Western Front*. Based on Erich Maria Remarque's heartbreaking autobiographical novel about World War I, the book was banned and burned in Germany. The 1930 film is still one of a handful of best war films ever made, and Lew Ayres' portrayal of young German soldier Paul Baumer has never been surpassed as a veteran portrayal. Baumer and his schoolmates go off to war to the jingoistic cheerleading of their schoolmaster Professor Kantorek, and after a predictably horrendous experience at the front Paul returns home on leave and walks by Kantorek's classroom. He overhears the familiar chauvinistic rhetoric coming out of the window, glorifying war and urging Kantorek's young charges to "save the Fatherland."

The professor introduces Paul to the students like a laboratory specimen as "one of the first to go, a lad who sat before me on these very benches. One of the Iron Youth who have made Germany invincible in the field. You must speak to them. You must tell them what it means to serve your Fatherland."

"No, no. I can't tell them anything."
"You must, Paul. Tell them how much they are needed out there. Tell them why you went and what it means to you."
"I can't say anything." Kantorek continues cajoling. Paul says dryly:
"I can't tell you anything you don't know. We live in the trenches out there. We fight. We try not to be killed. Sometimes we are. That's all."

The boys look confused and hostile. Kantorek keeps up the badgering. Paul finally breaks:

I heard you in here reciting the same old stuff, making more Iron Men, more young heroes. You still think it's beautiful and sweet to die for your country, don't you? We used to think you knew. The first bombardment taught us better. It's dirty and painful to die for your country. When it comes to dying for your country, it's better not to die at all. There are millions out there dying for their country, and what good is it?

Paul is booed by the students and returns to the front four days before his leave is due to expire, despite his mother's failing health. In the controversial concluding scene Paul is back at the front reaching out of the foxhole for a butterfly when he is shot. Milestone does not change the book's ending as Stallone did for Rambo. There is no sequel, one is left with only the infinite sadness of war, something Mike lived with in every moment:

War widow
Mother of an unborn son
Let surviving uncles
Teach the orphan of the gun
Cannon fodder
The unborn daughter
The stillborn father
Daddy, was it fun?
Widows weep and quiet their keep
From the machine that is the thief
As able bodies fight for peace
Tiny pensions, not to mention
Guidance never given
No one suffers from the war
Except the ones left livin'

World War II brought forth its own PTSD portrayals, notably William Wyler's 1946 Academy Award-winning *The Best Years of Our Lives*, a brilliantly woven homecoming narrative of three small-town veterans and their families. Nearly every conceivable readjustment challenge—unemployment, infidelity, alcoholism, PTSD symptoms and physical disability—occur among the veterans in their relationships with each other, with their wives, with their parents and with their girlfriends. A huge box office and critical success, the film is unique among veteran films in its complex structure. One reason *The Best Years of Our Lives* is easy to relate to is because it is about human relationships, and the human females (rare in war movies) are sympathetic if somewhat stereotyped characters: the faithful long-suffering wife, the floozy, the girlfriend whose love is tested by her fiancé's profound physical injury. Real-life maimed veteran Harold Russell received two Academy Awards for his portrayal of Homer Parrish. Myrna Loy as the storybook wife of banker Al Stephenson (Frederic March) is gracefully convincing in subtle ways as when she makes hash marks with a fork on a tablecloth at a fancy dinner keeping track of Al's drinks before his turn at the podium. By the time he gets up the count is five, and he gives a tipsy veteran speech using his war experience in part to criticize his bank manager boss' reluctance to give GI loans to veterans without collateral. Al invokes a combat analogy:

> So I said to the major, but that operation involves considerable risk. We haven't sufficient collateral. "I'm aware of that" said the major, "but the fact remains that there's a hill and you guys are going to take it." So I said to him "I'm sorry, Major, no collateral no hill." So we didn't take the hill and we lost the war.

Against unlikely odds, Al pulls off the speech to the satisfaction of his boss and the relief of his wife. Also defying off-screen probability the film has a quintessentially happy Hollywood ending, where the story lines wrap up in a gauzy bow. But the film's generous duration of three hours allows treatment of a nearly comprehensive range of veteran issues. The female characters are one-dimensional and there is no physical abuse, but the wives and girlfriends contribute pathos and depth to the veteran's stories. The tidy ending reflects the virtue of being a soldier in "The Good War" and presages the suburban nuclear family automobile fueled decade that followed.

In contrast to the World War II happy ending, the most noted Vietnam homecoming film conveys the turmoil, anger and confusion of its own era. Titled aptly *Coming Home* (Ashby 1978), Bruce Dern's compelling portrayal of a vet suffering from PTSD two years before the condition was formally recognized hit especially close to the mark for me. Jon Voight got an Academy Award and well-earned attention for his portrayal of the paraplegic vet Luke Martin. At the end of the movie Voight delivers a speech to a high school audience that is as powerful as any veteran monologue on film:

> You know, you want to be a part of it—be patriotic... Go out and get your licks in for the U.S. of A. And when you get over there it's a totally different situation... I wanted to be a

war hero. I wanted to go out and kill for my country… And now I'm here to tell you that I have killed for my country or whatever and I don't feel good about it… And I know some of you guys are gonna look at the uniform, man, and you're gonna remember all the films and you're gonna think about the glory of other wars and think about some vague patriotic feeling and go off and fight this turkey, too… And I'm telling you it ain't like it is in the movies. That's all I want to tell you because I didn't have a choice.

(Ashby 1978)

Voight/Luke is the logical speaker using reasoned if heartfelt discourse, but Bruce Dern's character Marine Captain Bob Hyde is pure pain and rage. One critic wrote about the "odd combination of jittery energy and menacing nonchalance" that got Dern typecast as a psycho in earlier films (Biskind 2008: 3). Dern's brief scene after he has discovered his wife Sally's (Jane Fonda) affair with Luke is gripping from the first frame where the bayonet of his locked and loaded weapon glistens as he prowls slowly through a doorway in total silence and into the room towards Fonda, who has been frozen in place by the sound of his approach. He enters gun first. She stands up slowly and reaches out to him.

"I wanted to talk to you. You seem so far away from me since you came back. I've been scared."
"Don't bullshit me. Don't bullshit me. Don't bullshit. If it's over it's over."
"What are you saying? That you're not even gonna make the effort?"
"What I am saying is that I do not belong in this house and they're saying I don't belong over there. I don't even deserve the medal they're going to give me tomorrow. How can they give you a medal for a war they don't even want you to fight?"
Luke arrives, wheeling in the door.
"I don't want to make things more complicated."
"It's actually very simple. I don't belong here."

Dern looks at the wall. Voight says he understands, and Dern whips around pointing the gun at Luke and Sally in firing position. Fonda holds her arms out defensively and keeps them there for a long time in an almost martial arts pose. Dern jabs in the air at both of them.

"You Jody fuck."
"Get back slope cunt."
"I understand because I'm a brother. I'm not the enemy. The enemy is the fucking war."

It is unclear throughout the scene just what Dern will do in his simmering fury alternating between a 1,000-yard stare and brief moments of intensely intimate vulnerability. The tension and terror in the scene are palpable, expressively captured by Fonda's body language, sometimes motionless with fear, then momentarily tender as she reaches out to stroke him as if to soothe the savage beast. That complicated dialectic between love and fear is something I learned about from Mike.

Ocean View Motel

One cool June twilight in the late 1980s I heard the sound of tires on gravel approaching my remote country retreat. I looked out the window to see Mike pulling in, driving a car I had never seen. I stopped breathing. Since the restraining order he was not supposed to be here, which didn't stop him from trying. He coaxed me out of the house by turning on the charm. "Come on out here, darlin'. There's somethin' I want to show you." I fell for it and went outside and around the back of the car as he flashed a grin and lifted the trunk, revealing a jumbled cache of assault weapons. I really stopped breathing. We had reached a new level of insanity. I can't remember how I maneuvered him into leaving, but it was the last night I stayed in my own house until he was admitted two months later to the newly created PTSD unit of the Menlo Park Veterans Administration Hospital.

In our three years together Mike had become increasingly agitated and verbally abusive. He knew I hated drugs, not that I hadn't tried them, and would not tolerate them at all when any kids were around, so he would disappear for days at a time to get high with his buddies. I never believed that those closest to an addict are often the last to know the extent of the problem until it happened to me. Mike made a meager living working at the local gas station, supplemented by disability payments from a back injury in Vietnam he had reinjured at Lordstown. He lived for his Panhead and for tinkering with cars or bikes of any kind. When we owned a body shop, I realized that he liked to talk about working on cars and bikes a lot more than he liked actually working on them. At one point we had two Harleys (his Panhead and my Sportster), a 1966 white Mustang convertible, a 1986 silver Camaro, a 1978 El Camino, a 1953 Ford pickup, and a Subaru wagon just to have something to actually drive. On the motorhead level life was good.

Mike had the rough way with words of a working class troubadour, untainted by the conventions one might learn in a poetry class in college. He turned me toward Buddhism when he asked simply "Who would you rather follow? Some bleeding guy with nails in his feet or a fat laughing guy with kids crawling all over?" What little equilibrium Mike was able to maintain was derived from his ability to put his feelings into lyrics, as in "Eat It."

> *More than ten years have come to pass*
> *Still my mind keeps drifting back to those kidnapped boys in rubber sacks*
> *Murdered in a foreign land and then shipped back*
> *To a mother who wasted affection*
> *Ten thousand dollars and a goddamn flag*
> *For a teenage corpse in a rubber bag*

A battlefield death on a foreign shore
To save a freedom that lives no more
I'd like to tell you just how I feel
About your phony patriots
And the cheapness of your deal
You can't bring that boy back to life
You stabbed him in the back with your best steak knife
Then imprisoned his brother for refusing to fight
How do you sleep at night?
I'll tell you what I'd like to do
I'd like to steal your eyes and piss on you
Just knowing you are alive makes me write this two-bit rhyme
Just knowing you are alive tells me there's a major crime
Not yet brought to justice
If there's a god, and I hope there is
Maybe some day he'll bust you for raping his kid

Poetry helped the healing but it was not enough and Mike steadily deteriorated, become more restless, sleepless, erratic, and addicted. I joined in the morbid dance of the codependent, unable to let go and unable to help even myself. I guess I should have realized sooner that I was living with a very angry man, but nature had to take its course. And when he wasn't angry he couldn't be more charming which amplified the confusion, but not for long.

Superior Court of California, County of Mendocino 12 July 1988 Injunctive Order: Restraint on Personal Conduct, Stay-Away Order, Property Restraint
The plaintiff has suffered ongoing verbal abuse from the respondent for the past two years. He is a Vietnam vet and suffers from post-traumatic stress disorder. He has punched out the walls in the house and on June 29 he assaulted the plaintiff by slapping her across the face, punching her with full force on her arm, and pushing her to the ground. The respondent is a chronic alcohol and drug abuser.

I grew up in a family that was dysfunctional in a 1950s garden-variety sort of way, but in no sense abusive. The most violent thing I witnessed at home were the skirmishes between my brothers Chuck and Tom when they watched *The Three Stooges*, airing daily after school. After that, no one ever had to convince me about the link between media and violence. But I had no context for the experience of the 29th of June in Room 7 of the Ocean View Motel.

Mike and I were separated and he had lured me to the motel using his characteristic charm offensive to exploit my confusion. I was unaware that by this time I was already well into the cycle of abuse. Though he had not yet laid a hand on me, I had developed a psychological and almost physical addiction to him that I learned later was typical of abuser-abused relationships. The good news about this obsessive behavior was that I learned that my erratic attention span was in fact infinite because I could not get Mike out of my mind for one minute, and I lost a lot of weight. The fear diet, effective but not recommended.

I entered the darkened motel room and Mike was already there sitting on the edge of the bed drinking a bottle of wine. I am sure I had some too, but things are blurry until the moment out of the blue when he backhanded me across the face, punched my right arm with his full force, and sent me flying across the room to land in a dizzy heap. Then he left.

For several days I was reeling as I hid in my house and watched the bruises bloom. I have never felt more completely vulnerable, scared or alone. And then somehow I did the smartest thing I have ever done in my life, the thing that saved it. The CAARE Project, an hour up the coast in Ft. Bragg, was a new domestic violence treatment center housed in a rickety little Victorian off the main drag. This was during a time when the police would still not necessarily even respond to domestic 911 calls. I am not sure the CAARE Project even had a sign, and I do not know what state of grace allowed me to turn up there a few days after the assault. I was in absolute denial. I had little self-awareness and less self-esteem and I was fighting the urge to turn around and run out of the door. Instead, the staff artfully led me to a group counseling session that had nothing touchy-feely about it. Alice, the leader, looked me dead in the eye and said, "We see three hundred women a year here, and the profile you are describing—a Vietnam vet with PTSD and substance abuse—is the most violent and dangerous man we see. He could kill you. He will kill you. It happened here not more than six months ago." I learned that abuse creates dependence and that "battery transmits PTSD," so I had it, too. But I was now armed with just a glimmer of self-awareness that continued to grow over the course of my visits to CAARE. They led me every step of the way through filing the restraining order and beyond. I was lucky.

In the 1980s, domestic violence was on the verge of being taken seriously. It is still the number one problem for women worldwide. The sheriff's deputy in my town (from whom I had bought my house) pointed out that there were only two officers at any one time patrolling 50 square miles, and 911 or not, an endangered woman without a weapon and a big dog was pretty much on her own. It was a long summer, and with my kids away, I spent the nights up the hill at my friends Bill and Andrea's house. Bill is a retired Los Angeles deputy sheriff, and he mercifully took me under his protective wing.

Still, it was a small town (population 485) and Mike was around, ostentatiously tooling around on his Harley with the local coke whore in tow. The restraining order had put him in something of a bind because his usual way of trying to punish me was to stop speaking. Now that he wasn't allowed to talk to me, his defiant self had to take any opportunity to catch my ear. Mike was so rebellious that he considered being held to what he himself said he was going to do an infringement of his constitutional rights. His strategies for communicating frustration were limited to silence and violence. The first time he edged near me in the General Store he said "they're toasting me at the bar for kicking your ass." Another time, looking at my giant arm bruise, ever the poet he said, "Want me to autograph your tattoo?" That did it for me. The spell was broken, though I could not help but appreciate the literary touch.

In September, Mike was admitted to the first PTSD unit in the country at the Veterans Administration Hospital in Menlo Park, complaining that he had been "rode hard and put away wet." He stayed at Menlo for a month, got better, got out, got worse, went back a few more times. I lost track, and the day finally came when it did not seem to matter any more. I was well on the way back to my own life. I was drained. I loved him and wanted to make his terrifying pain go away, but I couldn't. I could only become more of a PTSD carrier myself. During this period I was lucky to have as a therapist the singularly gifted John Weakland, an original member of Gregory Bateson's double bind team—which coincidentally had been housed at the same Menlo VA Hospital back in the 1950s. Weakland and CAARE are what pulled me back from the brink, especially John's ever-sardonic injunctions. When Mike was admitted to the VA, John said, "If he gets his act together what are you gonna' do for excitement? How are you gonna' shine?" By then I was ready to figure out something.

Figure 6.2: Veterans Administration Hospital, New York 2012.

PTSD The Family Disease

One of the visitors to our "Vietnam: Rhetoric and Realities" class during the Mike years was Le Ly Hayslip, who had just published her autobiography *When Heaven and Earth Changed Places*, later (1993) an Oliver Stone film. She was the first Vietnamese woman I ever heard speak, and at the time I did not know how much we had in common as women who were now in some sense PTSD carriers. In the wake of the Iraq and Afghanistan wars, the Veterans Administration built an extensive program for what they call IPV—Intimate Partner Violence—which they estimate is experienced by up to one-third of American women. Twenty years ago it was a shameful secret. One hopes that the mothers of veterans are included in the program—witness Tom Cruise as Ron Kovic verbally assault his mother in *Born on the Fourth of July* in his dramatic "penis" scene. In the film *Heaven and Earth*, Le Ly urges her husband (Tommy Lee Jones) to "tell me all." He responds:

> I'm a killer, baby. I killed so many out there... Sometimes three or four a night. All kinds. Rice farmers, rich fat cats bankrolling VC units. It was a complete mind fuck. Psy-ops, baby, knives, rip a man's guts, bite out his liver, drop it on his chest so he don't get into Buddha heaven... You know what it's like doing that? It's like being eaten alive from the inside out by a belly full of sharks... Well, one day I found you and it all changed, I thought. But nothing ever changes.

"One day I found you and it all changed, I thought. But nothing ever changes." PTSD is a family disease. Vietnam vet portrayals on screen get it right more often than not, maybe because the symptoms of the condition are theatrical to begin with. Patriotism, trauma, disillusionment, blame all together trace the arc of classical tragedy.

When PTSD is Like a Box of Chocolates

In the 1990s something peculiar happened to the cinematic image of Vietnam vets. Rambo is often thought of as the revisionist symbol of Vietnam, the soldier who is once again betrayed when he returns to find his POW buddies. "Do we get to win this time?" is his animating question. But in the decade following Rambo a stealth rewriting of Vietnam appeared in the immensely popular and successful movie *Forrest Gump* (Robert Zemeckis 1994). Starring the affable Tom Hanks along with screen-friendly Sally Fields and Robin Wright, Gump spun the irresistible yarn of a mentally challenged hero who accomplishes amazing things to a comfort-food musical score that sold 12 million albums. "An epic of human proportions," commented Hanks (DVD).

Forrest Gump is based loosely on the novel of the same name by Winston Groom. Sweet and simple minded (IQ 70) Forrest strolls through a life of blissful ignorance and down home values, unexpectedly becoming a superhero in any domain he enters—sports, combat, ping-pong, fishing (and in the book space flight, chess, and wrestling). The episodic story has been called a virtual reality theme park of the 1960s and 1970s, and despite its critical and commercial success and shelf of Academy Awards has attracted some fierce critics: "glib, shallow and monotonous"; "the message that stupidity is redemption is clearly what a lot of Americans want to hear"; "a dismayingly reactionary work"; "toeing the centerline like a motherfucker while Rome burns"; "a vile, irresponsible film whose massive success says some very frightening things about America"; and "a coffee table book celebrating the magic of special effects."

Fans of the movie might be surprised to learn that it ranks number four on *National Review's* list of "Best Conservative Movies." John Miller (2011) lauds Tom Hanks character as "an amiable dunce who is far too smart to embrace the lethal values of the 1960s while pointing to the cautionary tale of Forrest's love Jenny (Robin Wright) who "becomes a drug-addled hippie with disastrous results." In the book, Jenny marries another man and does not die of an inferred AIDS virus as in the movie, but her cinematic death bolsters the morality play that recasts the sixties as a collective bout of bad behavior that deserves and incurs wrath and retribution. Jennifer Wang has written in *Cinema Journal* about "how political conservatives have used the film to articulate a traditional version of recent America" and the death of Jenny as a result of her experimentation with sex and drugs "symbolizes the death of liberal America and the death of the protests that defined the decade" (2000: 96).

The Vietnam War makes a predictable appearance in the Gump story. While the Vietnam sequence was shot in full-on production mode, the broader theme-park context of the movie makes its treatment resemble the satiric *Tropic Thunder* (Stiller 2008) more than *Apocalypse Now* (Coppola 1979) or *Platoon* (Stone 1986). It is in the Vietnam episode that Forrest meets Lt. Dan Taylor (Gary Sinise) who delivers "a dark, bitter performance" (Maslin). Lt. Dan, who comes from a long line of soldiers killed in battle, is Gump's commanding officer. In the middle of a firefight Forrest tries to pick up the wounded (now legless) Lt. Dan, who barks "Goddamit! What are you doing! Leave me here! Get away! Just leave me here! Get out!"

Gump himself is wounded and he and Lt. Dan are evacuated to the same field hospital where Lt. Dan gives his version of the combat veteran speech:

> Now you listen to me. We all have a destiny. Nothing just happens. It's all part of a plan. I should have died out there with my men! But now I'm nothing but a goddamned cripple! A legless freak! Look! Look! Look at me! Do you see that? Do you know what it's like not to be able to use your legs?… You cheated me. I had a destiny. I was supposed to die in the field! With honor! That was my destiny! And you cheated me out of it! You understand what I'm saying, Gump? This wasn't supposed to happen. Not to me. I had a destiny.

To this point Lt. Dan's speech is virtually interchangeable with the classic veteran PTSD monologues of Lew Ayers, Bruce Dern, or Sylvester Stallone, but an interesting transformation occurs as the movie begins its denouement.

Forrest himself almost makes a "veteran's speech" when he is thrust to the front of an anti-war protest at the Washington Mall and urged by Abbie Hoffman to "tell us a little bit about the war, man..." Forrest begins "There was only one thing I could say about the war in Vietnam..." at which point a cop disables the audio and while Forrest continues to talk none of it is heard. At the end Hoffman says, "That's so right on, man. You said it all." In the book Forrest throws his Congressional Medal of Honor on the steps, so who knows what his silenced speech might have included. The few clues we are given like Hoffman's response suggest that hearing the actual content of Forrest's speech might have made it harder for conservatives to appropriate the movie for their agenda in the 1990s, but the significant erasure of the speech renders the point moot. Again, as in *First Blood* and *The Quiet American*, the filmmaker changes the ending to such a way as to reverse the message of the movie as compared to the original story.

When Forrest next encounters Lt. Dan he is living in a flophouse and drinking as much Ripple as he can get his hands on. Forrest tells Dan of his dream to be a shrimp boat captain in remembrance of their fallen comrade Bubba. Dan promises, "I tell you Gilligan, the day that you are a shrimp boat captain, I will come and be your first mate." This predictably comes to pass and not only are they wildly successful at shrimping but Dan invests their money in "a little fruit company" (Apple) that makes them obscenely rich. Dan turns up at Forrest and Jenny's wedding on "magic" titanium legs with his Vietnamese fiancé on his arm. "Magic" is the operative word here as it is in most of this special effects laden movie because Vietnam combat narratives rarely if ever have such a warm and fuzzy ending, let alone one in which a maimed soldier finds true love with the enemy and grows new legs. Forrest Gump bestows the 1960s in general and the veteran story in particular with a happy ending for those who served (Forrest, Dan) and tragedy for those like Jenny who rode the wave of social change, liberalism, and experimentation. And in another twist on the PTSD story convention, while Jenny is assaulted in the story (both book and movie) it is by her boyfriend the radical SDS leader and not by Forrest the combat vet. One serendipitous consequence of the movie is that it prompted Gary Sinise to form the "Lt. Dan Band," which plays for U.S. troops and charities around the world.

Happy movie endings notwithstanding, the problems of PTSD, family violence and veteran suicide continue unabated. All 1.1 million U.S. soldiers are now required to take a training course in "mental stress" in order to improve combat performance and reduce the mental health problems that affect so many Iraq and Afghanistan veterans. Paul Haggis' *In The Valley of Elah* (2007) is one film treatment based on a true story from the Iraq war where veterans suffering from PTSD actually murder one of their own. The cognitive therapy program for PTSD is modeled on techniques that have been tested primarily with middle school students. Cognitive therapy, an elaborate variant of the power of positive thinking, may help to improve overall life coping skills, but it remains to be seen how effective it will be in forestalling appropriately horrified reactions to direct experience of war. One note of optimism is that families are included in the training so that it may reduce the relationship violence that is epidemic in today's military. Still, it would be far better to do more to prevent situations that create the wounds of war in the first place and the family and cultural disease of PTSD that follows. War is forever.

The suffering of all movie combat veterans and many real ones keeps the Vietnam war alive, unresolved, incomplete. What should be a conversation has become a cliché. And then there is another war to depict, another war started under false pretenses against an exaggerated enemy in a country whose language and customs are unknown and whose people are underestimated. The movie has ended too soon without imparting a lesson, and the wars go on. We may never know the secrets in the heart of the wounded warrior, but we do know that every so often, when least expected, the undead war will arise again.

Who are these fools who pretend
That unjustified death will go unavenged?
A well blown mind never mends
For you and me, dude, the war never ends
The battles rage inside our heads
And I'm certain they will til the day we are dead

Chapter 7

Reinventing Rambo: *Flooding with Love for the Kid*

On a mild spring evening in lower Manhattan my daughter and I met at Soho Rep on Walker Street to experience a most unusual theatrical encounter, one that *New York Times* critic Charles Isherwood (2009) called "a winking shard of low-concept theater for downtown hipsters." I guess that meant us. *Rambo Solo*'s six-week run had been extended, and I stayed in the city an extra night that week so that we could attend whatever the winking shard was going to be. The Soho Rep space had been reconfigured especially for the one-man show. We were led downstairs through a subterranean passage and up again into a black box theater with floor cushions for seats and no visible exit signs. I headed for the sidewall to have something to lean against, having no interest in pillow-sitting in the dark for two hours. The hundred audience members wiggled on their own pillows trying to get comfortable. When the lights dimmed an amiable young man walked through the pillows up to the stage and began his strange story. The mood that emerged was like sitting around a campfire with a slightly deranged friend who nonetheless had a knack for spinning a good yarn. Everything that was about to come was simulated in the best Baudrillardian sense as we heard the Rambo story's myth and meaning bravely reimagined in both content and form.

Zachary Oberzan is a solid and earnest Ivy League grad who would make a perfect Clark Kent or an Alden Pyle in the next remake of *The Quiet American*, except that it is not Alden Pyle that preoccupies him, it is Rambo. When Oberzan was ten years old his family took advantage of an HBO free-all-weekend promotion, and he stayed up all night glued to the television watching *First Blood*. He told NPR (2009) "I was quite moved and taken by the story. I found the book at the supermarket, and read it about a dozen times." Years later Oberzan joined the experimental theater group Nature Theater of Oklahoma, named after the magical company Franz Kafka's hero in *Amerika* runs off to join. Nature Theater of Oklahoma has nothing to do with Oklahoma and a lot to do with the theater of everyday life, infused with what John Del Signore (2009) called "the aesthetics of amateurishness." The company's production immediately preceding *Rambo Solo*, called *No Dice*, featured seven actors dancing while reciting cell phone conversations.

Oberzan's 90-minute monologue is likewise constructed from a recorded phone conversation he had with director Pavol Liska, during which Oberzan breathlessly recited the story of *First Blood* scene by scene from memory. From this material Liska and Kelly Copper collaborated in the development of a stage piece where Oberzan performs his retelling of the novel. The carefully crafted presentation style is faux spontaneous, complete with hesitations and vocalized pauses. The backdrop is a triptych of three rumpled sheets hanging from a clothesline. In an ingenious lowbrow high-tech (or maybe high concept

Figure 7.1: Zachary Oberzan in *Rambo Solo*, 2009. Used by permission.

low-tech) staging, three nearly identical but separately recorded video versions of the same script are projected, each taped earlier by Oberzan in his apartment.

Among the few props is the *First Blood* paperback in a plastic bag, the better for safekeeping. Isherwood tells us that "Rambo Nut believes the best way to transmit his joy is to narrate the plot in precise detail, scene by deathless scene, image by image, as if describing for the blind each shot of a movie endlessly playing on a screen in his mind." The naturalistic delivery is contrived, aided by an earpiece Oberzan wears to stay in sync with the video images. Or mostly in sync. All three images and the live actor are almost always a beat or two off, giving the viewer a sense of stop-frame animation. It is weirdly captivating scanning the various Rambos for seconds of sync that provide a small pop of delight. Acknowledging the difficulty of his mission to get the work of his grand obsession taken seriously, Oberzan argues from the stage that "*First Blood* is not what many people would call grand literature ... but for me, it—it is just as grand and just as universal as—as—as Hamlet." Isherwood would call this part of Oberzan's course on "Literary Appreciation for Lunatics," but most critics were more sympathetic. *Variety's* Marilyn Stasio (2009) wrote that Oberzan's Nature Theater of Oklahoma "has hit the mother lode in *Rambo Solo*, an idiosyncratic one-man show performed with hilarious conviction." Critic David Lee (2009) called *Rambo Solo* "the best kind of art; it is simultaneously silly and profound, engaging and disparaging, able to embrace the material and its audiences while thumbing its nose at recognizable tropes, tricks, and conjectures." Lee points out how as a play about a film about a book, *Rambo Solo* "belies an intrinsic curiosity with our culture's relationship to the nature of storytelling."

Oberzan's *Rambo Solo* piece of appropriation stage art reinvents Rambo for a new generation while at the same time confirming the durability of the story it tells, the myth of the wounded warrior, man against man turning to nature, the emptiness of heroism. David Morrell published *First Blood* in 1972, two years before Zachary Oberzan was born. Morrell first got the idea as a graduate student at Penn State University in 1968 when a pair of CBS stories caught his eye. One was about a firefight in Vietnam, the other on city riots in the United States following the assassination of Martin Luther King. The juxtaposition of those stories made him want to write a novel that brought the Vietnam War home. *First Blood* was the result. Morrell was an English professor at the University of Iowa by the time *First Blood* was published. He had been struck by the Vietnam veterans he saw returning to campus. Rambo (first name John was added later) was drawn as an intentionally sympathetic character—the betrayed veteran/victim. Morrell acknowledges that while the character was based on real-life World War II hero Audie Murphy, the name Rambo was derived primarily from a variety of apple.

> In the early stages of composition I struggled to find a strong name for the character. One afternoon while I was writing, my wife came home from the grocery store and said that she'd found a new kind of apple that she thought was delicious. Apples were the farthest thing from my mind while I struggled to find the character's name, but politely I took a bite of the apple and discovered that it was in fact delicious. What's it called?' I asked. 'Rambo,' she replied. This was in Pennsylvania where the Rambo type of apple is grown and appreciated. Instantly, I recognized the sound of force. It also reminded me of the way some people pronounce the name of a French poet I'd been studying, Rimbaud, whose most famous work is *A Season in Hell*, which I felt was an apt metaphor for the prisoner-of-war experience that I imagined Rambo suffering (2008).

Rambo's first name "John" was added by the screenwriters, in one of many departures from the book where the name "Rambo" stood alone. Does "John" as a modifier add an everyman quality to the character? Does it invite sympathy by mitigating the force of "Rambo"? Does it point to the character's many contradictions by the pairing of a bland and a colorful word? How many Rambo fans can even identify his first name?

It would be ten years, 26 scripts, nine directors, and three production companies before *First Blood* was released as a movie in October 1982, but the timing ensured maximum impact. The United States was deep in the middle of a severe global economic recession. Unemployment topped 10 percent, interest rates soared, and more than 100 savings and loan companies failed. This "Reagan recession" sent his approval rating free falling to 35 percent. At the same time, the United States was still recovering from the long hangover of having lost the Vietnam War in 1975 when Saigon "fell" to the Communists in the words of the Americans or was "liberated" according to the Vietnamese. A few filmic treatments of the war had been released before 1982 (*Coming Home, The Deer Hunter, Apocalypse Now*) but most were yet to come. John Rambo blazed into this grim context as the veteran victim avenger, a symbol of America's lost power and respect and a one-man show of "getting to win this time." Rambo provided the ideal vehicle for displacement of the political and military wrongs onto the sympathetic victim veteran, foreshadowing the daunting hawkish response to protests against the first Iraq war: if you are against the war you are against the warrior. This has become such a master trope in U.S. culture that any anti-war rhetoric is subject to its silencing influence. Rambo was able to contribute to right-wing revisionism of the Vietnam catastrophe while at the same time valorizing the wounded warrior. It is seldom noted that Rambo-as-killing-machine emerged primarily from the second picture in the franchise—*Rambo: First Blood Part II*—which was a significant departure from the more complex and sophisticated *First Blood* ethos.

Rambo's Kill Chart

The central conflict of *First Blood* occurs when Rambo is unjustly harassed by small town Sheriff Will Teasle out to flex some muscle. Teasle is played by Brian Dennehy, himself a two-tour Vietnam veteran. Once incarcerated and further provoked by the petty nastiness of jail, Rambo flips into a flashback of his prisoner of war experience in Vietnam. At this point all hell and high energy break loose, Rambo escapes, and soon has everyone up to and including the National Guard on his tail. This play off of the lone drifter against the military establishment is the first place where the Rambo character becomes larger than life. At a critical point in the *First Blood* story, Rambo's former special forces commanding officer Colonel Trautman (Richard Crenna) appears, as he says, "to save the police from Rambo." In the end of the book Rambo dies, given the *coup de grace* by Colonel Trautman himself and securing his place as the wronged and sympathetic veteran/victim. In the film *First Blood*, Rambo lives, presumably to leave the door open for the sequel that became *Rambo: First Blood Part II*.

First Blood was a modest $27 million domestic box office success by Hollywood standards and made no notable waves in the critical establishment. Eventually *First Blood* grossed 125 million worldwide; Part II 300 million; Rambo III 188 million, and Rambo IV 200 million. Stallone's portrayal of Rambo in *First Blood* was as appealing as his script, and the single scene where he articulates his anguish to Colonel Trautman is powerful and moving in spite of itself. Not everyone was pleased with changing the end of the story. Kirk Douglas, originally cast as Colonel Trautman, left the project following multiple disagreements about the script with director Ted Kotcheff. Kotcheff claims that Douglas questioned every line in the script, stole other actors' lines, and did rewrites that sounded like a "1945 B-film." "It was him or me" (Kotcheff in St. Mary and White 2012).

The original ending shot was true to the book: Rambo dies. This played so poorly to test audiences that an alternative ending where Rambo lives—shot by Kotcheff almost as an afterthought—was substituted. Both endings are included in the DVD collectors set, which can be disconcerting for viewers familiar with the original film. Kotcheff was cautioned by one of the *Casablanca* screenwriters that "there are two battles you'll never win: titles and endings."

If Alden Pyle is the model of the fictional quiet American aggressor, John Rambo is the quintessential loud one; Pyle on steroids bombarded with gamma rays or some other mystery elixir that breeds superhuman strength. For evidence that Alden Pyle's image has endured one need only recall George W. Bush's 2007 invocation of him. But John Rambo is something else again. The Rambo movies were hands down the most popular war films among my students in Vietnam, especially the young men, despite the fact that in the first two movies of the franchise they are the enemy.

Morrell was right about the force of "Rambo." The Rambo image with all its iconicity and metaphorical weight made an instant and searing impression on the American cultural psyche with *First Blood* in 1982, an impact that increased exponentially with the release of *Rambo: First Blood Part II* in 1985. Two more Rambo films followed in 1988 and 2008, and the progression of the series is summarized by John Mueller's droll "Rambo Kill Chart":

	I: "First Blood" (1982)	II: "Rambo: First Blood Part II" (1985)	III: "Rambo III" (1988)	IV: "Rambo" (2008)
Number of bad guys killed by Rambo with his shirt on	1	12	33	83
Number of bad guys killed by Rambo with his shirt off	0	46	45	0
Number of bad guys killed by Rambo no matter how attired	1	58	78	83
Number of bad guys killed by accomplices of Rambo acting on their own	0	10	17	40
Number of good guys killed by bad guys	0	1	37	113
Total number of people killed	1	69	132	236
Number of people killed per minute	0.01	0.72	1.30	2.59
Time at which the first person is killed (mins:secs)	29:31	33:34	41:9	3:22
Number of people killed per minute from that point until the end of the film (not including the ending credits)	0.02	1.18	2.39	3.04
Sequences in which Rambo is shot at without significant result	12	24	38	2
Number of sequences in which good guys are tortured by bad guys	2	5	7	3
Number of sex scenes	0	0	0	0

JOHN MUELLER *holds the Woody Hayes Chair of National Security Studies at Ohio State University. Among his books are "The Remnants of War" and "Overblown: How Politicians and the Terrorism Industry Inflate National Security Threats, and Why We Believe Them."*

Figure 7.2: Rambo kill chart by John Mueller (2008).

Rambo IV (2008), shot in Thailand featuring Burmese as the bad guys, has twice the violence of even *Rambo III* and 100 times the violence of *First Blood* if measured by people killed per minute. Rambo followed the pattern of so many people as they age and just became an exaggerated version of himself, which is hard to do when you are hyperbolic to begin with. Yet at the same time Stallone was releasing *Rambo IV* in 2008 to a jaded public and mildly favorable reviews, two wildly different reinventions of the Rambo story were making their debuts. British filmmaker Garth Jennings released his coming-of-age film *Son of Rambow* (2007) and actor-writer-filmmaker Oberzan mounted his one-man show *Rambo Solo* and released the companion film *Flooding With Love for the Kid* that includes Oberzan's revised ending for *First Blood*. As heavy-handed as Rambo may be, both Jennings and Oberzan manage to reframe the story and the character with deft and nuanced sensibility and a refreshing lack of cynicism.

"They Drew First Blood, Sir."

What accounts for Rambo's enduring popularity even among those who should hate and fear him? All four Rambo films have been worldwide money machines, notwithstanding countries like India or the former Soviet Union where they have been censored. How does the style of Stallone's Rambo compare to the substance of Morrell's Rambo? In Morrell's original depiction, Rambo describes himself as a follower of Zen, a Buddhist. He is the son of an Italian father and a Navajo mother. He meditates daily. He has been celibate for 14 years because "after the horrors he'd endured, sex had ceased to be an urge" (1972). *Catch 22* is one of his favorite books. This is Rambo, who became John Rambo, who morphed into Sylvester Stallone Rambo, who turned into the second largest grossing film of 1985, and became a notorious icon for the decade. "They drew first blood, sir." "Do we get to win this time?" An icon so potent it shows no sign of fading away.

If this celibate Zen description plays against Rambo's popular image it is because the John Rambo character in its various manifestations is a jumble of contradictory features, most notably between the narrative substance of the Rambo story and the beefed-up style of Stallone's interpretation. Actors considered for the Rambo role included Al Pacino, Steve McQueen, Clint Eastwood, Robert DeNiro, Nick Nolte, and Michael Douglas. Paul Newman was considered for Teasle. The initial Rambo movie *First Blood* was a fundamentally supportive portrayal of Vietnam veterans, and the controversy that erupted upon the release of *Rambo: First Blood Part II* in June 1985 was at first puzzling. How did Rambo become such an instant symbol of testosterone run amok that after even 30 years inspires dozens of web sites, thousands of eBay transactions, numerous video games, a Facebook page, scholarly work such as Gordon Fellman's *Rambo and the Dalai Lama* (1998) as well as Garth Jennings movie and Zack Oberzan's multimedia *tour de force*. Rambo is even in the Random House dictionary—"a fanatically militant or violently aggressive person." According to the Social Security Administration, at least 64 baby boys were named Rambo the year after the movie came out.

Thirty years after *First Blood* barely a week goes by without some Rambo reference in popular culture, colorfully illustrated by Eli Manning as "Rambeau II" in 2012.

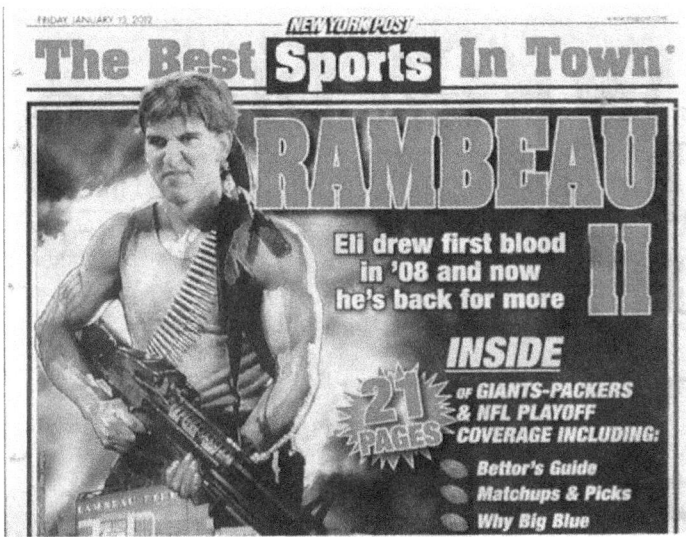

Figure 7.3: Eli Manning as Rambeau II, 2012. Used by permission.

The Rambo industry contributed to making Stallone Hollywood's most bankable star in the late 1980s, commanding at $12 million per film, more than twice the fee of his nearest rival. Stallone was considered the No. 1 box office star worldwide, and his movies grossed more than $1 billion from 1975 to 1985. He may strike some people as an opportunistic troglodyte, but he is very hard to ignore as a cultural and financial powerhouse, even decades later, tied as he is to the warlike behavior of a U.S. having in the words of George H.W. Bush, "kicked the Vietnam syndrome." The impressive bottom line of Stallone's success suggests that he struck a most responsive chord in the post-Vietnam pre-Gulf War period. Stallone himself spoke of his impact in a *Rolling Stone* interview. "What I try to do in films is to explore violence—not so much exploit it, but explore it, use it for a positive means." Interviewer Nancy Collins responds "A lot of critics didn't see Rambo as a positive exploration of violence." Stallone:

> I don't blame them. But it's important for everyone to get a sense of what's happening, especially when something has caught the imagination of the American public—if for nothing else just to study why this has caught fire. I think the intelligentsia should understand that this country now is functioning on emotional more than intellectual energy (1985: 132).

From the start, Rambo was a cultural force of nature so strong that during 1985 President Ronald Reagan repeatedly cited Rambo as a role model. The Rambo message in 1985 scattered over popular and political culture like a shotgun blast. At the time of the movie's release you might read the Rambo movie review in the newspaper, overhear colleagues in a hallway commenting on the movie, see on television that Vietnam veterans were protesting the film in a neighboring town, walk by a display of M-16 Rambo water guns on a visit to the local toy store, see a political cartoon about "Ronbo" Reagan in the paper, and even catch the Rambo/Ronbo cover of cultural touchstone *Mad* magazine.

Richard Dawkins concept of a "meme" was not yet in widespread use, but it could have been custom made for Rambo. You might even actually see the Rambo movie or read the book, but it was hardly necessary to either see the movie or read the book to have a strong impression of the Rambo figure. Around this time I surveyed a large class about Rambo, asking them to write a list of adjectives that came to mind when they heard the name. Those who had *not* seen the film generated a longer list than those who had, provoking a lively discussion of how that counterintuitive result could be explained. Rambo's creator Morrell remarked that Rambo is one of only five characters from thrillers that are internationally known, along with Sherlock Holmes, Tarzan, James Bond, and Harry Potter.

The matrix of the Rambo message emerged over time and space in an array of communication contexts. I was struck by the impact of Rambo from the day of the film's controversial release, and became a collector of message bits from single mentions to full reviews. Through an accumulation of these fragments I could track the symbol as it spread virally, saturating both

Figure 7.4: Rambo and Reagan on *Mad*, December 1982.

broadcast and print media. While such rapid diffusion is typically associated with "important" events like assassinations and natural disasters, the ubiquity of the Rambo symbol within weeks of the film's release suggests that a message need not be important in any conventional sense if it strikes a nerve, even in pre-Twitter trending culture.

Getting to Win This Time

Stallone claimed it was a letter he received from the wife of a soldier missing in action in Vietnam that inspired him to write the screenplay for *Rambo: First Blood Part II* along with James (*The Terminator*) Cameron. David Morrell also participated, and while Stallone and screenwriters Michael Kozoff and William Sackheim adapted *First Blood* from Morrell's novel, the second time around Morrell wrote the Rambo novel from the screenplay by Stallone and Cameron. Stallone has always considered himself to be first and foremost a writer. *Rambo: First Blood Part II* again centers on the betrayal of the individual veteran/victim by the establishment. Rambo, imprisoned and assigned to rock chopping duty as a result of his *First Blood* escapades, is offered relief in the form of a reconnaissance mission aimed at determining the presence or absence of American MIAs in a particular camp. Unknown to Rambo, the mission is primarily a grandstanding move by the opportunistic Congressman Murdock, a man so lacking in principle that he lies about his combat record. When Colonel Trautman learns of Murdock's betrayal, he exclaims: "The mission was a lie, wasn't it? Just like the whole damned war! A lie!"

While various interpretations can be extracted from the *First Blood* and *Rambo* plot and characterizations, it is virtually impossible to see them in the pro-war pro-American light cast upon them by Ronald Reagan's co-optation of Rambo as an anti-Communist saber-rattling symbol. Indeed, no less a source than Sylvester Stallone strongly refuted charges of anti-Soviet bias in his films.

> In Rambo I didn't sit there and say that every communist should die. What did I say? What did I say?... I put America down at the end! I put my own country down. I said I wanted it to love me as much as I love it. Don't [the critics] listen to the end of the movie? Do they leave before it's over?
>
> (Collins 1985)

In the month following its June 1985 release, *Rambo* brought in $100 million at the box office, making it the third most successful opening gross in history to that date behind only *Indiana Jones and the Temple of Doom* and *Return of the Jedi*. Almost immediately the film's "novelization" with 800,000 copies in print made *The New York Times* best seller list and Rambo achieved the mark of an American cultural phenomenon of its time—an hour on the Phil Donahue television show. Reviews of this second Rambo adventure were mixed. Andrew Kopkind writing in *The Nation* called it "at once hilarious and disgusting" (1985).

Pauline Kael's *New Yorker* review argued that "director George P. Cosmatos gives this near-psychotic material—a mixture of Catholic iconography and *Soldier of Fortune* pulp—a veneer of professionalism, but the looniness is always there" (1985: 117). Kael was also among the first to make the point that the movie exploits both Vietnam vets and MIA families with its "comic strip patriotism." Richard Schickel wrote in *Time* that "this childhood dream of glory vulgarizes a demonstrable anguish," and shames it for doing so (1985: 91). And *Variety* underestimated what it termed this "overwrought sequel" to *First Blood* by suggesting (wrongly, as we now know) that "the productions risible, comic book heroics seriously qualify its box-office durability" (1985).

Foreign critics were predictably even tougher. James Tye, Director General of the British Safety Council, called Rambo "truly sickening" and "96 minutes of mindless violence." India banned the film outright because of its anti-Soviet and anti-Vietnamese bias. Soviet critics condemned Rambo as "war-nography," alleging that it is part of a deliberate propaganda campaign to portray Russians as treacherous enemies, while other sources reported that despite the official Soviet criticism of Stallone and his movies, Moscovites said that videos of Stallone films were among the most sought after by Russians who owned VCRs. It has also been reported that Rambo was a smash hit in Beirut and that the Nicaraguan Contras took to sporting Rambo-style dress following the film's release. Rambo-garb was also popular within Poland's Solidarity Movement during the same period. The unsung costume designer of *First Blood* Tom Bronson deserves much of the credit for Rambo's iconicity. A bandolier, a headband and some leafy vines in the hair and anyone is good to go as our anti/hero.

Rejected by critics and embraced by record audiences, in 1986 Stallone received two contradictory awards: The Golden Raspberry for the worst motion picture and Harvard's Hasty Pudding Club Man of the Year. Vietnam veteran Paul Atwood was among 100 veterans and Asian Americans who picketed the Hasty Pudding ceremonies, saying "We are protesting the award and, by implication, Stallone's work. We think that rough, tough Rambo would have puked his guts out if he had to face what we did."

Rambo became an instant legend during the summer of its release, elevated to the highest levels when President Ronald Reagan, upon the release of 39 American hostages in June 1985 said, "After seeing Rambo last night, I know what to do next time this happens." Several months later, pleading for tax reform, Reagan said, "Let me tell you, in the spirit of Rambo, we're going to win this thing." These extraordinary references by an American president attest to the power and ubiquity of the Rambo phenomenon. In June 1985 both *Time* and *People* published accounts of what immediately came to be called "Rambomania." Vietnam veterans groups on both coasts, including Vietnam Veterans of America and the Veterans Speakers Alliance, picketed theaters screening *Rambo*. The War Resisters League protested on several occasions at Coleco Industries corporate headquarters in West Hartford, Connecticut, calling the company's Rambo doll "extremely racist, extremely sexist, and extremely simplistic."

Public figures lined up to weigh in on the Rambo juggernaut. Former Vice President Walter Mondale urged students at Brown University to avoid romanticizing war and violence, warning that "Rambo may be strong, but he is also a fool." Mondale suggested that in Rambo "complexity is blown away by simple violence," admonishing his young audience to "be careful, for this is history's most difficult lesson." Charles Haid, a Vietnam vet who played Officer Andy Renko on Hill Street Blues, called Rambo "entirely unrealistic," "an irresponsible fantasy," and "the shame of our industry." Then-U.S. Senator Bob Kerrey, a Vietnam Media of Honor recipient, stated that the movie "didn't tell about the war as I knew it. It made it look fun." Given the later revelations about Kerrey's controversial service as a Navy Seal, he knew what he was talking about.

David Halberstam, speaking at a "Rambo" colloquium at Stanford University, said the movie presents the "exact reverse of the real message of the Vietnam War," calling Stallone's statement that he made the film in support of Vietnam veterans "an obscenity." Halberstam termed Stallone a "cinematic Joseph McCarthy" and mocked the film's "this time we can win" theme as "a very bad example of how to obliterate history, to summon the worst kind of emotion" (Walsh 1986).

A Military Consumerist Icon

In the six months following Rambo's June 1985 release, hardly a day went by without some reference to Rambo in the popular media. *People, Time, Mad Magazine, Vanity Fair, Rolling Stone, Esquire, The National Enquirer*, and numerous other newspapers and magazines caught the virus. There was even a Rambo coloring book ("Find the matching assault helicopters.")

During this time a flood of Rambo merchandise appeared, from the predictable to the ridiculous: T-shirts, hats, bumper stickers ("This Car Protected by Rambo"), weapons sets (bows and arrows, guns, knives, grenades), headbands and even Rambo "Action Peanut Butter Cups" and "Rambo Black Flack Chewing Gum" for the ultimate in mixed messages.

Rambo also became a regular cartoon character. *Satellite TV Guide* published a Thanksgiving cartoon depicting a TV watcher with hatchet in hand and a turkey visible outside the window as he says to his wife "Let me watch a little more 'Rambo' and maybe I can do it." Funky Wunderbean showed a combat-geared dog with the caption "Neither rain nor snow nor sleet nor hail, they said, could stop the mail. But they didn't figure on Rexbo." *Mad* magazine presented a full spread on "Dumbo: More Blood Part II." Farley had a Christmas strip where a family is viewing a window display of elves, teddy bears and Mrs. Claus and the Rambo doll says "Bam! Bam! Rat-Tat-Tat! Eat Hot Lead Commie Elves!! Buda-Buda!" Bloom County's penguin Opus pounded on a foreign ship shouting "Out! Let Cutter John out you Rambo torturers." Rambo provided a field day for comics and cartoonists. Pornographers jumped on the bandwagon, too, with contributions like *Rambohhhh* and *Rambone*.

One linguistic feature of Rambo that inspired legions of satirists was the way that the second syllable "bo" can stand as metaphoric ground to just about any figure, as in Gary Larsen's

Figure 7.5: Rambo Coloring and Activity Book.

"Rexbo" and *Mad's* "Dumbo" cited earlier. Predictably, a "Ronbo" poster with Reagan's head on Stallone's body was one of the first "bo" creations in a nonstop line of offspring over the years and decades.

Colorado Governor Richard Lamm earned himself a "Lammbo" cartoon in the *Rocky Mountain News*. "Farmbo" depicts Grant Woods' American Gothic farmer on Stallone's body. Bizarro introduced "Bambo: First Fawn Part II… Finally! Violence the whole family can feel good about!!!" On Capitol Hill in 1985, the Gramm Rudman fiscal legislation was dubbed by its opponents "Grammbo." Another "Grambo" turned up on

Figure 7.6: Rambo Black Flak bubble gum.

greeting cards with the caption "She is Fighting a War Against Old Age." Then there was "Rambose," a Houston nightclub decorated with grenade launchers, camouflage netting and 50 caliber machine guns. In several cities one could send a "Rambo-gram" to friend or foe. And naturally there was "Rockybo," the sequel to Rocky/Rambo where Stallone beats himself to death. More recently there was Barack Obama's former chief of staff "Rahmbo" Emmanuel, and in a twist on the suffix-play Britain's Got Talent's "Susan Ramboyle."

Figure 7.7: Ronbo.

Figure 7.8: Susan Ramboyle. Used by permission: Andy Davey/The Sun.

I had an impressionable five-year-old little boy during the height of the Rambo craze, so I may have been more attentive than most to the decidedly ominous way that Rambo was marketed heavily to children and tied into the increase in privately owned weapons in the late 1980s. During this time, Americans became armed to the teeth not only with handguns (an estimated two for every three households) but also with military style assault weapons, with an estimated 500,000 in private hands. This personal firearms build-up was echoed in children's toys, which were increasingly combat related. Rambo and Commando toys alone accounted for more than $200 million in sales through only the end of 1985. Mom and Dad were shooting them up, too, as revealed in tabloids like the *Weekly World News*, which reported that "every Saturday night hubbies and wives and dating couples flock to the Bulletstop where they get their kicks playing Rambos and Rambettes by blowing away targets with the terrifying firepower of machine guns."

A chilling Rambo reference appeared in a *San Francisco Chronicle* report with the lead "Stalker May Be A Rambo Gone Awry." Paul Libertore (1986) reported that the Night Stalker might be a Rambo gone awry "who learned to kill in Vietnam," according to a well-known forensic psychiatrist. As it turned out, the Night Stalker was 24-year-old Richard Ramirez, who was barely out of elementary school when the Vietnam War ended. Here we have the Rambo character, whom Stallone alleges he developed to help the image of Vietnam vets, used as a symbol by a high credibility source who wrongly links the Vietnam vet image to a series of brutal murders. The double disservice done to veterans by this sort of speculation is typical of the double bind of Vietnam combat veterans' experience and allows us to simultaneously use him as a scapegoat and mythologize him as a hero. The sympathetic veteran/victim motif of Morrell's original novel was entirely lost and contradicted by the avenging Rambo symbol that emerged.

Rambo Reimagined

Imitation may be the sincerest form of flattery, but it is also the surest sign that an icon endures. Greg Jennings, *Son of Rambow*'s writer and director, had his formative *First Blood* moment at the age of ten or eleven, setting off with his father's video camera to make his own ten-minute action movie *Aron*, which is included in the *Son of Rambow* DVD and lends the main feature a sweet stroke of authenticity. While *Son of Rambow* is at its heart about two English schoolboys making their own version of *First Blood*, it is layered with enough themes and subplots to hold the fickle attention of the audience. Will Proudfoot (Bill Milner) has recently lost his father. Because his family's conservative religious beliefs forbid him from watching television, when his teacher screens a documentary in class Will is parked in the hallway outside when along comes school bully Lee Carter (Will Poulter). Both kids, first-time actors, are perfection in their roles.

Figure 7.9: Lee and Will in *Son of Rambow*.

Lee has a sideline of pirating movies from the theater by shooting them with his brother's video camera. One shot of him lounging over two rows of seats with the camera in one hand and a cigarette in the other (1980s England; smoking permitted) sets the cheeky tone.

In the early days of their relationship, Lee dominates Will completely, and when he shows him a pirated copy of *First Blood*, they are off and running. Will is the designated stuntman and nearly drowns imitating a Rambo feat that involves swinging out on a vine and dropping into the water. Lee shouts to Will who has plopped in the water and is bobbing "What do you mean you can't swim???" Other characters get into the act, including some droll oldsters and a French exchange student Didier, the coolest kid in school who practically steals the show.

Will becomes increasingly estranged from his conservative family, who represent the way media censorship often serves only to increase interest among those it is designed to shelter. *First Blood* is the first story Will has known outside of the *Bible*, and to him it becomes a quest to rescue his recently departed father. While Lee supplies much of the derring-do of the project, Will contributes fantasy elements with his genius at cartooning and the surreal sequences that emerge from it.

Son of Rambow is also a story about filmmaking itself: how difficult it is, how collaborative, how messy, how obsessive. Bits of actual filming are scattered throughout the movie, interspersed with other story lines, and so it is a surprise and delight to see it come together at the end as a *Son of Rambow* short within the *Son of Rambow* feature. The final short is full of unexpected moments that as viewers we knew were shot but led to believe were not intended for the film, such as Didier's antics. Director Jennings comes full circle to his own pre-teen short film, perhaps this time achieving the movie as he first imagined it before he had the filmmaking craft to carry it off.

Son of Rambow is a small ($4,500,000) movie that was well-received on the festival circuit (including Sundance, Newport Beach, Toronto, Glasgow, The British Film Institute, London Film Festival) and by the critics. Manohla Dargis called it "a likeable, lightly sticky valentine to childhood, the 1980s, and the dawning of movie love" (NYT 2 May 2008). *Son of Rambow* was even endorsed by Stallone himself in the DVD commentary. Director Jennings said that when he and producer Nick Goldsmith were first discussing the idea, which was eight years in development, they were "thinking back to that age when you have no fear and no concern for the consequences of your actions whether they're dangerous or stupid or cruel. You just kind of go for it."

Making a comedy about the making of a comedy about an action movie that's funny only in a campy way reimagines Rambo in a key that takes the sting out of the original narrative while at the same time demonstrating the archetypal reach of the story itself. The feral politics of the original are swallowed by a coming of age story with a film buff twist. But Jennings is not the only young filmmaker, nor the most original, whose Rambo inspiration takes the story into uncharted territory.

Flooding with Love for the Kid

Zachary Oberzan's staging of *First Blood* in *Rambo Solo* works as a manic campfire tale, but he takes the Rambo project to another level in the one-man film *Flooding with Love for the Kid* (2007). "Adapted, produced, directed, filmed, performed, edited, special effects and make up by Zachary Oberzan," the movie was shot for $96 in Oberzan's 220 square foot New York City apartment. Oberzan played all of the characters including three police dogs and two women. The kitchen stands in for the police station with the refrigerator serving double duty as the town diner. The bathtub is a muddy streambed, a sleeping loft a deadly cliff, a toaster serves as a police radio, a sideways ventilation fan with a plastic propeller makes do as a helicopter, and when Rambo gets hungry he kills, cooks, and eats a stuffed teddy bear.

Oberzan manages to move the story along at a watchable tempo with smart editing and clever animation, but the true originality of the matter is how he moves *First Blood* away from the famous film adaptation and closer to the original novel. The story becomes less about the wronged and deranged wounded warrior and more about the archetypal myth of the father-son relationship and how difficult it is to communicate as played out between Sargeant Teasle and Rambo. Andrew O'Hehir wrote in *Salon*:

> In fact, I feel like I understand what *First Blood* is really about much better after seeing this version. Having one man play both Rambo and Teasle … underscores the fact that

Figure 7.10: *Flooding with Love for the Kid* (2007) Used by permission.

they're a yin-yang pair of American males with crippled dreams, divided by generation and perhaps by ideology, but essentially similar in background and outlook. The Korea vet and Vietnam vet are literally joined by blood; they're both a metaphorical father-son pair and a homoerotic couple who cement their passionate union with guns rather than genitals (2010).

David Morrell said of Oberzan's film adaption that it is "an absolutely amazing concept … wildly creative and energetic." Garth Jennings should be acknowledged for reinventing Rambo without sarcasm in *Son of Rambow*, but Oberzan takes it one step further in reimagining Rambo without guile, attempting "to turn narrative on its side." Oberzan takes Rambo seriously and doesn't understand why others do not. Parts of *Rambo* are funny, he conceded in an NPR interview, "but parts of *Hamlet* are funny." The interviewer responds "We're not talking about Shakespeare, we're talking about Sylvester Stallone." Oberzan: "What's the difference between Agamemnon and Rambo? They're both about a bunch of dudes going to fight other dudes about women."

David Morrell takes the work seriously as well, pointing to its qualities as a Greek tragedy and to the Jungian influence he attributes to the fact that he was reading Joseph Campbell's *Hero With a Thousand Faces* at the time he was writing *First Blood*. This is a long way from Isherwood's snarky review of "Rambo Nut," where he concludes that despite some original moments, the project is "more conceit than character." Isherwood seems to miss the point of the significance of how the story is told, in multiple media as well as multiple simultaneous media. Oberzan: "With both *Rambo Solo* and *Flooding with Love for the Kid* the pieces aren't so much about the story but about how you tell the story." One commonality in all Rambo versions—books, films, stage, new films—is that there is a lot of heart in each one, which may go a long way in explaining the curious staying power of the story. The homoerotic undertones must also exert some gravitational pull on an unsuspecting audience and the transmedia versatility of the story suggests it will most likely outlive its critics.

Surely the medium is the message here, and several things can be said with some confidence about the Rambo text. For one, it is clear that Stallone's hyperbolic style prevailed over Morrell's more thoughtful substance in creation of the resultant Rambo symbol. In this case, style metacommunicates a message that contradicts and subsumes the substance, perhaps partly because the substantive message itself is awash in *pathos*, a dimension that plays well into the hands of nondiscursive elements of style. The *logos* of the narration is there, to be sure, but is not salient compared to the gut tone of the story. Rambo's trope is hyperbole and his canon is style. Was Rambo a prominent symptom of an age where style became increasingly divorced from substance, where it was not who you were but who you seemed to be? If a soap opera actor could establish credibility in a television commercial at the time by declaring "I'm not a doctor, but I play one on TV," then the possibilities for reframing roles and realities are endless.

This triumph of style over substance may be in part a function of the simplifying tendencies of the broadcast media and may be in part a function of the militaristic

Zeitgeist that Rambo both played into and perpetuated in the 1980s. The fact that much of the Rambo story was about going back and winning this time capitalized on the instant replay culture summarized in Tom Shales' (1986) piece on "The Re Decade." Shales argued that the time shifting capabilities of VCR technology meant that "we're all getting used to larger and larger parts of our lives being illusory... It's that old media theory talk about the line between fantasy and reality. In fact the talk is passé, because the blurring and the overlapping are things everyone is taking for granted now. If this is so, what does it mean for a movie to take us back in fantasy to a war we lost in reality? Perhaps the Rambo generation was being readied for service by this conspiracy of collective amnesia which glorifies war and romanticizes combat. Or maybe any message is trivialized by the sheer magnitude of the information tsunami of which it is a part.

One of the most provocative Rambo bits that appeared during his 1980s lifetime was an editorial cartoon depicting a male television viewer, cigar in mouth and remote control/beer can in hand, sitting in front of a TV with videocassettes stacked on top labeled "Rambo" and "Mad Violence." The message on the television screen reads "USA Raids Libya" (the first time) and the caption has the viewer calling to his wife "Heh Emma get in here, it's starting." The frame that distinguishes fantasy from reality is dissolved and why not? Television is a great credibility/reality leveler. Why should U.S. raids on Libya or Iraq or Afghanistan be any more real than the adventures of Rambo? The Contragate revelations of 1986 made those questions even more pertinent, and Desert Storm—Gulf War I was the perfect realization of the video game infotainment war. Ronald Reagan may have been the first president to make foreign policy decisions based upon the movies but he was not the last.

The dangers of this way of thinking have become obvious to nearly everyone over the past several decades with their succession of cruel and fruitless wars. Sylvester Stallone did not create the mediated culture he so cannily exploited, much less was he responsible for the blurred genres that came to characterize his prime decade. Even so, by portraying the betrayed veteran/victim with fraudulent hyperbole, Stallone himself contributed in no small measure to the jingoism of the Gulf War that shortly followed and the long line of U.S. military misadventures that have become a permanent feature of foreign policy. Rambo was born of the war in Vietnam but his continued relevance carries a wider if not encouraging message. Even if Rambo's narcissistic jingoism is partly offset by his anti-authoritarian, anti-government zendo leanings, the net effect remains troubling.

While it is tempting to attribute American aggression and the Bush Doctrine in particular to cultural influences that include Rambo-think, over the longer term it seems not so simple. It is hard to argue that Rambo has made any contribution to world peace, but at the same time fresh work like that of Jennings and Oberzan illustrate a deeper and more complex genealogy of the Rambo idea. In these ingenious reinventings, the implicit and explicit violence of the message is mitigated by reframing it as play, reminding us to never underestimate the power of a message that no one takes seriously. Not one or two but three endings to *First Blood* were shot: the first where Rambo dies, the second where Rambo lives to create a franchise, and a third ending where Stallone blows a line and he and Richard Crenna and the crew in the background break up laughing and Rambo says "Thanks a million."

While Rambo on the surface seems to be a trophy of the radical right, Oberzan's adaptations shows a softer side that comes into play in his relationship with Teasle, who feels likewise as the novel ends: "He thought about the kid, and flooded with love for him, and just a second before the empty shell would have completed its arc to the ground, he relaxed, accepted peacefully. And was dead" (1972: 284).

Oberzan has performed *Rambo Solo* around the United States and Europe, where he reports that audiences responded mostly to his "deep personal love for the story and its characters." Audiences on both continents shared a "sudden new appreciation for the depth of the story of Rambo." Oberzan:

> That certainly made me feel proud that I was offering this illumination. Spreading the gospel, as I like to think of it. It's like, imagine if everyone thought Hamlet was a dumb story with dumb characters because they had never taken the time to read it? And I was able to show them the true depth and humanity of Hamlet. So my attachment and love of the book grew even more, being this conduit. People understand these projects because of their form and passion. They personally couldn't care less about Rambo, but they appreciate it as a vehicle for excellent storytelling. And I can live with that, because I've done my job, and I have forever embedded myself in the world of *First Blood*, a world of tremendous struggle and bloodshed, but also a world of boundless love (2012).

Chapter 8

Murder on May 4th: The Case of the Missing Mob

Thomas M. Grace is trim and professorially dressed with serious blue eyes and a shock of sandy hair sprinkled with grey. Courteous and direct, he could pass for someone decades younger than his 62 years. It is only when he steps forward to greet you that a slight limp gives itself away, a reminder of the day his left heel was pierced by National Guard M-1 gunfire 40 years earlier. It was a day he expected to face nothing more challenging than a history exam, and history came easy to him. Little did he know that sunny morning he was about to become a part of history himself. His course instructor understood that the students were distracted by the growing commotion on campus and gave them the choice of postponing the test. Tom's girlfriend opted to leave; he stayed for the exam. When his next class ended at 11:30 a.m. he deliberated whether to check out the rally in progress on the Commons.

> I remember thinking to myself, this is too momentous; it's too important for me to stay away. Certainly I couldn't see any harm in my going over just to watch. It was only a five-minute walk to the Commons. I found several hundred students and some of my roommates, Alan Canfora and Jim Riggs, had flags, black flags I believe. Alan had spray painted "KENT" on it, and the other one was just a black flag, so I was drawn to them right away. There was some chanting going on: "One, two, three, four, we don't want your fucking war." And "Pigs off campus."
>
> (Morrison 1987: 330)

Students were congregating around the Victory Bell, usually rung for more festive occasions like football rallies. Four officials in a jeep ordered the crowd to disperse. KSU patrolman Harold Rice was on a bullhorn. Orders from the bullhorn were audible to the closely clustered protesters, but beyond the inner circle there was widespread confusion about the status of the right to assemble. Multiple contradictory messages had been given from the university administration and law enforcement officials at all levels, who were unclear among themselves just what was prohibited and permitted (Tompkins and Anderson 1971).

"The Guns Are Always Loaded."

The weekend had been filled with foreboding. Friday night May 1st I was on campus with a friend to see a stage adaptation of Leonid Andreyev's *The Serpent's Tale* directed by one of my students. On our way out of town, we stopped on Water Street for a beer. People were roaming around as usual for a balmy spring night, but when the noise level rose sharply and a cluster of bikers calling themselves The Chosen Few started performing wheelies in the street we decided it was time to head home. As it turned out it was a prudent decision, because from that point on the weekend unfolded with one disquieting event after another including the burning of the rickety ROTC building on campus, an inflammatory statement by Ohio Governor James Rhodes, and the summoning and arrival of the Ohio National Guard. Monday morning May 4th arrived and since Kent was a commuter campus half of the students had gone home for the weekend. Many of them were only vaguely aware of the events that had taken place since they departed the campus on Friday.

It was before the era of 24 hour news, let alone social media saturation. Student mailboxes were often not checked on Sunday or Monday. One student reported that she found the "special message" prohibiting assembly in her box only after students had been shot. I was a research associate on a study led by Phillip Tompkins (1971) based on 500 interviews of students, faculty and staff, in which it was reported that nearly one-half of the students were not aware that assembly had been prohibited. In any case, classes were in session and is not a class an assembly? The attitude of the students was that it was the guard who were the intruders, not the students who were rightfully on their own campus where teaching and other university functions were open for business. By about 11:45 a.m. somewhere from 500 to 2000 or 3000 students had gathered near the Commons, depending upon the source. The smallest and most active group of about 500 students was clustered near the Victory Bell. Most of the rest were observers ringing the large natural amphitheater of the Commons. The National Guard moved across the broad Commons lobbing tear gas, some of which was returned by students. Students threw rocks and chanted anti-guard slogans. This scene on the Commons involved the most guardsmen, the most students, and the most chanting and tear gas action of the morning. Film and photographic evidence suggests that the back and forth movements of the guard and the students were almost balletic, a *pas de deux* of death.

With most of the students effectively scattered, the guard marched over the top of Blanket Hill and down the other side to a football practice field. This is an entirely different site from the Commons; a separate sloping bowl. It is crucial to note that by this point most of the protesters had dispersed and only several hundred students remained near Taylor Hall and in the Prentice Hall parking lot. Some of the guard assumed a firing position aimed at students in the Prentice Hall parking lot but did not shoot and then regrouped to climb back up Blanket Hill. According to the official *President's Commission on Campus Unrest* (1970)—widely known as the Scranton Report—as the guard climbed the hill to the site of the fatal action "about 100 students stood on the terrace of Taylor Hall, watching the guardsmen approach the adjacent hill. They are not known to have thrown any rocks and seem to have been spectators throughout. In the Prentice Hall parking lot there were 100 to 200 students, some throwing rocks, others carrying books" (271). The final maneuver that resulted in opening fire was sudden. Tom Grace remembers:

> When the National Guard got to the top of the hill, all of a sudden there was just a quick movement, a flurry of activity, and then a crack or two cracks of rifle fire, and I thought,

Oh, my God! I turned and started running as fast as I could. I don't think I got more than a step or two, and all of sudden I was on the ground. It was just like somebody had come over and given me a body blow and knocked me right down... It seemed like the bullets were going by within inches of my head. I can remember seeing people behind me, farther down the hill in the parking lot, dropping. I didn't know if they were being hit by bullets or they were just hugging the ground. We know today that it only lasted thirteen seconds, but it seemed like it kept going and going and going. And I remember thinking, When is this going to stop?

(Morrison 1987: 332)

It stopped when the guard had expended 67 rounds, killing four students and wounding nine in the worst military violence against students in U.S. history. *A crucial and often overlooked fact is that the shooting did not occur in the Commons where the guard earlier faced thousands of students, but rather later on the other side of the hill with only several hundred students in range.* Carole Barbato and Laura Davis, in "This We Know: Chronology of the Shootings at Kent State May 1970" report that an 8mm student film shows that

a member of Troop G [the firing squad], looking over his shoulder and down toward the parking lot, would have seen five students at a distance of 60 to 85 feet, 24 students between 85 and 175 feet, and 30 students between 175 and 325 feet... The evidence of the film is that at no time before Troop G opened fire were they being approached by more than 17 students, that none of the approaching students was closer than 85 feet, and that 10 of them were more than 175 feet away... The film provides conclusive evidence that the guardsmen had not been rushed (2012: 215).

Those killed and wounded that day were all full-time students at Kent. The dead and wounded students were on average more than 300 feet from the soldiers who shot them. Tom Grace was one of the closer wounded students at 225 feet. Two students were shot from the front, seven from the side, and four in the back. 19-year-old ROTC cadet William Schroeder was shot in the back at the seventh rib while lying prone 390 feet from the Guard. Twenty-year-old Sandra Scheuer was shot in the front side of her neck on her way to class, also from 390 feet. Twenty-year-old Jeffrey Miller was shot in the mouth while facing the guard 265 feet away. Allison Krause, 19, was diving for cover when she was shot 343 feet away from the line of fire. Despite these striking facts, the impression lingers that the guardsmen fired to defend themselves against marauding masses of students.

Does the fact that common memory mistakenly conflates the heavily populated Commons scene with the sparsely populated shooting site on the other side of the hill help to account for the mystery of the missing mob when the guard opened fire?

Tom Grace (2011) recalls that some students at the scene were hysterical. Some fled in terror. Many more seemed shocked. Still others focused on treating the injured or carrying them to dorms and ambulances. A significant number erupted in anger, screaming oaths at the Ohio National Guard. When hundreds reassembled on the Commons, others urged a suicide charge on the guardsmen. One can only imagine what would have resulted from that.

A story that made the rounds following the shootings tells of two girls sobbing "The guns were loaded. The guns were loaded. We didn't know the guns were loaded." A black student in the Afro hair and dashiki style of the day passes by and says coolly: "The guns are always loaded."

"Unnecessary, Unwarranted, and Inexcusable."

Tin soldiers and Nixon comin'
We're finally on our own
This summer I hear the drummin'
Four dead in Ohio

– Neil Young

Four oblong granite stones line up like giant caskets one behind the other atop a leafy knoll high above the Commons. They are the centerpiece of the site commemorating Sandra

Figure 8.1: KSU Memorial to May 4th Dead.

Scheuer, Jeffrey Miller, William Schroeder, and Allison Krause, the "martyrs" of May 4th, as some survivors of the event call them.

Almost immediately after the Kent State shootings, five million American college students went out on strike for the rest of the term. Classes met in church basements and professors homes to complete the work of the semester. Active "Kent State in Exile" communities sprang up at Case Western Reserve University and Oberlin College. It was a strikingly intimate time, not unlike after 9/11 in New York, where for weeks it seemed the closeness that came out of being a part of the traumatic event erased the interpersonal barriers we maintain in daily life. Survival suddenly depended more on community than the individual. Even now May 4th is a, if not the, defining event of the Vietnam generation, uniting millions of young people. If there was any silver lining to the event, it is that it marked the beginning of the end for Richard Nixon and his descent into the hell of Watergate.

Early news reports identified the dead as guardsmen. State officials reported that the shooting started when a rooftop sniper opened fire on the guardsmen. General Sylvester Del Corso said "guardsmen facing almost certain injury and death were forced to open fire on the attackers." None of these statements was accurate. The presidential commission later determined that "the indiscriminate firing of rifles into a crowd of students and the deaths that followed were unnecessary, unwarranted, and inexcusable" (1970: 289). It took 20 years, until 1990, for a memorial to be completed on the campus, following years of fractious debate and protest between activists and parents determined to remember and a university administration that would just as soon forget. It took another 20 years for the 17 acres of the site to be added to the National Historic Register, and several years more, until 2012, for a proper museum to be completed and opened to the public.

I am an accidental expert on May 4th, having been a graduate student and Teaching Fellow at Kent in 1970. I completed undergraduate studies at Miami University and had heard the aspersion "if you can't go to college go to Kent," but I was a young mother in Cleveland with no option to leave the area. Kent was the best choice within commuting distance where I could study the emerging field of media and communication, and it was a progressive program that integrated social science and humanities approaches. May 4th bestowed a morbid cachet on a school and place whose very ordinariness created the dramatic irony. Kent State? Not Berkeley, Columbia, Wisconsin? I entered a cow college as a complete political innocent and graduated from the place where the Vietnam War literally came home.

I began Ph.D. studies in 1969 with courses on Plato and Aristotle and Attic Greek and a year later had made a complete shift to a lifelong fascination with how language is used and information is managed in social and political change. As a suburban Ohio girl with a baby I had been little involved in the late 1960s revolution, but May 4th changed that and my life became driven by the questions: How could such a thing happen? Why? What didn't I know and why didn't I know it? It is a short step from these questions to an interest in media and politics, and despite the soft spot that remains for all things classical, media and political communication have been the focus of my academic and much of my personal life. Most importantly May 4th is how I got an unexpected short and intense course on Vietnam and developed a passion for learning about how the Vietnam War was reported and represented in American media, politics and culture.

Death by Semantics

One way to understand how language is used for political ends is to focus on words themselves. Word choice is a political act. More often than not, a writer has a repertoire of near-synonyms that can be invoked to express a thought and almost always these choices carry different connotations and points of view: citizen, patriot, protestor, freedom fighter, revolutionary, terrorist. May 4th has suffered a slow death by semantics over the years. In 1995, the Kent State University Publications Office requested that the word "shooting" be changed to "events" in a college newsletter. In the year 2000, an invitation I received from the Coordinator of Public Relations to speak at the 30th commemoration ceremonies, prescribed the topic: "The Mediated Reality of the Kent State Incident." It continued: "The panel will examine the various histories and interpretations ... and how specific audiences have accepted interpretations that make sense to their respective value systems." In my talk I addressed the value system that chose the neutered term "incident" to describe May 4th at its very own commemoration ceremony, making the point that words do matter. Why "incident"? Why not even the plainly descriptive "shootings" or "killings"? You don't have to call it a "murder" or a "massacre," neither of which is a stretch, to know that it was more than an "incident." It is worrisome enough that among Kent students at that time (2000), only two-thirds knew the year of the shootings, 58 percent could identify Nixon as the president at that time, and 16 percent knew the name of even one of the dead (Hallowell 1990).

To my surprise, the mothers of slain students William Schroeder and Jeffrey Miller were in the front row when I stepped up to the podium for my presentation. As the mother myself then of a 20-year-old son, the age their boys were when they died, I was shaken. I wish I could report that I threw away my prepared remarks and said something profound, but all I managed in the heavy heart of the moment was to thank them for attending and for the inspiration of their strength. Thirty years later they were there, tending the flame. I wondered if Mrs. Schroeder and Mrs. Miller talked about May 4th as the "incident."

Not long ago, a fellow graduate student from those days, now a university provost, told me she ran into the KSU president at an alumni event and the subject of May 4th came up. He said "Is that all you people ever think about?" Clearly those closest to ground zero of the event are among the most eager to forget.

Tom Grace remembers that on May 4th a nursing student applied a tourniquet to his leg. "The bullet blew the shoe right off my foot, and there was a bone sticking through my green sock. It looked like somebody had put my foot through a meat grinder." Finally, the ambulances came, and the attendants put Grace on the top tier.

> They had the back doors closed by this time, and the ambulance was speeding away from the campus and I looked down and saw Sandy Scheuer ... she had a gaping bullet wound in the neck and the ambulance attendants were tearing away the top two buttons of her blouse and then doing heart massage. I remember their saying that it's no use, she's dead. And they just pulled the sheet up over her head.
>
> (Morrison 1987: 333)

In 1999, memorials were dedicated to each of the slain students at the precise spot in the parking lot where they fell. It is an unexpected sight because the rest of the lot is still in use for parking, and the memorial rectangles are slightly off kilter as parking places. It is a grass roots memento that evolved from annual spontaneous gatherings each May 3rd during a midnight candlelight walk that ends in this unlikely place, where caretaking students maintain a vigil at each site and others leave poems, flowers, tokens, toys, candles. This is where the secret ritual, the real ritual of remembrance of May 4th is enacted. It is a solemn line of mourners who walk through the night by candlelight around the campus and then from one to the other of these very personal sites of remembrance. If you ever want to

Figure 8.2: Allison Krause Parking Lot Memorial.

understand Kent State as living history, join the solemn witnessing some May 3rd at midnight in the parking lot behind Prentice Hall.

"Troops Fight with Rioters"

May 4th is most often remembered, when at all, by a flat and shallow summation like "National Guard troops killed four and wounded nine anti-war protesters on the Kent State Campus." None of the context, the choreography, the temporality, the geography, the rhythm or the punctuation of the event is carried by that description. What succinct representation would constitute a more accurate account, a richer memory, a deeper understanding, a more accessible and enduring impression? What metaphor or mapping would etch the outlines of the event in a way that the outrage of it could be apprehended immediately, viscerally, completely?

John Gaddis (2002) addresses the challenge of remembrance in his lectures on the *Landscape of History*.

> We know the future only by the past we project onto it. History, in this sense, is all we have. But the past, in another sense, is something we can never have. For by the time we become aware of what has happened it's already inaccessible to us: we can not relive, retrieve, or rerun it as we might some laboratory experiment or computer simulation. We can only represent it (3).

The vehicles of representation are words, images, and sounds, and while the signifier bears no necessary relationship to the thing signified, the correspondence of word and referent can still achieve greater or lesser fidelity. The semiotic triad of thought, symbol, and referent is iterative and dynamic. Living words are subject to continual evolution. They don't stay still. At the same time, words, sounds and images matter. Whether I refer to May 4th as an "incident" or a "massacre," whether the students fired upon are "rioters" "victims" or "martyrs" makes a difference in how the event is signified, interpreted, repeated, remembered, memorialized, acted upon. Tom Grace is interested in similar challenges of representation when he calls attention to "the battle over how the shootings have been and ought to be remembered" (2009).

If journalism is the first draft of history, then a look at early coverage of a front page story can be revealing. The *Chicago Tribune* was then as now one of the largest daily newspapers in the United States. The banner headline on 5 May 1970 blared "4 STUDENTS SLAIN AT KENT." We already find a loaded word choice in "slain," which evokes the myth of George the Dragon Slayer, where the slain dragon is the evildoer and George is the hero. In this connotation to be "slain" is to be rightfully killed because the victim is a threat. One half of the front page above the fold is filled by John Filo's iconic photograph of teenager Mary Ann Vecchio wailing over the body of Jeffrey Miller. A two-column spread on the right is headlined "Troops Fight With Rioters."

Figure 8.3: May 4th, 1970, media coverage.

Compare headlines "4 Students Slain at Kent" with "Troops Fight with Rioters." "4 Students Slain at Kent" is almost denotative by comparison. A less loaded word could be substituted for "slain" (killed, shot) that would preserve the meaning. Still other words ("murdered" "gunned down") would shift the meaning to suggest more accountability on the part of the shooters, but those words were not chosen. By contrast consider "Troops Fight with Rioters." "Troops" almost has the friendly feel of a troop of acrobats or actors. It is a word lacking menace. Alternatives are "soldiers," "Ohio National Guard," "Shooters," "Guardsmen," "Gunmen." And these troops do not "shoot at unarmed students," they "fight with rioters." In the first place, a "fight" implies a two-sided conflict, when clearly soldiers with M-1 rifles are not equivalent to students with random rocks. There was no "fight"; the shooting was a one-sided assault against unarmed civilians. And last—the "rioters." The suggestion here is that the students were out of control and creating a chaotic and dangerous situation. All evidence suggests that at the time of the shooting the protest was controlled if fluid and at no time were the students a threat to the Ohio National Guard. "Troops Fight with Rioters?" More true to say "Soldiers Fire at Unarmed Protesters."

The *Tribune* article that follows the "Troops Fight with Rioters" headline continues with questionable representations. "Four students were shot to death and at least fifteen other persons wounded or injured, four seriously, in a confrontation today between 3,000 students and Ohio national guardsmen and police at Kent State University." The inaccurate number of wounded (it was nine) can be expected in early reports; the 3,000 number is many times the number of students actively involved in the protest, especially at the time of the shooting.

The next allegation, common to early reports, was never supported: "A state official said the shooting started when a rooftop sniper open fire on the guardsmen." Then: "The gunfire broke out as guardsmen dispersed an anti-war rally on the campus." It would be more accurate to say that gunfire broke out *after* guardsmen dispersed the rally. Even more subtly, the term "broke out" here makes it sound like the gunfire just happened spontaneously like a case of poison ivy. In fact, "guardsmen opened fire" would place the accountability where it belongs. Also: "Adjt Gen. S.T. Del Corso said guardsmen were forced to open fire on their attackers." This construction completely reframes the accountability for the shooting by alleging that guardsmen were "forced to open fire" on their (unarmed) "attackers." "Regrettably but unavoidably several individuals were killed and a number of others were wounded" he said in a statement. "Unavoidably?" There is not an alternative scenario Mr. Del Corso could imagine? What would make these shootings "unavoidable"? If students were likewise armed and the guard had been surrounded?

Other prominent newspapers of the day offered more measured accounts. *The New York Times* led with: "Four students at Kent State University, two of them women, were shot to death this afternoon by a volley of National Guard gunfire. At least eight other students were wounded." The identification of the gender of the dead is an interesting detail. It would be equally true that "two of them were walking to class and were not part of the protest" or "two of them were men," or "three of the four dead students were Jewish." The *Times'* focus on gender may reflect the media prominence of the Women's Liberation Movement in 1970. Of the 17 students killed on U.S. Campuses between 1967 and 1971 the only female fatalities were at Kent State.

The Times quotes President Richard Nixon's Kent reaction statement:

> This should remind us all once again that when dissent turns to violence it invites tragedy. It is my hope that this tragic and unfortunate incident will strengthen the determination of all the nation's campuses, administrators, faculty, and students alike to stand firmly for the right which exists in this country of peaceful dissent and just as strong against the resort to violence as a means of such expression.

Comparing this statement to the facts of the situation, at what point did "dissent turn to violence" unless it was the moment of National Guard gunfire? And the determination that needs to be strengthened "to stand firmly for the right which exists in this country of peaceful dissent"—is that not the right that was being exercised by the Kent State protestors? And does not opposition to "violence as a means of such expression" apply to the M-1 shooters and not the unarmed victims? Nixon's looking-glass rhetoric smoothly inverts accountability by giving the impression that a statement that at first glance supports the rights of the protestors actually blames them for their own deaths.

While the *Chicago Tribune, New York Times*, and *Cleveland Plain Dealer* featured slightly different headlines ("4 Students Slain at Kent," "4 Kent State Students Killed by Troops," "4 Dead, 10 Hurt at KSU"), all three papers featured John Filo's archetypal photograph of an anguished Mary Vecchio over the body of Jeff Miller. As KSU Professor Jerry Lewis has pointed out, both the composition and content bear an eerie resemblance to Michaelangelo's *Pieta*, where in a similar triadic structure the dead Jesus is draped in the arms of a young Mary. There is no blame in Filo's image; no history, no context, no suggestion of how it happened that this grief stricken girl reacts to the horror of a blood soaked corpse. There is only the moment of shock and terror. The consequence of the act tells more than the story of its execution. A single image can encapsulate the story beyond words. Filo's Pulitzer Prize winning picture is among the most memorable of the twentieth century, and remains associated with the May 4th story more closely than the dozens of books and several movies that followed, which played to small audiences and had no discernible lasting effect on raising public knowledge or consciousness about the facts or significance of the shootings.

"They Should Have Shot More of Them"

Some mainstream media coverage of May 4th ran counter to the neutral to negative characterizations, notably *Life* magazine, which had dramatically turned the corner toward an anti-war stance in 1969s *One Week's Dead*. Its extensive 15 May 1970 spread on May 4th "Tragedy at Kent" was anything but neutral:

> The upheaval in Kent seemed at its outset to be merely another of the scores of student demonstrations that have rocked U.S. campuses. But before it ended, in senseless and brutal murder at point-blank range, Kent State had become a symbol of the fearful hazards latent in dissent and in the policies that cause it.

Still, *Life* got it wrong. No one was shot at "point-blank range": on the contrary the ranges were extraordinarily long.

But *Life* was an exception in its use of "murder." A Gallup poll published in *Newsweek* on 18 May 1970 found that 58 percent of the public blamed the students themselves, while only 11 percent blamed the National Guardsmen. Public opinion as expressed in letters to the editor was often along these lines. Consider these letters to the *Cleveland Plain Dealer*.

10 May 1970:

Why must the news media give space and air time reporting the violence at universities and elsewhere? If these students at Kent State University hadn't been so busy protesting, there would not have been any killings. This is a democratic society and if the students don't like our national policies the place to protest is in the voting booth—not on the campuses and on Euclid Avenue.

And:

I don't think we can condemn the Ohio National Guard for doing their job at Kent State University because they were on campus because someone felt the situation was serious enough to bring them. They were obviously trying to do their job and no one likes to be pelted by rocks the size of baseballs or otherwise. Those men are just as human as those of us sitting at home reading about the situation, and most of us would or could panic if put in the same situation.

And the occasional alternative opinion:

Protest peacefully, you say? How soon you forget the hundreds of thousands of peaceful demonstrators against the war in Washington last November. And where did it get the cause of peace? Into Laos, Cambodia, and the resumed bombing of North Vietnam. I don't condone violence; it is a disturbing philosophical contradiction in the name of peace. But since when in this country do sticks and stones warrant, without warning, bloodshed and death in return?

That last letter was actually from me, probably my first words in print beyond the college newspaper, and likely the first overt sign of rising political awareness, although the use of "philosophical contradiction" betrays some graduate student striving.

The "M" Word

The most notorious semantic meltdown following May 4th, at least in Northeast Ohio media, came from the unlikely source of a 77-year-old television commentator with a closer resemblance to Dame Edna than Diane Sawyer. Dorothy Fuldheim worked her way up through radio, where she was the first female commentator for the ABC Radio Network. Called "The First Lady of Television News," Fuldheim famously interviewed Mussolini and Hitler and just about everyone else who mattered, becoming the first woman in the United States to anchor a television news broadcast. Her on-camera commentaries began at the age of 54 and continued until she was felled by a stroke at the age of 91. Fuldheim's strong and incisive commentaries on issues of the day paved the way in broadcast news analysis for both women and men. She packed brains and gutsiness into a five-foot frame crowned by a thick halo of bright red hair. Fuldheim did not shy from unpopular causes or contentious interviews. On one occasion she threw 60s activist Jerry Rubin off the show for calling policemen "pigs." "I've a got a shock for you. Some of

Figure 8.4: Dorothy Fuldheim.

my friends are policemen." Rubin replied "Well, I've got a shock for you. Some of my friends are Black Panthers." "Out! Stop the interview!" Fuldheim insisted as the cameras rolled.

On 4 May 1970, Fuldheim followed her usual morning routine, reading the papers and eating breakfast in time to be driven to the WEWS studios at Thirtieth and Euclid Avenue arriving promptly at 9:30 a.m. She called the wire services and began writing the three commentaries she would deliver that day. Her habit was to organize her thoughts in the morning and then write the commentaries after lunch on a small tablet. When she was about to begin writing the day's commentaries word reached the newsroom that there had been gunfire at Kent State and two guardsmen and several students were dead or wounded. She tried unsuccessfully to place a call to Kent, whose phone system had gone down. When the first UPI report came through at 1:30 p.m. Confirming 15 people shot, Fuldheim decided she had to go to Kent to see for herself. Cook reports that the scene at Kent looked less like rural Ohio and more like the many military dictatorships she had seen while reporting overseas. The WEWS car was stopped by a roadblock north of town; khaki-clad soldiers with menacing M-1 semi-automatic rifles at the checkpoint reinforced the surrealism. Fuldheim later described how she felt when she arrived upon the scene:

> What had they done, what crime that they should meet death? Their eyes were innocent; their hands bore no weapons; their hearts were pure with the hope of peace in Vietnam; and for this hope they died, indiscriminately shot by the National Guard. I call your names: Allison Krause, William Schroeder, Jeffrey Miller, and Sandy Scheuer, so that we remember that on this day the blood of the very young, not much older than children, stained the earth of our land because they dreamed, these young, of a world without war. (1974: 75)

Fuldheim returned to Cleveland and went on the air, tearfully calling the killings "murder." "Who gave the National Guard the bullets? Who ordered the use of them? Since when do we shoot our own children. What is wrong with our country? We're killing our own children!" The switchboard lit up like a Christmas tree. "Too bad the National Guard didn't kill more." "Those good for nothing smart-aleck bums. It's about time someone put them in their place." "Good for the National Guard" (Mote 1997). Fuldheim was flabbergasted by the vehemence directed at her. Ninety-five percent of the calls were against the students. Death threats against her were serious enough to warrant police protection. The barrage did not let up for days. Fuldheim went to General Manager Donald Perris, for whom she had worked for 25 years, and offered to resign. He turned her down. "Nonsense, Dorothy. You are nine feet tall" (Mote 1997: 137). Loyalty worked both ways in those days between journalists and management. Other local broadcast news outlets did not share WEWS' problem, for the simple reason that they put no commentary on air.

> In my twenty-four years on television, nothing that I ever said drew such an avalanche of disapproval, and some of it couched in savage and brutal words. I admit to being emotional about this matter, but I am still bewildered at the intensity of the feeling against the students and the support of the shooting by the National Guard, who undoubtedly were unnerved by the whole bizarre situation.

Fuldheim continued to deliver May 4th commentaries until 1979, when the last civil proceeding stemming from the event was settled.

Murder on May 4th

ALLISON B. KRAUSE

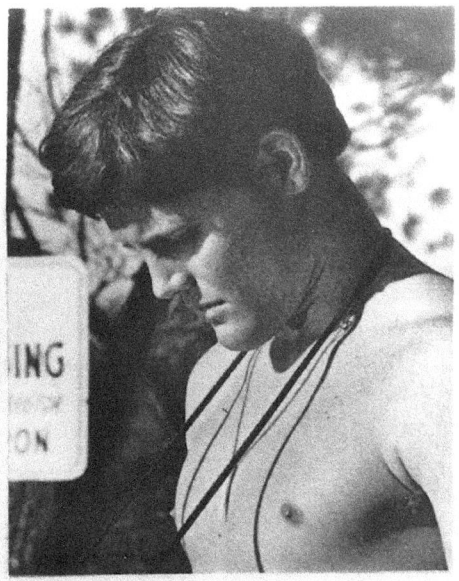
WILLIAM K. SCHROEDER

JEFFREY G. MILLER

SANDRA L. SCHEUER

Figure 8.5: Kent State Dead, KSU special collections.

When the Map Is Not Even a Map

A few years after the Kent State killings, having moved far away, my husband and daughter and I were half way down the Baja California peninsula in our green Dodge van when we pulled over at a little "Coca-Cola" shack. In addition to selling refreshments, the waddling woman was selling maps—beautiful hand drawn road maps rendered in multiple colors over an official United States Geological Survey topographical survey. Since by this time we had no idea where we were, the map was as welcome as the Coke, and we drove off following its directions toward the sea. Or so we thought. Several hours and many circles and dead ends later we were completely lost. I began to panic; surely we were moments away from death by bandits who were on the run like in a B-movie. By some miracle of dumb luck with no thanks to my hyperventilation we eventually found ourselves back to where we had started. We looked at each other at the same moment with the same epiphany: the colorful roads drawn onto the topographical survey bore no relation to the roads that existed. We knew that the map was not the territory, but this map was not even a map of the territory in any recognizable sense. I have never read a map with complete confidence since.

The Baja incident came to mind as I prepared for a presentation at the 40th anniversary of May 4th commemoration events in Ohio. I had asked that my presentation feature a public conversation with Tom Grace, with whom I had struck up an email correspondence several years earlier when he came across some obscure writing I had done on Kent. Six of the seven surviving casualties were in attendance at the 40th year ceremonies. To prepare for my conversation with Tom I tried to collect as much background as possible on him

Figure 8.6: Tom Grace at The Victory Bell. Photo: David King.

and his role in the protest. Tom was an activist before and since May 4th. He is a history professor who values his privacy, so I began with published maps that I could find of the shootings.

I have never been satisfied with documentary representations of the Kent State shootings because they often give the impression that it was some sort of World War I trench warfare between thousands of students lined up with rocks on one hand and a handful of soldiers lined up with rifles facing them like *All Quiet on the Western Front*. It was not like that at all. The terrain at Kent is steep and hilly, the core interaction between the guard and the students took place over about 30 minutes and had a complex choreography, involving tear gas canisters being lobbed back and forth, the guard moving around the area in serpentine formations and kneeling in firing position but not firing, and minutes later, having gone back up a hill, turning 135 degrees and firing 67 shots without warning. The nearest student hit was 60 feet away; the farthest more than 700. The word "massacre" is often used to describe the shootings, and to understand the context is to see how this fits. Gaddis suggests that mapmakers "go through a three-stage process of connecting reality, representation, and persuasion" (2002: 45). I have yet to come across a map of May 4th that meets these criteria.

In preparing for my conversation with Tom, I had three maps of the shootings and noticed that he was indicated as having fallen in a significantly different place on each map. One map was from the official *President's Commission on Campus Unrest*. In this document Grace is close to Taylor Hall and about 60 feet from the guard, where in the other two maps (one from *Wikipedia*, one from the 1990 *Akron Beacon Journal*) he is more than 200 feet away in an entirely different location. Other casualties were placed in different locations on different maps as well. During our public conversation, I asked Tom about the discrepancy regarding what seemed like a fundamental fact. He told me that after the shooting he was in Robinson Memorial Hospital with his father in his room when the FBI appeared to interview him. Tom was a seasoned protester, and he knew that while you could get in a lot of trouble by talking to the FBI, you wouldn't get in trouble by remaining silent, so he declined to speak to them. They applied some pressure, until Tom's father said "Don't you hear what he is saying? He won't talk to you." And that is how Tom Grace ended up in the wrong place on the early maps of the shootings; failure to cooperate with the FBI. In the interest of accuracy, Tom supports the 2010 map published by the May 4th Visitor Center, on which he consulted. It is the most accurate and comprehensive map to date.

Words and Things

Words are fundamental building blocks of representation. The arbitrary relationship between words and the things they represent notwithstanding, words can denote or connote, frame or blame, clarify or obfuscate, wound or heal. Images inhabit a more complex grammar, the language of the visual, adding richness and variegation to verbal representation and calling into being a whole new vocabulary for analysis. Maps fall somewhere between words and images, typically incorporating elements of words and numbers and illustrations to make a word picture that is less abstract than a painting, and more concrete than a poem. The Kent State shooting was an irresistible topic for mapping from the start because of the geographical complexity of the physical site, the choreography of students and guardsmen during the fateful last minutes, and the distances between the guardsmen and the students who were shot.

Mapping is more than lines on paper; it is a rhetorical activity, as Mark Monmonier's social history of the Mercator Projection winningly illustrates.

> Any attempt to show how map projections work must include their rhetorical role, which involves goals markedly different from traditional cartographic tasks like describing boundaries, exploring patterns, and getting around. This rhetorical prowess, rooted at least as much in the symbols and generalizations as in its projection, makes the map vulnerable to diverse ideological interpretations (2003: xii).

While Monmonier is primarily interested in the highly charged case of the Mercator versus the Gall-Peters world map projections, he recognizes the ideological value of maps more

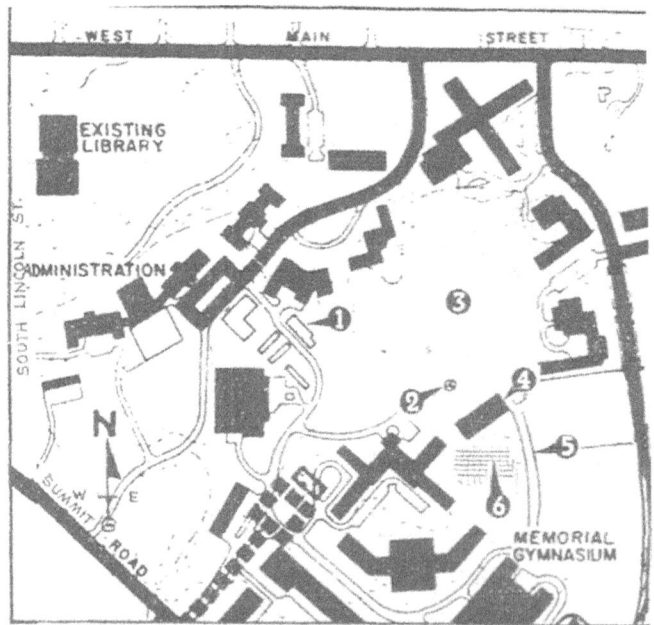

Figure 8.7: *Cleveland Plain Dealer,* 5 May 1970.

generally, "including their persuasiveness in dramatizing problems and setting agendas." The May 4th killings have proven to be an irresistible challenge to a whole range of would-be cartographers over the years, with results ranging from wildly inaccurate and misleading to nominally accurate if less than rhetorically compelling.

The first map of the shootings appeared 5 May 1970 in the *Cleveland Plain Dealer*. On the accompanying legend (1) indicates the ROTC building that was burned the previous Saturday night; (2) is the Victory Bell used for campus gatherings; (3) is the campus commons; (4) Taylor Hall; (5) Portage Path; and (6) the Prentice Hall parking lot. The actual shooting took place from one end of Taylor Hall (location of Guard is not noted) in the direction of the parking lot, which is misplaced as being next to Taylor Hall rather than next to Prentice Hall (one building to the right). Without laboriously deconstructing this image, it is fair to say that no one could possibly understand the guard's firing position let alone their movement from this drawing. Important physical features like the parking lot are significantly misplaced, and the position of the National Guard is not indicated at all. The placement of elements in the terrain could give the impression that students were 30 feet from the National Guard rather than 300, which was the case. These are facts that matter.

In the *Plain Dealer* map, note how it indicates the Prentice Hall Parking Lot (labeled 6) as adjacent to Taylor Hall (4), when in fact the aerial photograph (Fig. 8.8) shows that the parking lot is a separate unrelated area that extends at an angle. The guard opened fire from the top left corner of Taylor Hall, aiming into the parking lot that extended more than 700 feet away. A perspective on the distance of the shooting is a critical feature of representation of this event.

Figure 8.8: Aerial Campus View, Scranton Commission Report, 1970.

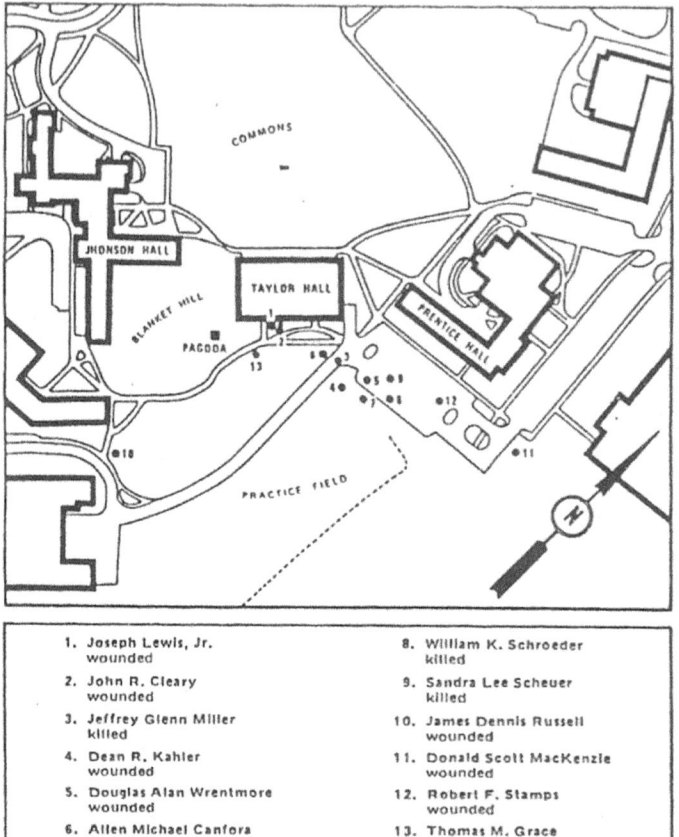

Figure 8.9: Scranton Commission Report Casualty Map.

Toward the end of 1970, the President's Commission on Campus Unrest published their findings on Kent State. The report included numerous photographs from May 4th accompanied by maps. Taken together in sequence the photographs represent the most accurate visual series available. The Scranton Commission report is also the first to include a map with distances of the fallen, inaccurate though they are.

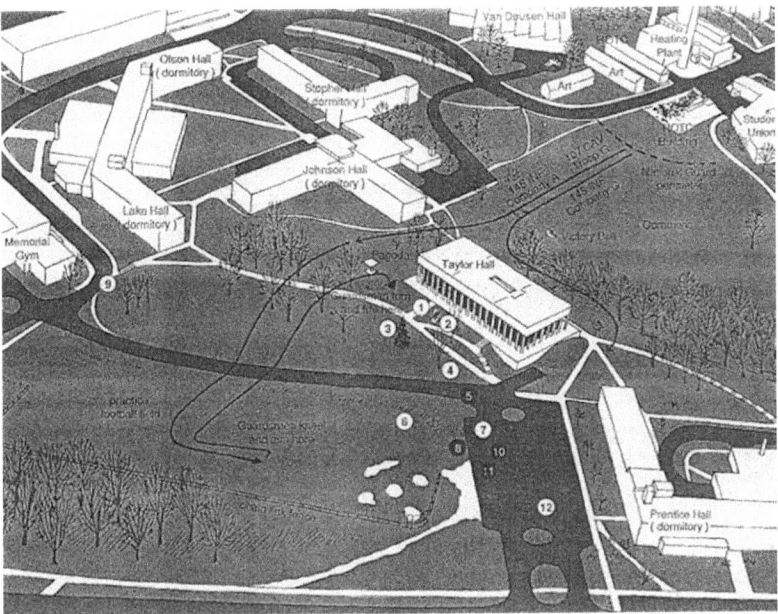

Figure 8.10: *Akron Beacon Journal*, 4 May 1990.

The Scranton Commission map must be credited with its attempt to place the bodies of the victims, yet the position of the firing guardsmen (next to the pagoda noted on the map) is not represented. Nor is there any sense of the minutes leading up to the barrage where there was considerable movement of the guard within the area depicted. Placement of some of the victims, including Tom Grace, is incorrect in this representation, for the reason noted earlier.

In 1990, on the occasion of the twentieth anniversary of the shootings the *Akron Beacon Journal* published a more detailed map than earlier attempts, with an accompanying legend.

To the cartographer's credit, the trajectory of the guard's movements are traced to allow for some sense of time and the physical features of the buildings landscape are accurate. The point of view looking from the outermost shot students toward the point of gunfire simulates the real time action of the shooting. As in the Scranton report, several casualties are misplaced.

Other maps have been published over the years, including by Kevin Subella of the Ohio Geographically Referenced Information Program (OGRIP). No doubt, the most widely referenced current map was published in 2007 by *Wikipedia*.

This map uses a cartoon-style of illustration and gets nearly everything factual wrong. Physical and geographical features are distorted, the point of view does not reflect that of any participant, the timeline of the guard trajectory is unclear, the scale and distances are unspecified, and several victims are misplaced. This may be the most familiar and widely

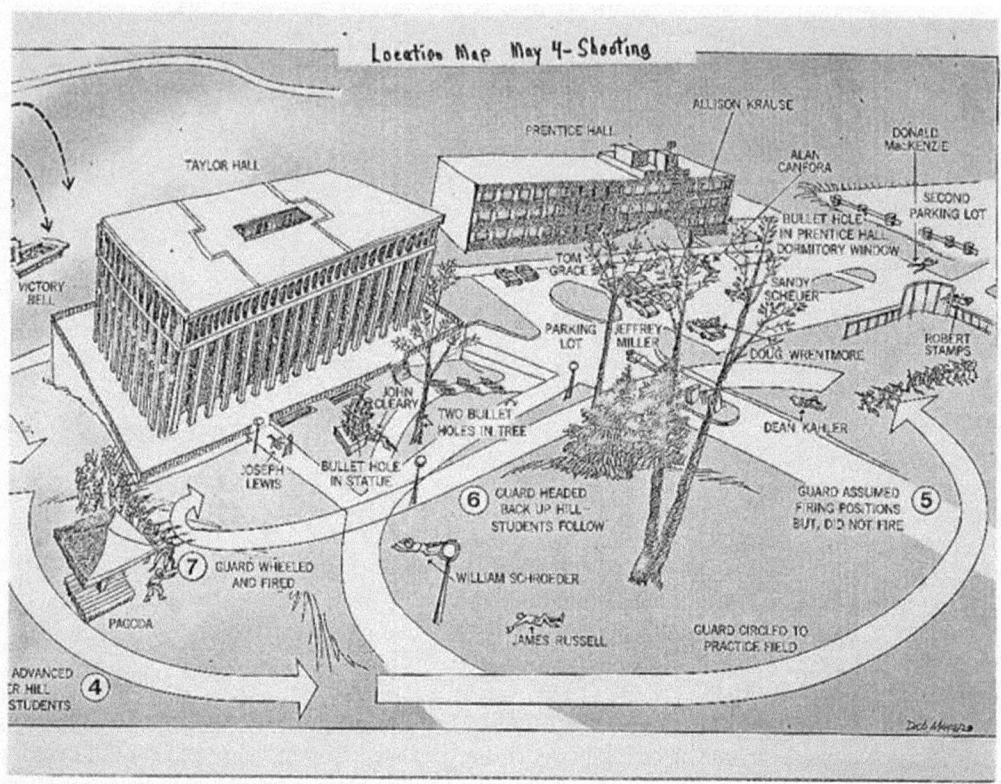

Figure 8.11: May 4th Map from Wikipedia, 2007.

reproduced map because of its user-friendly illustration style and ready availability, but it is also the most misleading.

There is a popular cartography story from a book by Jorge Luis Borges (1999), where the art of cartography had attained such perfection that the Cartographers Guilds struck a map of the Empire whose size was that of the Empire, and which coincided point for point with it. "The following generation, who were not so fond of the study of cartography, saw that vast Map was Useless and … they delivered it up to the inclemencies of Sun and Winters."

We try to avoid being too literal in making maps because "to do otherwise would be not to represent at all but rather to replicate. We'd be drowning in detail" (325).

This is a lesson that was lost on the mapmakers from the *Cleveland Plain Dealer*, on the occasion of another anniversary in 2010. So much detail is crammed into this rendering that the essential throughline is lost entirely. The mapmaker succumbed to the temptation to tell the whole time-based story in a stop-frame image, with the result that less would have been more.

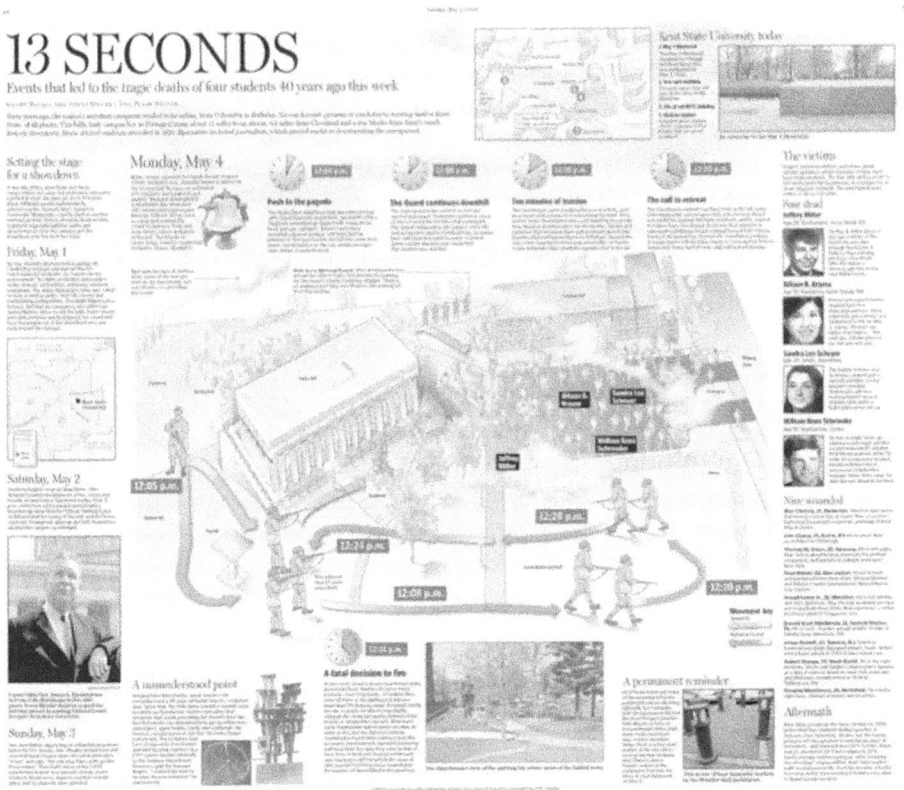

Figure 8.12: *Cleveland Plain Dealer*, May 2010.

The legend of this map includes a timeline from 12:05 p.m. to the shooting at 12:24. National Guard movements during that period are indicated, signified by large illustrations of one or two guardsmen. Point of view is omniscient and not from the perspective of any participant in the event. The perspective is similar if not identical to the Wikipedia map. Only one guardsman is represented at the shooting spot, and lines of fire are not indicated. The Prentice Hall parking lot appears populated by zombies, who are not looking toward or away from the line of fire. Dead students are indicated but wounded are not. Crucially, this map lacks the information of who (National Guard troops) did what (shoot M-1 rifles) to whom (13 students) from where (Pagoda to beyond Prentice Hall parking lot). With all of the surrounding explanatory copy on the map, it fails to tell the fundamental story.

In 2010 a map of the shootings was published by the Kent State May 4th Center. This representation provides context, history, and illustration that most fully tells the story.

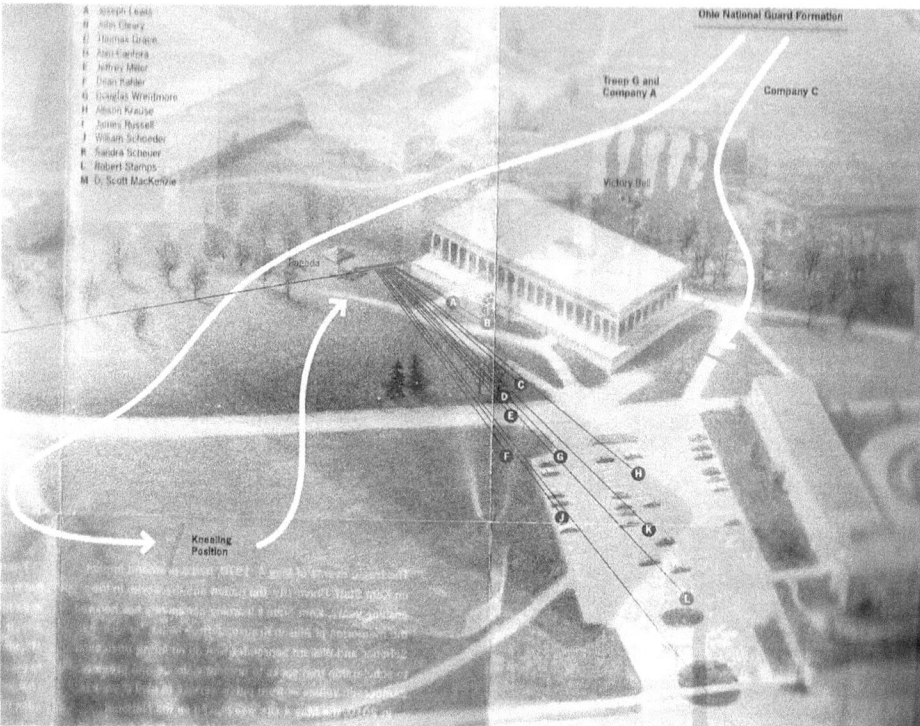

Figure 8.13: May 4th Center map 2010.

This map is physically accurate and surrounded by a narrative timeline of 1 to 4 May. The movements of the National Guard are clearly depicted. Above all, the position of the guard, lines of fire and the position of the victims are clearly marked in a way that gives the viewer a sense of distance and scale, although the map reproduces poorly. The point of view is close to that of the students. What this map lacks, as do the others, is a depiction of the other protestors on the scene. Headlines like "troops fight with rioters" surely give the impressions that thousands of students were surrounding the soldiers. Was this the case? Should the protestors be part of the map?

The Missing Mob

Observe Fig. 8.14 of the National Guard firing which does not include any surrounding students or area, leaving the physical context indeterminate. Where is the mob?

Providing more context, Fig. 8.15 is taken from behind the guard immediately following the shooting. Where is the mob?

Figure 8.14: National guard firing.

Fig. 8.16 is a picture of Joe Lewis, injured student closest to the guard. Where is the mob?

Fig. 8.17 is a picture of the Prentice Hall parking lot immediately before the shooting. The guard can be seen in the upper left hand corner. The line of fire was close to the point of view of this photograph. Where is the mob?

Is there evidence in any of these photographs that "troops were fighting with rioters," or that there were any "rioters" at all? Where are the thousands of protesters? Could it be that they had dispersed earlier? The striking thing about these landscapes is the absence of protesters and the distances at which students were killed and wounded. This documentary evidence does

Figure 8.15: Immediately following shooting behind guard.

Figure 8.16: Injured Student Joe Lewis, Closest to Guard.

not support the impression that "troops were fighting with rioters," and none of the maps of the event depict the small numbers of student protesters present when the guard opened fire. We can imagine the fateful minutes of May 4th as a compressed three-act tragedy. Act I takes place from about 11:45 to noon on the Commons, a wide natural amphitheater. Five hundred or so protesters cluster near the middle of the site at the Victory Bell. Up to several thousand more students ring the natural bowl, many of them near the West side of Taylor Hall. The National Guard advances across the Commons lobbing tear gas, scattering the students. Act

Figure 8.17: Prentice Hall Parking Lot where most injuries occurred. Guard can barely be seen in upper left. The figure in right foreground is near where students were killed.

II begins with the guard ascending Blanket Hill and going over the top and down again to a football practice field within sight of the East side of Taylor Hall. Several guardsmen assume firing position but do not fire, before advancing back up to the crest of Blanket Hill, making a half turn, and opening fire in the direction of the Prentice Hall parking lot. Act III, the dénouement, is a montage of ambulances and stunned professors trying to calm distraught students. What these three acts reveal is that the thousands of protesters appearing in Act I are confined to a specific geographic site—the Commons. In the shooting sequence on the other side of the hill on a different site, they have virtually vanished. The "mobs of rioters" were nowhere to be seen when the guard actually opened fire. No more than several hundred students—none closer than 60 feet away—were in the actual line of fire.

History Misremembered

Tom Grace and I presented our talk on May 3rd and May 4th was the day of ceremonies on the Kent State Commons. Thousands of people ringed the hillside to listen to speeches by survivors Gerald Casale (a founder of Devo) and Chic Canfora, as well as the mother of casualty William Schroeder and the boyfriend of Allison Kause. Notable sixties radicals Mark Rudd and Bernadine Dohrn also spoke. While sitting on the hillside I opened that day's edition of the *Daily Kent Stater*, the campus newspaper, to see a large splashy graphic of the shooting, a blowup of the least accurate map of all, from Wikipedia.

I could not believe my eyes to see this huge error when an accurate map was being published out of the May 4th Center on their own campus, indeed in the same building as the journalism department. I wrote to the editor, saying in part "You might want to take another look at the splashy map of the shootings in our May 4th issue. It is the most misleading of all

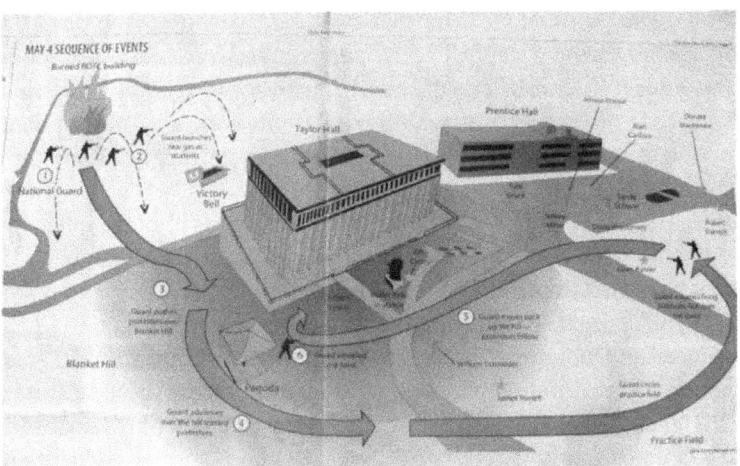

Figure 8.18: *Daily Kent Stater* 4 May 2010.

maps I have consulted and is from Wikipedia. A correct map of the shootings is published by the May 4th Center..." The editor replied:

> Thank you for the email. We noticed the exact same mistake yesterday and ran a correction in today's location. In addition to Thomas Grace's mistaken location, there were a few more that we noticed... We regret the error and have printed a correction to the map.

A reader had to look hard to find the correction: "In yesterday's graphic showing the May 4 sequence of events the locations of William Schroeder, Thomas Grace, Alan Canfora and Robert Stamps were incorrect. The errors occurred during the design process."

The design process, indeed. More like Wikipedia copying process? If the Kent State campus paper can get a map this wrong on the 40th anniversary commemoration of the shootings, does anyone care enough to get it right? And does it matter? Is it just wonky history or does accuracy make a difference in representation? How "wrong" can a representation be and still maintain verisimilitude and fidelity? Does it matter whether Tom Grace was 60 feet or 225 feet from the soldiers who shot him with M1 rifles that can shoot a mile? "Is that all you people think about?" The answer is yes if you care at all about the integrity of history and memory. The answer is also yes if you are trying to understand the event and the behavior of participants and all of the implications that follow. The same goes for other documentary representations such as film and photography. As Susan Sontag (2003) wrote, a photograph always has truth but it also always has a point of view. In the larger scheme of things, a few feet one way or the other or a changing point of view might not mean much, but such errors aggregate and suggest a carelessness that can be amplified in the broader interpretation of an event. When maps are the text to be analyzed, every element of representation reflects a choice on the part of the source and a lesson learned on the part of the audience. Point of view, for instance, is a rhetorical choice that has persuasive consequences. In a May 4th illustration, should the point of view be that of the guardsmen? The dead and wounded? Should it be omniscient from a neutral aerial perspective? What does each of these choices imply about the interpretation of events? And returning to Gaddis' idea that mapmakers go through a process of connecting reality, representation, and persuasion, what is the persuasive function of mapping May 4th? To educate, to encourage activism and engagement, to make an emotional connection with the past?

How is May 4th memorialized? Without question John Filo's photograph is the preeminent artifact of the event. As compelling and enduring as the image has been, it might also qualify for what Grace had in mind as "a permanent part of the American historical tableau, though a sense of the context surrounding the images may easily slip away" (2009: 246). The metaphorical power and ubiquity of the Filo image has appropriated the memory of May 4th to the exclusion of documentary representations that might provide a more descriptive recollection. The gruesome romanticism of the Filo image discourages and distracts from more didactic representations. There is no image of the National Guard firing with their victims in the picture. There is no document that shows both the guard and the protesters

Murder on May 4th

Figure 8.19: Representation of position of closest fatality from point of view of National Guard shooters. Photo: Tom Wilder.

who were in the line of fire. Such an image would allow a very different remembrance from Filo's devotional Madonna and child, but in the absence of such documentary confirmation Filo's photograph retains the imprimatur of history.

Do-It-Yourself Cartography

In order to satisfy my own curiosity about how May 4th might be remembered, I persuaded my brother Tom, a photographer, to join me at the local high school football field. It has always seemed to me that if people understood the *distances* of those shot and killed from the National Guard troops who fired at them, it might provide an "aha" moment. We measured the distance from the shooters to the closest fatality at about 270 feet. (The other three fatalities were *beyond* the far goal post between 330 and 390 feet and would not have been visible.) I stood where the closest fatality would have been and my brother stood by the goal post, where the guard would have been. He shot the picture with a 50mm lens to capture the point of view of the guard as accurately as possible. Representing one detail (distance from guard to victim) using the familiar context of a football field may show more about the essence and egregiousness of the shooting than more elaborate but less strategic arguments.

This simulation process got me thinking about what it would take to do a full reenactment, like Civil War battles, and what various camera angles and audio would tell us that is currently "unseen." Maybe for the 50th anniversary commemoration. There remains a lot to be learned about this moment when the curtain was pulled back to reveal, however, fleetingly the military state that the United States rapidly became following World War II.

State of Grace

Tom Grace has learned to live with his May 4th legacy while not being defined by it, taking his fate in stride. "I was an activist before the killings. I knew full well that military authorities killed protesters and had done so at least as far back as 1877 when many dozens of workers were shot to death during a national railroad strike. What was surprising to me was that the National Guard would open fire during the day, in full view of hundreds of witnesses, and with television cameras and still photographers documenting it all. Usually in such circumstances these things happen either at night or without many witnesses" (Gorman 2010). Grace approaches his public lectures on the subject not as a victim "but as a witness to a terrible act of unpunished violence against unarmed civilians." To Grace, the most important lesson of May 4th is the "vital necessity to stand up and speak out against the use of state terrorism. Millions of students and young people, and some workers, did just that and it shocked the entire system of American higher education."

To carry this legacy forward, all we are left with is representation. Cartography, like history, is not reality itself; Gaddis writes "indeed, if truth be told it's a pitiful approximation of a reality that, even with the greatest skill on the part of the historian, would seem very strange to anyone who's actually lived through it. And yet, with the passage of time, our representations become reality in the sense that they compete with, insinuate themselves into, and eventually replace the firsthand memories people have of the events through which they've lived" (2002: 136). Before eyewitness testimony and memory of May 4th are beyond reach, may multiple faithful maps be rendered that at least do justice to the complex territory.

The 2010 decision to include 17 acres of the Kent State Campus on the National Historic Register was welcomed by those who want the memory preserved, but became a bittersweet victory when in 2012 the U.S. Department of Justice declined to reopen an investigation of the case despite new evidence and the pleas of journalists, casualties and supporters citing "insurmountable legal and evidentiary barriers to bringing a second federal case in this matter" (Mangels 24 April 2012).

Case closed? May 4th remains a domestic wound that resists both remembering and forgetting the stark cautionary tale it tells, a moral close to activist S. Brian Willson's sentiment that "you are free to dissent in this country as long as you are not effective."

Chapter 9

Long Bien Story: Giving and Taking Away

Carol Wilder with Douglas Jardine

To Mai Lien remembers when she first heard that a media class was coming to Hanu, as the students call Hanoi University. She was a graduate teaching assistant with the Faculty of International Studies when she overheard the dean say that a filmmaking class was going to be taught by a visiting American Fulbright. "My curiosity was raised with questions about all kinds of media, filmmaking, and of course the professor. We had nothing like a media course at Hanu, and I wondered if we would really make a film. I asked the dean if I could join the class with the students and she agreed." As fate would have it, the teaching assistant assigned to the class had a scheduling conflict and Lien was asked to take over. "I couldn't wait!"

Lien was born in Hanoi in 1988, two years after the beginning of *doi moi* reforms. She was told by her mother that living conditions were much better than when her brother had arrived six years earlier. Lien was raised in a traditional northern Vietnamese family. Her grandfather made all of the decisions and her parents were expected to take care of him and her grandmother. Three generations lived together in a house that Lien still calls home with her grandmother. It was always expected that Lien would go to university, which she believed would help her to be more "independent, more trusted by my parents, and have a louder voice in my family." After successful completion of the grueling national qualifying exam for university, Lien enrolled in Hanoi's Vietnam National University where she received a B.A. in International Studies. This pleased her parents, who had always hoped she would become a diplomat, a calling at which she would excel.

Invincible Ignorance, Mine

Part of my Fulbright project for 2007–2008 was to establish a small media lab at Hanoi University, a hilariously improbable and even insane idea if I had known what was awaiting me on the other end. I quickly found myself operating on a variant of invincible ignorance, where you accomplish something only because you do not know it is impossible and should have never been started in the first place. The idea of a six-station Mac lab is simple enough in theory. I had participated in the creation of dozens of similar and larger facilities at my university. The challenge of trying to do it half a world and several cultural light years away begins with wrangling money and donations of equipment that then need to be somehow transported 10,000 miles, cleared through a notoriously sticky customs wicket, and set up in working order at the other end in a country where hardly anyone had seen a Mac, especially the university technology director. Add to this the fact that my personal technical expertise was largely limited at home to knowing the right person to holler for. "Jed!! There's something wrong with my computer!" Years as an administrator with a capable staff had left me afflicted with the familiar executive condition of learned helplessness. I have come a long way since.

The Fulbright Program has many wonderful features, one of which is its affiliation with the U.S. State Department. And one of the wonderful things about the U.S. State Department is that it is able to transport things via diplomatic pouch, bypassing the vagaries of customs and appearing magically at the intended destination unscathed, or almost unscathed. Our one hundred pounds of video and computer equipment appeared at the U.S. Embassy during my first month in Hanoi a little the worse for wear but intact and operational. I knew the lore about drugs and guns being sent via diplomatic pouch, and under the circumstances video equipment seemed almost as subversive.

Within a month the little lab was up and running thanks largely to student Pham Viet Ha who adopted it like a second home. I had banked on the probability that there would be a student who would fall in love with the Macs and want to put in some work hours in the lab in exchange for a small stipend and unlimited access. I had seen it happen many times at home. Ha was more than thrilled with the opportunity, which eventually helped him land a job at Vietnam's top television station. Still, the first year of the lab was rocky, and since university President Nguyen Xuan Vang requested that we shoot short films about the

Figure 9.1: To Mai Lien with the author, 2011.

Long Bien Story

Figure 9.2: Hanu (Hanoi University) Media Lab 2010.

university, despite my reluctance to assign topics to beginning students, that is what we did. The charmingly amateurish results were a big hit in our final screening a short three months after we started, but would not be mistaken for the broadcast quality public relations films I think Dr. Vang hoped for. Still, he was pleased with the movies despite realizing that he did not have a slick new advertising operation under his roof.

By my third time back to Vietnam to run a film class in the lab, which remained pristine but padlocked in my absence, I had a system. That is when Lien first joined us. While I have cut my teeth making several short films, I lay no claim to being a professional filmmaker. The invincible ignorance of thinking I could teach filmmaking may have helped me come up with a curriculum that resulted in nice tight short student films that tell a story. By spending time on storytelling, emphasizing mastery of a short list of camera and editing techniques, banishing special effects and shots of more than 30 seconds and requiring the inclusion of elements like interviews and a variety of camera movements, I stumbled on a pedagogy that may strike some as prescriptive or simplistic but demonstrably produces results in the form of smart and watchable short student films. I was also committed to using the simple iMovie editing platform, which had plenty of features for a beginning filmmaker with only a few weeks time to invest despite the fact that the filmmaking faculty back home considered iMovie beneath them. The masterstroke of thematically unifying the films around one broad topic was the idea of Douglas Jardine, who taught on the Faculty of International Studies and was responsible for my introduction to that department and our subsequent partnership. We liked to refer to ourselves as co-conspirators, against what or who did not matter. It was just the general idea of subversion that attracted us to each other.

Figure 9.3: Douglas Jardine and students on Long Bien Bridge, 2010.

Douglas had a fascination with Long Bien Bridge and had already done some writing about it and extensive photography. Doug thought that Long Bien would be a good topic for a series of short films and he suggested we make a visit. The bridge carries architectural, cultural, historical, agricultural and political meaning, making it among the richest sites in Vietnam. We expected some resistance when we told the students of our chosen subject, yet they showed nothing but enthusiasm. Douglas was so charming and persuasive he could probably sell rice to the Vietnamese. In any case, it did not take much selling. I have never known a student who did not jump at the prospect of a field trip. Early one foggy morning a few days later we were all meeting at the bridge and trudging around for hours while Douglas expounded on the many wonders of Long Bien.

Pont Doumer

The class assembled on the bridge as Douglas explained:

> Every city has its story to tell, and in every city the best way to hear its story is to understand the cultural and social symbols and the spaces that comprise the urban landscape. The most noted spaces like Hoa Lo Prison are complex with many layers of meaning. To understand the complexities of even one such space is to see the city in a new way, to begin to *hear* the city.

The meanings and memories of Long Bien have evolved from the French colonial period of its creation to the American War when the colonial meanings of the bridge were overwritten, to the contemporary meanings of the bridge after the *doi moi* reforms. Douglas taught us to *hear* Long Bien Bridge.

Douglas enjoyed talking about "assimilation" and "association," and how the French colonial urbanism in Hanoi, as in other major Indochinese cities, was an attempt to arrive at an ideal colonial city politically, socially, and physically.

> Assimilation was driven by an attempt to make Vietnam as much like France as possible, and association was marked by an effort to encourage cooperation and cultural sensitivity between the colonizers and the colonized. In the association model, ideally Vietnamese culture and institutions would remain largely intact and the French colonial presence would exist along side it, benefitting both societies.

While the policies of assimilation and association overlapped, both were ultimately for the sole benefit of the French colonial project.

The results of assimilation and association can readily be seen in the colonial architecture of Hanoi. The Hanoi Opera House and the Presidential Palace are such fine examples of assimilation that one might be in Paris or Versailles. Both structures try to create a metropole on the periphery—the home world in the colony. On the other hand, the History Museum and other structures created by Ernst Hebrard with his high Orientalism are a clear example of association. Initially, Long Bien Bridge was a powerful example of assimilation, strategically built over the Red River to connect Hanoi to the major port of Haiphong. The bridge was designed by the French and built by 3000 Vietnamese workers. It was completed in 1903 and originally named Pont Doumer (Paul Doumer Bridge) after the Governor General of Indochina (1897–1902) and later President of France. The 2500-meter span was a technological marvel and the longest bridge in Asia. The belief in progress it embodied as a guiding principle was a fetish of the colonial project and high modernism.

Reinforcing the modernist meaning of the bridge, its supposed creator was that great hero of the modernist ethos Gustave Eiffel. Eiffel's actual involvement in the design of the bridge is unclear. Construction of the bridge took place between 1898 and 1903 by Dayde and Pille, allegedly built to an Eiffel Company blueprint. Even if the bridge was designed by the Eiffel Company, Eiffel himself had left the firm in 1893 after he was implicated in a Panama Canal scandal. Nonetheless, the association of Eiffel with the bridge was wholly accepted and promoted by the French colonial residents of Hanoi.

At the conclusion of the French War (and the colonial era) the original meaning of Pont Doumer begins to change as it becomes a site of Vietnamese triumph over the French. In 1945, the triumphant Vietnamese revolutionary forces marched across the bridge to liberate Hanoi from Japan. After the end of the French War on 10 October 1954, the bridge was again the scene of Vietnamese triumph as the victorious Vietminh were greeted on the bridge by cheering crowds from Hanoi. Some months later the French would rendezvous at the bridge to evacuate Hanoi and Vietnam. To symbolize the transfer of power, the bridge was renamed Long Bien Bridge (*Cau Long Bien*) after a small village located on the far side of the river from Hanoi.

"We're Going to Bomb Them Back into the Stone Age"

U. S. General Curtis LeMay's notorious Stone Age remark saw its almost perfect realization in the bombing strikes of Long Bien Bridge during the American War. As a result of this conflict, the meaning of national resistance would be added to national triumph. The bombing of North Vietnam began in 1965 as "Operation Rolling Thunder," a key part of Lyndon Johnson's "Americanization" of the war. In all 300,000 sorties were flown and 860,000 tons of bombs were dropped on northern Vietnam. Some cities in the North such as Haiphong were slated for destruction and severely damaged. The attacks on Hanoi were never meant to destroy the city, but to destroy its will through the disruption of essential services.

The bombing of Hanoi began in 1966 as a special provision of Operation Rolling Thunder called "Rolling Thunder 52." Before then Hanoi had been off limits as a target. Some of the bombing of the city such as the destruction wrought upon *Pho Nguyen Thiep* (Nguyen Thiep Street) which runs near the Hanoi entrance to the bridge was obviously intended for the bridge. Anti-war activist and visitor to Hanoi Mary McCarthy (1968) actually urged the destruction of the bridge as a suitably military target as opposed to civilian targets.

It was not until 11 August 1967 that the Long Bien Bridge took major damage. The U.S. Air Force dropped 100 tons of bombs and a central span of the bridge was taken out. It was quickly replaced by bamboo gangplanks and later a pontoon section. The bridge reopened on 5 October. The bombing continued on the 25th and 28th of October and more

Figure 9.4: Pont Doumer (Long Bien Bridge), c. 1902.

Long Bien Story

Figure 9.5: Long Bien Bridge after U.S. bombing, 1972.

attacks followed in November and December. Johnson called off the bombings in April of 1968.

The Christmas Bombing of 1972 ordered by Richard M. Nixon, known as "Operation Linebacker II," also did extensive damage to the bridge. The bridge was repaired over the years in an ad hoc manner with whatever resources were at hand. About one half of the

Figure 9.6: Bridge supports after U.S. bombing. (Left to Right: replacement and original.)

Figure 9.7: Replacement Bridge support after U.S. bombing.

original supports are missing, and some of the replacements are ingenious such as a chicken wire cage filled with cement pieces in Fig. 9.7.

The bridge has never been completely repaired and is open to trains, bicycles and pedestrians but not car and truck traffic. The scars of Long Bien Bridge have elevated it to almost mythic status in Vietnamese culture as a symbol of resistance and triumph. The repeated bombings and attempted repairs of Long Bien Bridge came to symbolize to Hanoi, Vietnam and the world the will of the Vietnamese people to resist a more technologically advanced aggressor. The act of repairing the bridge even after repeated massive attacks was seen as a commitment to victory and national reunification and a continuation of a history of resistance to foreign domination. This message was not lost in the U.S., either. A *Time* magazine article in 1972 quoted General Giap referring to the bombing of Hanoi saying that "we will be the only ones to stop the Americans in the 20th century." And he was right.

"Shanghai Port"

Long Bien is no longer the sole vital link across the Red River. Thanh Tri Bridge, Thang Long Bridge, Nhat Tan Bridge and Vinh Tuy Bridge serve as alternative crossings. Long Bien still provides an important rail link and facilitates motorbike traffic on two roadways hung on either side of the bridge in 1925. To find the meanings that Long Bien holds today entails walking the bridge and the warrens and spaces that it gives life to. The bridge has tremendous

Long Bien Story

Figure 9.8: *Van Chai Thuy Cu* (Floating Village) Red River.

presence not only as a discrete structure, but it also has a profound effect on the area around it. This is especially true of the island that the bridge spans in the middle of the Red River. The bridge is the only link to this island except by boat, and access is open through two steep stairways on either side of the bridge. The island is mostly devoted to agriculture, primarily corn, but there are also long-time residents and dwellings and a random collection of drug addicts who gather under the bridge for shelter. The island is also home to about 40 families who live in floating shacks (*van chai*) and who do what fishing is to be done but for the most part collect recyclable garbage from all over the city. There is an almost identical community of *van chai* on the Hanoi bank of the island. Both communities are desperately poor, though those on the Long Bien side are eligible for government aid.

Long Bien Bridge also serves as an informal market, with women selling mostly fruit or corn along the sidewalk next to the roadway. Finally, the bridge provides a happy unexpected function for young lovers who find privacy in Hanoi in short supply. The bridge becomes a destination to meet and spend some time alone, thus its nickname "Shanghai Port," a symbol of romance for young Vietnamese.

Our class walked the pedestrian span of the bridge, past lovers and vendors and bicycles piled sky high with goods as only the Vietnamese seem to know how to balance. At the bottom of a walk down the steep steps to the island below were tons of trash, mostly plastic bags, strewn among the now dry corn fields. Some years the island is entirely flooded, but in recent years the building of a dam upriver has created the opposite problem of drought. We walked up the island curving around to see the community of floating houses that would later be the subject of one of our films. We came unexpectedly upon a small graveyard as well as inhabited shacks dotting the island. We ran into no apparent drug users, but ample evidence of their presence. The cool misty weather was invigorating, but dragging ourselves back up the stairs hours later we knew it was time to go.

Hearing Long Bien Bridge

Back at the university we had a brainstorming session about possible topics for short documentaries. We considered the history and architecture of the bridge, its importance as a site of resistance and triumph against the French and later the Americans, the corn and vegetable growers, the rubbish collectors, the trains that run nonstop, its darker side as a refuge for addicts and the homeless, future plans for the bridge, the upriver dams, the pollution of the Red River, and other environmental challenges. Within an hour the students had naturally divided into four small groups for the project and left for the day to produce a written proposal with a synopsis, production plan and other standard items. We had less than three weeks of part-time meetings to finish the project and the pressure was on. Lien remembers:

> The first participation in the course was eye opening. Thanks to the equipment and instructions we received, my teammates and I got first-hand experience in the process of mediamaking that was beyond all expectation. Afterwards, I knew how to write a proposal, to film with different shots, how to make an argument or statement with an image, what is required to make a video. But above all my perspective towards media shifted from passive to active. That made me so much more confident.

The students I have encountered in Vietnam are extraordinary. I am not the first to observe that as a culture the Vietnamese are exceptionally attentive and engaging. Vietnam has more than 50 ethnic minorities, but most university students are part of the Kinh majority ethnic group. They are graceful and small boned. To put it another way, Americans are Yetis by comparison. I gasped the first time I looked down to see my hand next to that of a Vietnamese girl. My students always seem to be smiling that Vietnamese smile. I was once told by a Vietnamese woman that the smile is a mask cultivated over centuries in the presence of invaders in order to protect one's true feelings. Fact or not, it is a disarming smile that at the same time lacks any suggestion of submission. Most students wear eyeglasses, and I wonder why. About three-quarters of my students were women because International Studies is a "girl subject." The boys are off doing science, engineering and business.

Maybe it is because most education entails rote learning in Vietnam that the students so delight in a creative endeavor like filmmaking, but they have an incredible aptitude. The results we achieved in three weeks were better than I have sometimes attained in the United States in a full semester. I would like to think that my prescriptive pedagogy played a part. The Vietnamese students have a natural sense of editing rhythm, and an uncanny ability to mix narration and music and to cue the violins at precisely the right moment. Their aesthetic seems inbred and ancient. While their Western musical taste runs toward Yanni, they know how and when swelling strings are called for. Moreover, the students I have worked with have a deep social consciousness that shows everywhere in their documentation of the less advantaged. They produced social documentaries with a bite but with no blame and no stridency. While many of the films could be read as highly skeptical of the government treatment of various social subjects, the presentation is framed as more compassion than critique and achieves a rhetorical balance that bespeaks informed and sophisticated thinking.

Living on Rubbish

A good example of this is the film *Living on Rubbish*. Behind sweeping images of endless rows of garbage bags, the narration begins:

> The charming peaceful Red River and the historic Long Bien Bridge are classic symbols of Hanoi, but as the city prospers people have also been damaging it. Long Bien is now suffering from heavy pollution. Walking along the river bank and the island it is easy to see that the rubbish is piling higher and higher on this contaminated land. However there are still people living meager lives. The poor residents of these communities are used to living with pollution. Their fragile handmade shanties make up the floating

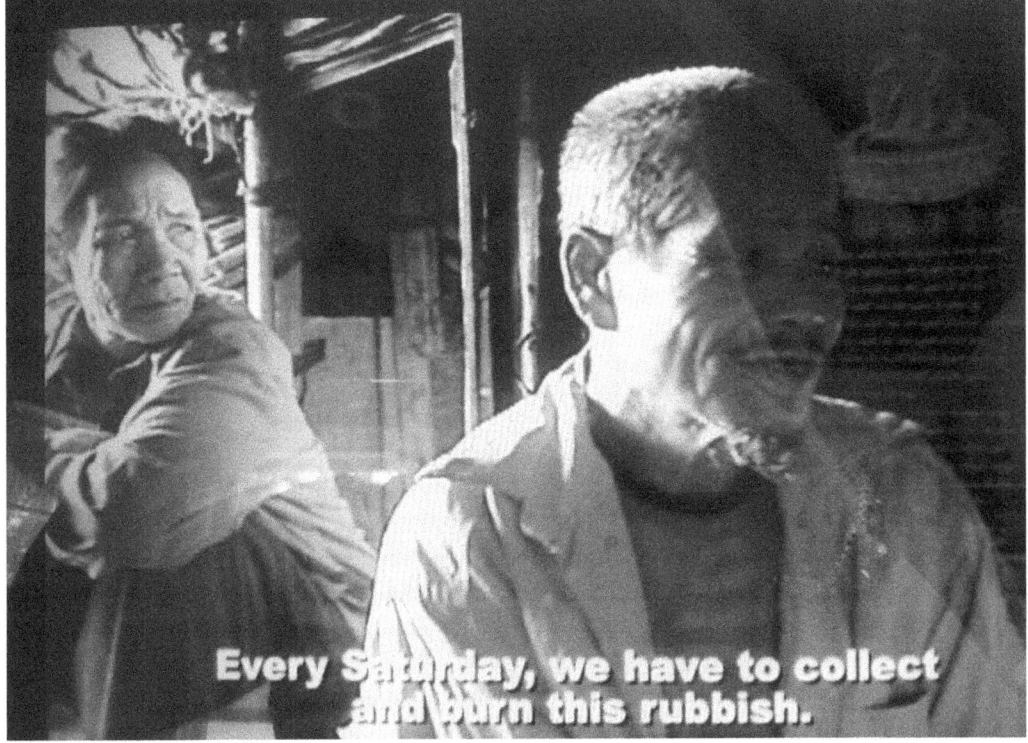

Figure 9.9: Mr. Tang and Mrs. Tui in Living on Rubbish (2010).

communities on the Red River. They play on the polluted ground, they grow polluted vegetables, they use polluted water to wash their dishes and even relax in the polluted river. They try to make the most of things that have been discarded as useless by others.

(Doan Thu Nga 2010)

The filmmakers interview 76-year-old Mr. Tang who shares his ten square meter floating house with his wife Mrs. Tui. Like other houses in the community it is made of rubbish. Tang and Tui are emigrants from another province who were among the first residents in this area 12 years ago. They have no children to look after them and their job of collecting garbage has become too difficult for the old couple. They collect garbage for about five or ten days until they have enough to sell. They can collect only 2000 to 3000 VND per day worth of trash, the equivalent of about 20 cents U.S. "We wish nothing but health to keep on collecting rubbish to earn our living."

Mr. Tang and his wife are assisted by the local authorities, other residents and visiting students, but they worry about the children of other families in their community who should be able to look forward to "a future where they will not have to wait for rubbish even if their lives will still be floating on the Red River like their parents and their grandparents before them." A companion film *Floating Futures* examined family life in the floating village with a focus on the plight of children who live and play among the rubbish and discarded hypodermic needles. The story begins:

Long Bien Bridge was the proud symbol of Hanoi after the American War. Despite repeated bombings, it is still standing. Many years after the war life is changing very quickly. Buildings are becoming higher. The pace is becoming quicker. Most of Vietnam is prospering, but is it true that everyone today is enjoying a better life? There is a place right in the center of Hanoi that is not yet sharing this good life…

(Vu Minh Huyen 2011)

The rhetorical nuance here is typical of the way the students approach delicate social subject matter. Rather than an accusatory stance, it is framed that this *van chai* is not prospering "yet." Similarly, a film from an earlier class on *Floating Lives* (Nguyen Thi Van Anh 2008) looks at how the *van chai* must buy electricity from their slightly less destitute neighbors up the riverbank who sell it at an exorbitant profit. While the average resident earns about 16,000 VN (about one US dollar) a day, the charge for electricity is 300,000 VND per month, more than half their income. Still, the narrator of the film after laying bare the poverty and exploitation ends on a glass-half-full note:

Narrator: Their life is full of hardship, but those things can't stop them from laughing.
Man: We come to each others' houses every evening.
Woman: Chatting with each other and laughing raises us up.

> Narrator: Seeing them laugh, watching the children innocently playing, we have the feeling that poverty or depression have never come to this place. Looking at the eyes of the women we see the light of hope. I hope for the children to have a full education and to have a better life.

The modes of expression the students crafted in their films confirm awareness of urgent social problems while at the same time sidestepping a confrontational tone. Given that the students are operating within a Confucian social context and a one-party political system, both of which discourage discord, their ability to nonetheless combine images and words to convey powerful social and political messages is inspiring.

In better days, the most delicious corn in Vietnam was grown by farmers on the island beneath Long Bien Bridge. Both climate and technology changes are phasing out this way of life, as illustrated in the film *Behind the Corn*, where the student filmmakers interview a corn farmer whose family has lived on the island for generations.

> Narrator: How long have you been living on this island?
> Farmer: Since a very long time ago.
> Narrator: Since your grandfather's time?
> Farmer: Yes, all my family has lived on this island. In 1971 we had the biggest flood on record. People have stayed in a refugee camp since then. It's hard. We depend on the weather. If the rain doesn't come the crops will die. Since the building of the Da River Dam the water has been blocked. There has only been a little water for several months. Without a good flood we don't get silt. The river used to flood the island. The land is getting drier and not as fertile as before… I don't have title to the land and it's zoned only for agriculture. The government can repossess the land at any time.
> Narrator: Do you look forward to any change in the future?
> Farmer: Oh, god. If life remains the same we will have to move on. There is no other way.
> (To Mai Lien 2010)

Long Bien Story

The most remarked upon of all of the small films we have made in Vietnam came out of the Long Bien project with the simple name *Long Bien Story*. The film is narrated from the point of view of the bridge itself—this bridge is a woman—and for whatever reason a device that could seem so clichéd instead lends enchantment to the story.

> I was born in 1902 as the great work of Gustave Eiffel and thousands of industrious and clever Vietnamese workers… Being a part of Hanoi I witnessed and participated in every historical event here, fighting with the patriots and sharing happiness with the triumphant revolutionary forces … the war has been over for thirty-five years but its remains still

Figure 9.10: Lam, 57, replanting after losing crop to flood on Bai Giua. Photo: Jamie Maxtone-Graham

exist… When the central span broke down[from U.S. bombing] brave residents did their best to fix me with everything they had therefore I still stand proudly as the new society changes. Day by day life continues peacefully…

(Do Thu Huong 2010)

The film acknowledges the people who call Long Bien home to catch fish, raise cows, and grow corn. The bridge is also a friend of commuters and tourists, who enjoy the bridge as "a destination of people who love beauty." As a romantic "Shanghai Port for couples," the filmmakers interview a strolling couple, where the young man says to the delight of his blushing girlfriend, "I find this place peaceful and romantic. It makes love grow." It is not often one finds a place that embodies war, work and love in such tangible ways, and the filmmakers capture the feeling as well as the fact. [All films available at YouTube: hanoiumedialab]

Plans have been underway for some time to restore or replace the bridge. France is working with Vietnam to preserve this historic site with possible plans of converting the bridge to a museum or a hanging garden or an artisan marketplace or some combination.

In any case the future of Long Bien Bridge is more secure than its past now that this great monument to architecture and revolution has been embraced for its priceless part in a heroic history.

Giving and Taking Away

My mother used to quote Job 1:21, "The Lord giveth and the Lord taketh away." While I do not know about the lord part, I certainly believe about the giving and taking away, and the Long Bien story led to both. The exhilaration of the student films was tempered by the knowledge that once I left Vietnam the lab would be locked until I returned or until Douglas could find time in his packed schedule to do a class for which he would likely not be paid. The secret to sustainability had to be local. Hanoi University needed to grow its own media program and faculty. The spirit was certainly willing, but the resources were nonexistent until we managed to persuade Lien to consider media study in the United States and were able to arrange with the Ministry of Education and Training in Hanoi and the Media Studies and International Affairs programs at The New School in New York to offer her a

Figure 9.11: Lovers at Long Bien Bridge.

Figure 9.12: Douglas Jardine at St. Joseph Cathedral 2011.

comprehensive fellowship to study for the M.A. in media studies. Lien remembers when she heard the news:

> I was so thrilled to learn that I got admitted and would be offered a fellowship. I remember waiting for the official acceptance letter and the anticipation of a whole new horizon. It was one of the most memorable experiences of my life and I am grateful for the opportunities it has brought.

Lien arrived in New York in August 2011 to begin the transition to her new life with a dream of leading the media program back at Hanoi University. Less than two months after her arrival, in early October 2011, we received news from Hanoi that the irrepressible Douglas had died suddenly of a massive heart attack at the age of 49, leaving his loving Connecticut family, his beautiful Vietnamese wife Huong, and hundreds of grieving friends and students. The shock waves went through the Hanoi educational community as well as through this book. Making Douglas a part of this chapter is a way of keeping his spirit close. Few teachers I have known were so truly beloved. In Fig. 9.12 Doug the adventure photographer is seen in typical garb trying to get the right angle for a shot.

Figure 9.13: Doug and students at Duong Lam Ancient Village, 2010.

Douglas embodied the spirit of many Americans who have found their way to Vietnam while not under the duress of the military draft. He was smart, energetic, talented, a little eccentric, larger than life, and madly in love with the people and places of Vietnam he captured so beautifully in his photography. Many of the images he took were of the ancient village of Duong Lam, where he led a community project through Hanoi University's International Affairs Program. I am so happy that I captured this moment of him at ease with his students.

Giving and taking away. That cruel war brought aching loss but has also introduced grace and beauty into many lives by opening a portal between two cultures that would not otherwise exist. When Thomas Fowler says in the film adaptation of *The Quiet American* "They say whatever you're looking for you will find here. They say you come to Vietnam and you understand a lot in a few minutes, but the rest has got to be lived," he spoke for anyone who has ever surrendered to this rugged and ravishing land.

Afterword: A Note on Theory

In graduate school I learned to appreciate, if not exactly love, theory. First Plato and Aristotle, then Marx and Weber, Kenneth Burke and Marshall McLuhan, and eventually Gregory Bateson and the whole world of cybernetic thought. I tired of abstraction and obfuscation during the years of the French invasion of all things theoretical, but I have always been happy to come across a good idea that sheds light upon something inchoate. It seems to me as a teacher it is my job to make the obvious even more so, make the transparent opaque, stopping short of smothering everything with erudition. I have always loved words, and it is only a short step from words to concepts, and a another step from concepts of things to the pattern that connects them in relationships, as Bateson taught. I am enamored with elegance and explanatory power and have little patience for theorists I cannot understand even with due diligence.

Good ideas have staying power. Plato's concern about the new fangled medium of writing, expressed at the end of the *Phaedrus,* is a classic of media critique. Aristotle's case for the primacy of *ethos*, or credibility, in human communication, is irrefutable millennia later. His introduction of the *enthymeme* as an interactive rhetorical syllogism presaged our participatory culture, and that is not even to mention the staggering influence of his codification of logic on Western thinking. More recently, the notion of "framing" or creating context is also a revelatory idea, first introduced by Bateson in "A Theory of Play and Fantasy" in 1956 and achieving virtual ubiquity decades later. "Metacommunication"—Bateson again—is another indispensable idea. Bateson's idea of double binds and related notions of symmetry and complementarity, paradox, contradiction, ambiguity, and irony tap into the many splendored complexity of human communication. For a time the working title of this book was *Paradox Lost*. The genius of Marx made a profound intervention and his credibility should be restored now that the seeds of destruction are undeniably sprouting. I think Norbert Weiner's notion of feedback (and more elaborated forms of recursion) was the most underrated idea of the middle of the twentieth century. Like many graduate students, I was enamored by the concept of entropy from thermodynamics. There was a long stretch of my life where the second law of thermodynamics was my first principle, but that wasn't the end of it. Baudrillard's hyperreality, Adorno's culture industry, Confucius' rectification of names, Satre's alienation and engagement, Barthe's *studium* and *punctum*, and the intoxicating vision of feminism. Agenda setting, dramatism, thick description, cultivation theory, disinformation, and onward down a long and ever growing list. I cannot imagine teaching about media and communication without these thoughts and thinkers and I have inflicted them upon many a skeptical student, converting some and turning others glassy eyed. Still, while I try not to wear theory on my sleeve, in this chapter I share some of the ideas that have helped me better understand political communication in general and Vietnam in media and popular culture in particular, giving a nod to scholars who have thought seriously and with useful results about the matters addressed in this book. If I had to point to one thinker who most influenced me and this work it would be Gregory Bateson, although the influence is more often between the lines than within them. I have written about Bateson in the past (1978, 1982) and commend his work to anyone who is inclined to think about thinking.

We live in a media environment as deeply and surely as we live in the ecology of the natural world. This may seem painfully obvious today, but it is really a very recent notion. Technology, geography, ideology and culture combine to create the limits and possibilities of our media consciousness, and we are often as not like the fish trying to understand the water. Part of the construction of this media world is volitional: we are what we choose to read, view, hear, make, say, do. But an equally or more important part of its construction is determined by others who provide the content options that are in varying degrees available, legible, attractive, and convenient. It is well established that we tend to seek out information that conforms to our existing attitudes, beliefs, and values. At the same time we are indisputably awash in a swirling sea of bits and some of us have firmer control of the rudder than others.

At the very dawn of the current information age, in 1922, Walter Lippman observed that "the real environment is altogether too big, too complex, and too fleeting for direct acquaintance," leading people to construct an abridged mental image of the world that constitutes a pseudo-environment. We "live in the same world but think and feel in different ones." Plato was making a similar case when he wrote about our inability to apprehend reality directly, relegating us to the spectatorship of seeing only passing shadows of puppets on the wall. This renders the human psyche vulnerable to infinite delusion and manipulation. Lippman coined the phrase "manufacture of consent" to refer to the process by which consensus is constructed by leaders who seek to create public opinion rather than follow it. Noam Chomsky and Edward Herman (1988) introduced the term to a new generation of readers when they used it as the title of their classic work on propaganda that explicates the ways that news is biased by the filters of concentrated corporate ownership, dependence on advertising revenue, reliance on official sources, orchestrated flak, and construction of an enemy. Chomsky first made the transition from being a distinguished linguist to being a prolific, renowned, and controversial social critic because of his objection to the war in Vietnam. Despite a wide following, Chomsky has managed to remain a permanent inhabitant of the sphere of deviance when it comes to the mainstream media, although more of our incoming graduate students are familiar with his name than perhaps any other.

Prior to the 1960s and 1970s models of communication and mass media were based on linear cause and effect thinking, where a source sent a message to a receiver. The source could be a person or a magazine or a television network or a community organization. Messages could be print or visual or audible but in any case they were typically understood as unitary and discrete and capable of individual impact. If feedback occurred at all it was often delayed in time and place. The occasion for the communication might be considered, but not in an ecological sense. This model is not unhelpful, but as it turns out any single message seldom creates variance in belief or action. More likely in any situation we are responding to an aggregate of messages that somehow stick to each other topically or psychologically or both. Samuel Becker was one of the first to write with this in mind when in 1971, around the midpoint of the Vietnam War, he introduced a mosaic model of communication. Becker argued that "our traditional concept of the message has severely limited usefulness for understanding contemporary communication." To illustrate, Becker uses the example of message patterns of the Vietnam War:

> The Vietnam War message prepared by a source is relatively free of redundancy, it is organized it is short. The message to which the receiver is exposed is scattered through time and space, disorganized, has large gaps; he is exposed to parts of it again and again, and there is great variance with the message to which other receivers are exposed (1971).

Thus it is that despite the efforts of sources, as receivers we each have a different aggregated experience of the "message." This is as true for interpersonal communication as for political issues. My Vietnam War message might include conversations overheard at the office, television news reports, the stories of friends just back from the war, and hundreds of other fragments. Becker suggests that these message sets are

> Overlayed to form the large complex communication environment or mosaic in which each of us exists. This mosaic consists of an immense number of fragments or bits of information on an immense number of topics ... scattered over time and space and modes of communication.

The thinking of Becker and others was ecological in the sense that we live in a media environment analogous to the natural environment, where televisions and fountain pens stand in as trees and water to create an environment that has an identifiable ecosystem. In the way that natural elements combine to create weather, media systems interact with audiences to create informational and political atmospherics. Becker pointed out that since any single message creates little variance in attitudes or behavior, it is the aggregation of multiple message bits and pieces that results in thought and action. Attitude change researchers of the 1960s and 1970s tried with limited success to invent formulas that would predict attitudes and with even less success making predictions about behavior. How my students and I loved the wacky social psychology experiments of Phillip Zimbardo (Stanford Prison Experiment) and Stanley Milgrim (Obedience to Authority) which showed if nothing else that context is king. I imagine they also get the lion's share of the credit for the creation of Institutional Review Boards looking out for the treatment of human subjects.

The nature of the media environment in the first instance depends upon prevailing and emergent media technologies. In *Orality and Literacy: The Technologizing of the Word*, Walter Ong (2002) laid the groundwork for understanding how the introduction of a new medium can change culture and consciousness. The media world of the 1965–1975 Vietnam War era was initially dominated by print with 1,750 newspapers publishing in the United States, but the period was marked by the ascent of television. From 1965 to 1973 an average of 51 million people watched one of the three network newscasts, 38 million read one of the three major news magazines, and 9 million listened to the radio. Network news went from 15 to 30 minutes in 1963 and it was not until 1967 that all three networks were broadcasting in color. The first 30-minute network news was anchored by Walter Cronkhite on 2 September 1963 and featured an interview with President Kennedy, who would be dead less than three months later. The Roper report in 1964 had television and print about even in the number of people saying they got most of their news from each medium: 58 percent said television, 56 percent newspapers, 26 percent radio, and 8 percent magazines. By 1972, television led newspapers 64 to 50 percent. Television achieved its dominance both during the Vietnam War and partly because of it with former print journalists like Peter Arnett and Dan Rather distinguishing themselves as television war correspondents.

When Michael Arlen (1968) called Vietnam the "living room war" it was because it was indeed the first war to be televised into people's homes. Arlen wrote brilliant media criticism of the war for *The New Yorker*, eventually reporting from there himself.

> Vietnam is often referred to as "television's war," in the sense that it is the first war that has been brought to the people preponderantly by television. They really look at it. They look at Dick Van Dyke and become his friend. They look at a new Pontiac in a commercial and go out and buy it… They look at Vietnam, it seems, as a child kneeling in the corridor, his eye to the keyhole, looks at two grownups arguing in a locked room—the aperture of the keyhole small, the figures shadowy, mostly out of sight, the voices indistinct, isolated threats without meaning; isolated glimpses… (83).

This was a perfect vantage point for someone in Marilyn Young's "twilight sleep." Arlen wonders what people who run television think about the war because "we have given them the airwaves, and now, at this critical time, they have given us back this keyhole view." Arlen's observations on the limitations of television's communicating about the war is in contrast to more widely held beliefs that television made the war ubiquitous in the public mind. He sees its function as a framing technology that shapes the message rather than as a neutral information pass-through, a radical new idea at the time.

Television was in its adolescence in the 1960s. Vietnam War reporting censorship was limited both by the difficult logistics of confining reporters and by the fact that the war was undeclared. Prior to about 1968 Vietnam War correspondents for the most part supported the American effort. The problems posed by some young journalists who reported stories that displeased the White House were isolated, as when CBS aired Morley Safer's 1965 report on U.S. soldiers torching huts in Cam Ne. President Kennedy tried to remove David Halberstam, but a look at *The Making of a Quagmire* (1965) documents that on the contrary Halberstam was a loyal cold warrior in the early years. Phillip Knightly writes that in general "the correspondents were not questioning the American intervention itself, but only its effectiveness." Halberstam affirmed that "we would have liked nothing better than to believe the war was going well, and that it could eventually be won. But it was impossible to believe these things without denying the evidence of our senses" (2004: 417). This observation concurs with Lawrence LeShan's (1992) distinction between the "sensory reality" of the world as we normally experience it and the "mythic reality" typically constructed in advance of war in order to create an enemy who can be demonized at will and killed without reservation or regret. The mythic reality that Halberstam went to Vietnam in 1961 expecting to find eventually crumbled under the weight of the daily sensory reality he encountered once he got there, much like the attitude arc of the American people. That docile public opinion took a sharp turn in 1968 when Walter Cronkhite historically called the war a "stalemate."

The "Uncensored War"

Daniel Hallin distinguishes between the messages conveyed by newspapers and by television in his classic 1986 study *The "Uncensored War": The Media and Vietnam*. At the beginning of 1966, he found a dramatic contrast between television and prestige print media. While print media for the most part reported official statements just outside the sphere of consensus at face value, television made the peace offensive of the period into a morality play between good and evil. Television's visual nature and intrinsic attraction to conflict and drama led it to more thematic coverage over time and gave it superior (if unwarranted) credibility with the audience. It is easy to overlook Hallin's ironic stance on "the uncensored war" unless one notes the double quotes around his title.

Television was a great consensus-generating medium of the policy makers, but it was also beginning to be recognized as an effective tool for social change. Youth International Party (Yippie) founder and colorful sixties activist Jerry Rubin (1970) makes this point:

> Walter Cronkhite is SDS's best organizer. Uncle Walter brings out the map of the United States with circles around the campuses that blew up today. The battle reports. Every kid out there is thinking "Wow! I wanna see *my* campus on that map!"...
>
> The media does not *report* "news," it *creates* it. An event *happens* when it goes on TV and becomes myth. The media is not "neutral." The presence of a camera transforms a demonstration, turning us into heroes. We take more chances when the press is there because we know that whatever happens will be known to the entire world within hours.

Television keeps us escalating our tactics; a tactic becomes ineffective when it stops generating gossip or interest—"news"...

I've never seen "bad" coverage of a demonstration. It makes no difference what they *say* about us. The pictures tell the story.

Our power lies in our ability to strike fear in the enemy's heart: so the more the media exaggerate the better. When the media start saying nice things about us, we should get worried...

You can't be a revolutionary today without a television set—it's as important as a gun. Every guerilla must know how to use the terrain of the culture he is trying to destroy (1970: 106–108).

Rubin was fatally injured by a car while crossing Wilshire Boulevard in Los Angeles in 1994. As a result of this untimely demise, his observations about the social media revolution will never be known, but it is fair to speculate that he would have loved every electronic bit of it.

Television was not the only important technology of the Vietnam era. The 1957 launch of Sputnik by the U.S.S.R. created panic in Washington and contributed in no small measure to the anti-communist fever that fueled the domino theory and the subsequent invasion of Vietnam. Sputnik also motivated the more spectacular and benign race to the moon, but space travel did not seem to have the staying power of war.

Cold War ideology drove much of the policy-making about Vietnam and dominated the message spin and framing emanating from Washington. Hallin points out, for instance, that every escalation in Vietnam was either preceded by an announced estimate of a much higher number or accompanied by a statement that it represented "no change of policy." He writes incisively that "it was essential that major policy decisions appear routine, incremental and automatic," and offers multiple illustrations of this strategy in action (1986: 62). Phillip Knightley observed similarly that in the mid-1960s

> The United States tried either flatly to deny what it was doing or to minimize the effects or to conceal the results behind a torrent of questionable statistics, a bewildering range of euphemisms, and a vocabulary of specially created words that debased the English language (2004: 418).

Cold War ideology was so pervasive in the United States that it was not open to legitimate discussion—a twilight sleep, indeed. The infamous deceptively conveyed Gulf of Tonkin incident that provided a pretext for the invasion of Vietnam was capable of manufacturing consent for war in part because of the ubiquity of Cold War thinking combined with a general trust of government that existed at the time.

To help explain how this all came to pass, Hallin posits a powerful and deceptively simple media discourse model that consists of two concentric circles. The inner circle he calls the sphere of consensus—the zone of motherhood and apple pie where there is no discussion to speak of because everyone in agreement. In the ring just outside the sphere

Afterword

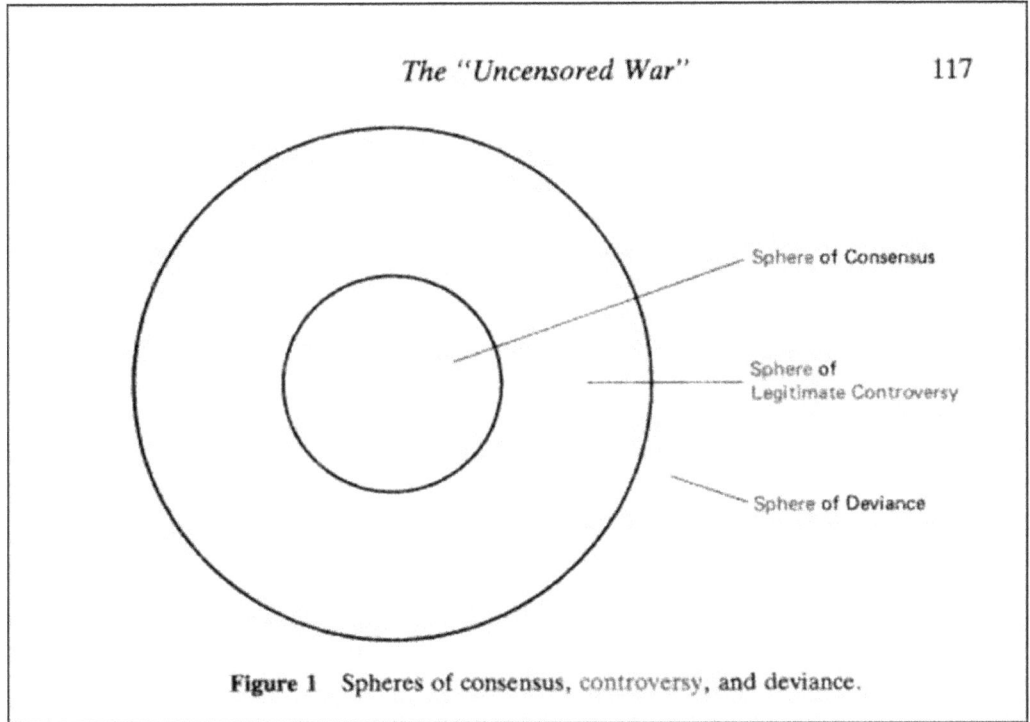

Figure 10.1: Daniel Hallin's spheres of discourse.

is consensus is the sphere of legitimate controversy—topics that are active in the public discourse— the public sphere, if you will. Outside of this band is the sphere of deviance, where messages are either marginalized, ignored or suppressed. While these spheres are permeable and their boundaries shift over time, for the most part the mainstream media confine themselves to the sphere of legitimate controversy. It gets interesting when the discourse shifts spheres. For instance, when the anti-Vietnam War movement shifted from deviance to legitimate controversy. More recently gay marriage is a topic that has shifted from deviance to legitimate controversy. The Occupy Wall Street protest has been credited with moving the conversation about income inequality into the realm of legitimate controversy. Breaking out of the marginalized sphere of deviance is a sign that a conversation is becoming mainstream, and regardless of the outcome of the argument the mere exposure and visibility confer huge benefits.

A wide and creative range of tactics are engaged by the media to marginalize messages that do not fall within the sphere of legitimate controversy. One of my own rules of thumb is the "Page A18" theory, which comes into play when a story which by any logic should appear on page one is relegated to the back pages of the front section. *New York Times* coverage of the

U.N. report on the Mavi Marmara flotilla attack in May 2010 is one example of a story that was buried in the back pages. More systematically, writing about the large 1967 March on Washington anti-war demonstration, Todd Gitlin (1980) points out that the *Times* deprecated the size and significance of the march, marginalized it as youthful deviance, trivialized it by failing to cover the speeches, polarized it by equivalent reference to its inconsequential right wing counterpart, and framed it as generational. This marginalization is more the rule than the exception when mainstream media cover dissent.

Michael Parenti (1993) outlines a compatible array of methods of misrepesentation that includes false balancing (giving two disproportionate sides of an argument equal weight, as in climate change discourse), face value framing (when something patently false is reported without comment by an official source), and the illusion of alternatives or no alternatives when the opposite is the case. Part of the problem is embedded in the routines of objective journalism itself with its privileging of official sources and absence of analysis or interpretation. During the twentieth century, the value of objectivity served an increasingly important mechanism for the legitimacy of journalism, resulting in a set of tenets that exalted independence, objectivity and balance. These admirable goals came to cut both ways and made journalists especially vulnerable to attempts by policy makers to frame the news to suit their political agenda. Sometimes there was sheer lying, but as often as not other strategies sufficed such as deluging reporters with briefing papers that would keep them buried until deadline. Eventually reporters stop asking questions that will not be answered and pitching stories that will not be approved. Finally, Parenti tells us, there is "no sensation of a leash around your neck if you sit by the peg. It is only when you stray that you feel the restraining tug."

The media environment of the Vietnam era was also influenced by the cultural revolution in music, drugs, and lifestyle that marked the late 1960s. The original "information wants to be free" generation produced a nonstop stream of alternative media, although it was available primarily to those in the counterculture network that included most colleges, some churches, and many urban centers. Social activists devoted considerable attention to the ways the existing media could be used to create favorable climates for social change. Handbooks like *The Media Works* (1973) and periodicals such as *Radical Software* (1973) not only advised readers on ways to use the existing media to their advantage, but also offered the information necessary to create and implement alternative media channels. More general social activism handbooks like *The Organizer's Manual* (1971) included thoughtful advice on the use of establishment media structures for the dissemination of social change. In *Subject to Change: Guerrilla Television Revisited* (1997) Deirdre Boyle traces the rich story of early experiments with video for social change, presenting three very different independent video collectives complete with funding struggles, in-fighting and artistic differences.

Another indispensible book on strategy appeared in 1970. *The Rhetoric of Agitation and Control* by John Waite Bowers and Donovan Ochs is now in its fourth edition. *Agitation and Control* offers a simple but powerful model of strategies of protest and control based on variables such as membership, control and rhetorical sophistication. Agitation strategies range across a continuum from petition to revolution; control strategies are avoidance, suppression, adjustment, and capitulation. Bowers and Ochs offer case studies to illustrate what happens when these variables interact.

Still, the conventional wisdom that "the media lost the war in Vietnam" is true at least in the ironic sense that access to television reports in particular made it clear that the war was not particularly winnable. When America's most trusted man Walter Cronkhite intoned from Vietnam "to say that we are mired in stalemate seems the only realistic yet unsatisfactory conclusion," President Lyndon Johnson is reported to have reacted "if I've lost Cronkhite I've lost Middle America." David Halberstam noted that it was the first time a war was declared over by a television anchorman. Little more than two months later Johnson made the shocking announcement that "I shall not seek, and I will not accept, the nomination of my party for another term as your president."

When I think about how my twilight sleep persisted to the extent that I was mostly oblivious of politics until 1970, it helps to understand that not only was I subject to all the filters of gender, geography and social class, but the media that were available to me overwhelmingly reinforced the status quo and alternative voices were either absent or marginalized. The importance of trust in the U.S. government in the decades after World War II can hardly be overstated. When Cold War thinking began to permeate the 1950s and led to the invasion of Vietnam ten years later, foreign policy was executed in the name of a trusting public in a way that is unlikely to happen again. The current level of public mistrust requires more sophisticated means of persuasion drawn from the dark arts of propaganda.

Defense Secretary Donald Rumsfeld got a lot of attention in 2002 when he said:

There are known knowns; there are things we know we know. We also know there are known unknowns; that is to say we know there are some things we do not know. But there are also unknown unknowns—there are things we do not know we don't know (2012).

Criticized for being outlandishly opaque, Rumsfeld's statement is also undeniably profound, especially when applied to managing information. If there is one hallmark of effective propaganda it is invisibility. Propaganda seldom works if I can see you trying to trick me, whether it is through withholding information, repetition, emotional appeals, managing expectations, or any of a hundred other ways humans have created to communicate deceptively. Lying is an obvious strategy, but practically for amateurs. War rhetoric takes far more stealth and creativity; the art of the half-truth. War leaders all have the same dilemma: how to communicate to the enemy that we will bear any cost and at the same time communicate to the home population that sacrifice will be small. War rhetoric also needs to keep public opinion off guard so an opposition movement cannot build momentum. It is truly the case, as Senator Hiram Johnson said in 1917, that "the first casualty when war comes, is truth."

I observed all of this happening during the "first Gulf War" in 1990–1991. During the buildup to the war I felt kept off balance by the daily headlines, which one day would be "war"(30 November 1990 "U.N. Offers Ultimatum to Iraq") and the next day "peace" (1 December 1990 "Bush Offers to Talk with Iraq"). Just when it seemed that war was inevitable (which it was), there would be a day or two of headlines where peace would seem to break out. One effect of this was to deflate any anti-war activism, which was brilliantly effective if it was intentional. This oscillating effect continued throughout the Fall of 1990, and with Adam Colby I charted the "war-peace" message of the newspaper headlines over three months to find a nearly perfect rhetorical roller coaster to war (1992). Of course we don't have the Pentagon Papers for the Gulf War yet, but the story of public opinion management leading up to that war will be a blockbuster some day and I am betting that the strategy of keeping public opinion off-balance through the use of mixed messages will be front and center. Invisible, yet hiding in plain sight.

It is often possible to see through these ruses, but it takes a lot of work and attention. In Hallin's study of coverage of the Vietnam War in the mid-1960s, he concludes that a "faithful reader of *The New York Times*—someone who read it thoroughly every day could follow the policy debate and see that escalation was immanent" (1986: 77). But what about everyone else? As late as 1964, two-thirds of all Americans had given "little thought" to Vietnam.

In the end, like Albert Speer, we didn't know but we could have known. Or could we, in the twilight sleep? Much has been said and written about politics, media, propaganda and war, but little has been heeded. Our natural propensities for distraction and denial have been exacerbated by post-9/11 fear, the rise of medication nation, and the trivialization of communication by social media. If Vietnam was not a lesson learned, one shudders at what it will take. But I suppose we should be darkly grateful to that sinful episode for introducing us to a land of such beauty and courage.

Acknowledgements

I wondered why some authors thank so many people until I wrote this book. Because its creation spanned the country and the globe as well as several decades, many kind and inspiring souls have joined me for some part of the journey. From my days as a student at Kent State until his death in 2010 my Ph.D. advisor D. Ray Heisey provided a moral compass that I was on occasion wise enough to follow. Hank McGuckin and Nancy McDermid at San Francisco State did the same for my political and professional sensibilities. During the years I lived in San Francisco the friendship of veterans like Paul Cox, Michael Blecker, Peggy Akers, Tama Adelman, Michael McDonell, Dan Ellsberg, and S. Brian Willson deepened my understanding of war and peace and led me to believe that while the former may be everywhere the latter is possible and worth the struggle.

In Vietnam special thanks go to my dear friends and mentors Nguyen Ngoc Hung and Nguyen Xuan Vang. I hope I have done justice to your kindness and example. Also in Vietnam, thanks to Nguyen Thien Nhan, Nguyen Huy Quang, Nguyen Thi Thanh Huyen, Truong Van Khoi, Tran Xuan Thao, Do Thu Huong, Nguyen Xuan Tue, Le Viet Hoa, Christopher Hodges, Gerry Herman, Pham Viet Ha, Tuyen Le, and former Ambassador Michael Michalak.

The staff of Kent State University Library Special Collections was cheerful and efficient negotiating their enormous holdings as I searched in vain for an image of the shooting from the National Guard perspective. Professor Carole Barbato of Kent State, a scholar of May 4th from the start, was gracious and helpful.

Eric Rothenbuhler gave welcome feedback on early versions of several chapters. John Waite Bowers read it all more than once, and provided his uniquely meticulous observations. Kevin and Jennifer McCoy, Annie Howell, Ladette Randolph, and Barbara Anello were supportive at key moments. My friend Bill Grimes was the first to read and respond to the full manuscript with an impressive 48 hour turnaround. My pal Joanie Hauswald was more responsible than anyone for the turn toward a more personal approach in my writing by encouraging me to include some of the content of my 2007–2008 letters home from Hanoi. Thanks also to New School colleagues Nina Khruscheva, Elizabeth Ellsworth, Carin Kuoni, Shannon Mattern, Eleni Litt, David Scobey, and Robert Polito. Jackson Taylor offered special encouragement. Along the way I contacted William Logan and Cathy Davidson whose work has been an inspiration, and both had kind words to offer. During the solitary months of writing my neighbors Jack and Kelly Reardon were always ready with a warm smile and a cold glass of wine to endure yet another update.

I have met many talented students over the years, but none more memorable than those who came to share my interest in Vietnam. Five intrepid graduate students have traveled with me to work in the Hanoi University Media Lab: Maria Byck, John Coogan, Alex Kelly,

Chris Rogy, and Ndelea Simama. Coogan was also my go-to guy in Hanoi and manned the camera for our moving interview of Mme. Hang. Unforgettable hardly describes our experiences, and I came to think of them as family.

I am indebted beyond measure to the people whose stories animate this book: Mme. Nguyen Thi Phuc Hang, Nguyen Ngoc Hung, Stephen Tace, Zachary Oberzan, To Mai Lien, Douglas Jardine, Thomas Grace, and the combat veteran I call Mike. They made Vietnam in its many manifestations real for me as I hope they do for you. Each one of them offers lessons in strength and hope and in some cases heroism as well. In several instances it is sadly their survivors who remain to be thanked: Dave and Joan Jardine, Huong Jardine, and Heather Tace. To Mai Lien provided support in many ways, including serving as my able interpreter with Mme. Hang and proofreading Vietnamese vocabulary, but in a wide-ranging project such as this any errors of fact or language are my own.

Fulbright awarded me a Senior Scholar grant in 2007–2008 and a Senior Specialist grant in 2011. I thank Peter Davis and Bob Kerrey for their crucial support of my original candidacy and the Fulbright Program, especially David Adams, for a life changing opportunity. My Fulbright cohort of 2007–2008 helped get us all through a challenging if spectacular year, especially Jamie Maxtone-Graham, Cary Trexler, Josh Glasser, and Jim Cobbe.

The New School Media Studies Program has provided a variety of research assistance and I thank Adele Ray, Phuong Thuy Pham, Chris Trice, and Danielle Fichera for their willingness to help and tolerate me even at times when I was not sure what I was doing. Rachel Morrissey became involved during the last year of the project and brought her fine mind and good humor to bear on myriad details large and small, including images, permissions, and web site. A New School Provost Innovation Grant sponsored by the office of Tim Marshall helped to fund Graduate Fellows in Hanoi. Janelle McKenzie, Dylan Fisher, Greg Griffith and Charles Whitcroft in the Media Studies office were always ready to lend a hand. And thanks to Christiane Paul for recommending Intellect as a publisher. I have nothing but highest praise for their people and process, especially Tim Mitchell, Alice Gillam, and Melanie Marshall. My brother Tom Wilder and his son Thomas both lent their professional eyes to the many images in the book.

Angels appear when least expected, and one appeared to me on a Friday afternoon midway through my 15-year administrative tour of duty when Lewis Lapham called my office to tell me he had come across something I had written and "I am calling to tell you that you are a good writer. I know writers need to hear that." Indeed, especially from the venerable Mr. Lapham and at a moment when the only genres I could manage were memos and reports. I don't know if Lewis even remembers this conversation, but it has meant a lot to me over the years of this project and I am very grateful for the gesture, which I have in turn extended to other writers in need of encouragement.

My children Casey and Elissa have always been the light of my life, a status they are happy to share with my four-legged youngest child Koby and our other dear family members Tiny, Styles, and Hazel.

Carol Wilder
New York City,
May 2013

References

Anderegg, Michael (ed.) (1991), *Inventing Vietnam: The War in Film and Television*, Philadelphia: Temple University Press.
Appy, Christian (2004), *Patriots: The Vietnam War Remembered from All Sides*, New York: Penguin.
Aristotle (336 BCE), *Rhetoric*.
Arlen, Michael J. (1968), *The Living Room War*, New York: Penguin.
Aronson, J. (1970), *The Press and the Cold War*, Indianapolis: Bobbs-Merrill.
Barbato, Carole and Laura Davis (2012), *Democratic Narrative, History and Memory*, Kent, Ohio: Kent State University Press.
Bateson, Gregory (1972), *Steps to an Ecology of Mind*, New York: Ballantine.
Baudrillard, Jean (1982), *In the Silence of the Silent Majorities*, Los Angeles: Semiotext(e).
Becker, Samuel L. (1971), "Rhetorical Studies for a Contemporary World," in Lloyd Bitzer and E. Black (eds), *The Prospect of Rhetoric*, Englewood Cliffs: Prentice Hall.
Blaire, Carole, G. Dickenson, and B. L. Ott (2010), *Places of Public Memory: The Rhetoric of Museums and Memorials*, Tuscaloosa: University of Alabama Press.
Bleakney, J. (2006), *Revisiting Vietnam: Memoirs, Memorials, Museums*, New York: Routledge.
Bloom, Harold (ed.) (2009), *Erich Maria Remarque's All Quiet on the Western Front*, New York: Bloom's Literary Criticism.
Borges, Jorge Luis and Hurley, A. (1999), *Collected Fictions*, New York: Penguin Books.
Bowers, John Waite, Donovan Ochs, Richard Jensen, and David Schulz (2009), *The Rhetoric of Agitation and Control*, 3rd ed., Long Grove, Illinois: Waveland Press.
Boyle, Deirdre (1997), *Subject to Change: Guerrilla Television Revisited*, New York: Oxford University Press.
Brinkley, Alan (2010), *The Publisher: Henry Luce and His American Century*, New York: Knopf.
Broeski, P. H. (28 September 1986), "Hurt Stallone Fires Back at His Critics," *San Francisco Examiner Datebook*, pp. 32–35.
Burke, Kenneth (1969), *A Rhetoric of Motives*, Berkeley: University of California Press.
CBS (19 March 1989), [television program] *60 Minutes: The Enemy*.
Chomsky, Noam and Edward Herman (1988), *Manufacturing Consent: The Political Economy of the Mass Media*, New York: Pantheon.
Collective, O. M. (1971). *The Organizers Manual*, New York: Bantam Books.
Collins, David (1986), *Vietnam Love Songs*, Pt. Arena, CA: Pt. Moot Press.
Collins, Nancy (19 December 1985), "The Rolling Stone Interview: Sylvester Stallone," *Rolling Stone Magazine*, pp. 126–130.
Combs, Steven C. (2006), *The Dao of Rhetoric*, Albany: State University of New York Press.

Cook, Russell (1991), "Dorothy Fuldheim's Activist Journalism and the Kent State Shootings," AEJMC (Association for Education in Journalism and Mass Communication), Boston.

Crow, Joan and Jean Valdes (1973), *The Media Works*, Dayton: Cebco Standard Publishing.

Currey, Cecil B. (March 1994), "An Officer and a Gentleman: General Vo Nguyen Giap as Military Man and Poet," in *Nobody Gets off the Bus: The Viet Nam Generation Big Book*, Volume 5, pp. 1–4.

Dargis, Manohla (2008), "Lonely Boy's 'First Blood' and First Pal," http://movies.nytimes.com/2008/05/02/movies/02ramb.html?p. Accessed 3 December 2012.

Davidson, Cathy (1994) *36 Views of Mount Fuji: On Finding Myself in Japan*, New York: Penguin.

Davis, Peter (1975), *Hearts and Minds* [film].

Dawson, Tom (9 August 2002), "*The Quiet American* Review," Channel 4.

DeCaro, Peter (2003), *The Rhetoric of Revolt: Ho Chi Minh's Discourse for Revolution*, Westport: Praeger.

Dillard, D. H. W. (1987), "Night of the Living Dead: It's Not Just a Wind That's Passing Through," in Gregory Waller, *American Horrors: Essays on the Modern American Horror Film*. Urbana-Champaign: University of Illinois Press.

Dittmar, Linda and Gene Michaud (1990), *From Hanoi to Hollywood: The Vietnam War in American Film*. New Brunswick: Rutgers University Press.

Do, Thu Huong, Le Thanh Hang, Do Phuong Linh (2010), *Long Bien Story* [film], Hanoi University.

Doan, Thu Nga, Mai Hai Nam, Nguyen Thi Hoan An (2010), *Living on Rubbish* [film], Hanoi University.

Doss, Erika (ed.) (2001), *Looking at Life Magazine*, Washington: Smithsonian Institution Press.

Duiker, William J. (2000), *Ho Chi Minh*, New York: Hyperion.

Eco, Uberto (1984), *The Role of the Reader: Explorations in the Semiotics of Texts*, Bloomington: Indiana University Press.

Ellsberg, Daniel (1972), *Papers on the War*, New York: Simon and Schuster.

Falludi, Susan (1999), *Stiffed: The Betrayal of the American Man*, Morrow and Company: New York.

Fellman, Gordon (1998), *Rambo and the Dalai Lama: The Compulsion to Win and Its Threat to Human Survival*, Albany: State University of New York Press.

Fitzgerald, Francis (2000), "Half Lenin, Half Gandhi," http://www.nytimes.com/books/00/10/15/reviews/001015.15fitzget.html. Accessed 3 December 2012.

—— (1972), *Fire in the Lake: The Vietnamese and the Americans in Vietnam*, New York: Little Brown and Company.

Fraser, Brendan (2012), "Personal Communication," New York.

Friedman, Simon (2009), "Opinionist: Rambo Solo." http://gothamist.com/2009/03/29/opinionist_rambo_solo.php. Accessed 20 December 2010.

Fuldheim, Dorothy (1974), *A Thousand Friends*, New York: Doubleday.

Gaddis, John (2002), *The Landscape of History: How Historians Map the Past*, New York: Oxford University Press.

Gardner, Lloyd and Marilyn B. Young (2007), *Iraq and the Lessons of Vietnam: Or, How Not to Learn from the Past*, New York: New Press.

References

Gitlin, Todd (1980), *The Whole World Is Watching*, Berkeley: University of California Press.
Gleiberman, Owen (1994) "Forrest Gump," *Entertainment Weekly*, 15 July.
Grace, Thomas (2003), "As Much as We Hated the War…," in C. Appy (ed.), *Patriots: The Vietnam War Remembered From All Sides*, New York: Penguin, pp. 384–389.
—— (2009), "Kent State: The Struggle for Memory and Meaning," *The Sixties: A Journal of History, Politics and Culture* 2: 2, pp. 245–249.
—— (2010), "Personal Interview," New York.
Graves, Ralph (2001), "Personal Interview," New York.
—— (2010), *The LIFE I Led*. New York: Tiasquam Press.
Greene, Graham (1955), *The Quiet American*, London: Penguin.
Groom, Winston (1986), *Forrest Gump*, New York: Washington Square Press.
Haggis, Paul (2007), *In the Valley of Elah* [film].
Haid, Charles (1986), "Renko vs Rambo," http://articles.sun-sentinel.com/1985-09-21/news/8502090849_1_famine-actor-charles-haid-bob-geldof. Accessed 15 August, 2012.
Halberstam, David (1988), *The Making of a Quagmire: America and Vietnam During the Kennedy Era*, New York: Knopf.
Hallin, Daniel (1986), *The 'Uncensored War': The Media and Vietnam*, New York: Oxford University Press.
Hallowell, Elizabeth (1990), "Mirror, Mirror: Were those who died so different from those who live," *Akron Beacon Journal Magazine*, 29 April, pp. 6–25.
Hanyok, Robert J. (2002), *Spartans in Darkness*, Washington, D.C.: Center for Cryptographic History, NSA.
Harris, David (1996), *Our War*, New York: Random House.
Hartocollis, A. (2001), "10 Years and a Diagnosis Later, 9/11 Demons Haunt Thousand," *New York Times*, 8 August.
Hayslip, Le Le and Jay Wurts (1993), *When Heaven and Earth Changed Places*, New York: Plume.
Hedges, Chris (2003), *War Is a Force That Gives Us Meaning*, New York: Random House.
Hellman, J. (1991), "Rambo's Vietnam and Kennedy's New Frontier," in Michael Andregg (ed.), *Inventing Vietnam: The War in Film and Television*, Philadelphia: Temple University Press, pp. 140–152.
Hendrickson, Paul (1997), *The Living and the Dead: Robert McNamara and Five Lives of a Lost War*, New York: Vintage.
Herring, George (2001) *America's Longest War: The United States and Vietnam 1950–1975*, 4th ed., New York: McGraw Hill.
Ho Chi Minh (1971) *The Prison Diary of Ho Chi Minh*, New York: Bantam.
—— (1977), *Selected Writings 1920–1969*, Hanoi: Foreign Languages Publishing House.
—— (2010), "Declaration of Independence of the Democratic Republic of Viet Nam," in O. Gregory (ed.), *Landmark Speeches on the Vietnam War*, College Station: Texas A&M University Press.
Hoa Lo Video (2009), "The Road to Hoa Lo," Hanoi: Vietnam Ministry of Culture and Information.
Hue-Tam Ho Tai (2001), *The Country of Memory: Remaking the Past in Late Socialist Vietnam*, Berkeley: University of California Press.

Huyssen, Andreas (2003), *Present Pasts: Urban Palimpsests and the Politics of Memory*, Palo Alto: Stanford University Press.
Isherwood, Charles (2009), "'First Blood': Obesssion: No Man, No Law, No War Can Stop It," http://theater.nytimes.com/2009/03/23/theater/reviews/23rambo.html. Accessed 20 December 2010.
Iyer, Pico (2012), The Man Within my Head, New York: Knopf.
—— (1993), *Falling Off the Map: Some Lonely Places of the World*, New York: Knopf.
Jamieson, Neil (1995), *Understanding Vietnam*, Berkeley: University of California Press.
Jardine, Douglas (2005), "The Past and Contemporary Meanings of Long Bien Bridge," Unpublished Paper, Hanoi University.
Jennings, Peter and Todd Brewster (1998), *The Century*, New York: Doubleday.
Kael, Pauline (June 1985), "Rambo: First Blood Part II," *The New Yorker*, p. 117.
King, Martin Luther (1967), "Declaration of Independence from the War in Vietnam," *Ramparts*, pp. 33–37.
Klinger, R. (26 November 1985), "Machine Gun Mania," New York: *Weekly World News*.
Knightley, Phillip (2004), *The First Casualty: The War Correspondent as Hero and Myth-Maker from the Crimea to Iraq*, Baltimore: John Hopkins University Press.
Kopkind, Andrew (22 June 1985), "Rambo: First Blood Part II," New York: *The Nation*.
Kozol, Wendy (1994), *Life's America: Family and Nation in Postwar Photojournalism*, Philadelphia: Temple University Press.
Kubrick, Stanley (1957), *Paths of Glory* [film].
Kwon, Heonik (2008), *Ghosts of War in Vietnam*, Cambridge: Cambridge University Press.
Laderman, Scott (2009), *Tours of Vietnam: War, Travel Guides and Memory*, Durham: Duke University Press.
Lamb, David. (2001), "Chopstick and an egg - the psychic way to find a missing brother's body," http://www.allpowmia.com/inter21/in010801psy.html. Accessed 31 July 2009.
Landers, James (2004), *The Weekly War: Newsmagazines and Vietnam*, Columbia: University of Missouri Press.
Lee A. D. (2009) Rambo Solo, *New York Times,* 20 March, p.n.a.
Leow, Rachel (2009), "The Puntastic Poetics of Ho Chi Minh," www.idlethink.wordpress.com/2009/11/16/chaizi/ Accessed 15 August 2012.
LeShan, Lawrence (1992), *The Psychology of War*, New York: Helios Press.
Libertore, Paul (24 April 1986), "Stalker May Be A 'Rambo Gone Awry,'" San Francisco: *San Francisco Chronicle*.
Liebling, A. J. (7 April 1956), "A Talkative Something-or-Other," *The New Yorker*, pp. 148–154.
Letters to the Editor (1970), "Irate Writers Take Both Sides on Kent State Rebellion," *The Cleveland Plain Dealer*, 10 May, p. 7-A.
Life Magazine. Various. 1965–1970.
Linfield, Susie (2010), *The Cruel Radiance: Photography and Political Violence*, Chicago: University of Chicago Press.
Lippman, Walter (1922), *Public Opinion*, New York: Harcourt Brace.
Logan, William S. (2000), *Hanoi: Biography of a City*, Seattle: University of Washington Press.

—— (2005), "Hoa Lo: A Vietnamese Approach to Preserving Places of Pain and Injustice," in N. Garnham and K. Jeffrey (eds), *Culture, Place, and Identity*, Dublin: University College Dublin Press, pp. 152–160.

—— (2009), "Hoa Lo Museum, Hanoi: Changing Attitudes to a Vietnamese Place of Pain and Shame," in W. Logan and K. Reeves (eds), *Places of Pain and Shame: Dealing with Difficult Heritage*, London: Routledge, pp. 182–197.

Lu, Xing (1998), *Rhetoric in Ancient China, Fifth to Third Century B.C.E.*, Columbia: University of South Carolina Press.

Lyman, Rick (18 November 2002), "British Star Speaks Up For 'Quiet American'; Michael Caine's Latest, In Time for Oscar Race," *New York Times*.

MacArthur, John R. (2004), *Second Front: Censorship and Propaganda in the 1991 Gulf War*, Berkeley: University of California Press.

Mangels, John (2012), "Justice Department Won't Reopen Probe of 1970 Kent State Shootings," *The Plain Dealer*, 24 April.

McCain, John S. (1973), "John McCain, Prisoner of War: A First-Person Account," in *U.S. News & World Report*, 14 May.

McGuckin, Henry (1986), *Memoirs of a Wobbly*, Chicago: Charles Kerr.

—— (2012), "Personal Communication."

McLuhan, Marshall (1994), *Understanding Media: The Extensions of Man*, Cambridge: MIT Press.

McNamara, Robert (1996), *In Retrospect: The Tragedy and Lessons of Vietnam*, New York: Vintage.

Michener, James (1971), *Kent State: What Happened and Why*, New York: Random House.

Milestone, Lewis (1930), *All Quiet on the Western Front* [film].

Miller, John (2011), "The Best Conservative Movies: National Review Online," http://www.nationalreview.com/nrd/article/?q=YWQ4MDlhMWRkZDQ5YmViMDM1YzcOMTE3ZTllY2E3MGM=. Accessed 20 December 2011.

Monmonier, Mark (2004), *Rhumb Lines and Map Wars: A Social History of the Mercator Projection*, Chicago: University of Chicago Press.

Morgan, Edward P. (2010), *What Really Happened to the 1960s: How Mass Media Culture Failed American Democracy*, Lawrence: University Press of Kansas.

Mock, Freida Lee and Sanders, Terry (1998), *Return with Honor: The American Experience*, Santa Monica: American Film Foundation [film].

Morrell, David (1972), *First Blood*, New York: Warner Books.

—— (1985), *Rambo: First Blood Part II*, New York: Jove Books.

Morris, Errol (2003), *The Fog of War* [film].

Morris-Suzuki, Tessa (2005), *The Past within Us: Media, Memory, History*, London: Verso Books.

Morrison, Joan and Robert K. Morrison (1987), *From Camelot to Kent State: The Sixties Experience in the Words of Those Who Lived It*, New York: Oxford University Press.

Morrissey, Rachel (2012), "Personal Interview," New York.

Mote, Patricia (1997), *Dorothy Fuldheim: The First Lady of Television News*, Berea: Quixote Publications.

Nguyen, T. (n.d.), *Hoa Lo Prison: Historic Vestige*, Administration Board of Hoa Lo Prison.

Nguyen Chi Thien (2007), *Hoa Lo Stories: Hanoi Hilton Stories*, New Haven: Yale Southeast Asia Studies.
Nguyen Thi Phuc Hang (2011), "Personal Interview," Hanoi.
Nguyen, Thi Van Anh, Tranh Ngoc Diep, and Dang Thanh Huong (2008), *Floating Lives* [film], Hanoi University.
Nisbett, Richard E. (2003), *The Geography of Thought: How Asians and Westerners Think Differently and Why*, New York: Free Press.
Oberzan, Zachary (2007), *Flooding with Love for the Kid* [film].
——— (2009), *Rambo Solo* [stage performance], Soho Rep, New York.
——— (2012), "Personal Interview," New York.
O'Hehir, Andrew (2010), "Rambo's Origin Story - Made for $96," www.salon.com/topic/flooding_with_love_for_the_kid. Accessed 3 December 2012.
Ong, Walter (2002), *Orality and Literacy: The Technologizing of the Word*, 2nd ed., New York: Routledge.
Palmer, William J. (1993), *The Films of the Eighties: A Social History*, Carbondale: University of Illinois Press.
Parenti, Michael (1992), *Inventing Reality: The Politics of the News Media*, 2nd ed., Belmont: Wadsworth.
Pham, Andrew X. (1999), *Catfish and Mandala: A Two-Wheeled Voyage Through the Landscape and Memory of Vietnam*. New York: Farrar, Straus and Giroux.
Pollack, Amanda and Steven Ives (2003), *Reporting America at War* [film] New York: Insignia Films.
Pratt, John Clark (1996), *The Quiet American: Text and Criticism*, New York: Penguin.
Prochnau, William (1996), *Once upon a Distant War: David Halberstam, Neil Sheehan, Peter Arnett—Young War Correspondents and Their Early Vietnam Battles*, New York: Vintage Books.
Quintilian (c.96), *Institutes of Oratory*.
Raindance Collective (1973), *Radical Software*, New York: Raindance Collective.
Remarque, Erich Maria (1929; 1996), *All Quiet on the Western Front*, New York: Random House Reissue Edition.
Ricouer, Paul (2004), *Memory, History, Forgetting*, Chicago: University of Chicago Press.
Rubin, Jerry (1970), *DO IT: Scenarios of the Revolution*, New York: Ballantine Books.
Rumsfeld, Donald (2012), *Known and Unknown: A Memoir*, New York: Sentinel.
Sachs, Dana (2000), *The House on Dream Street: Memoir of an American Woman in Vietnam*, Chapel Hill: Algonquin Books.
Safer, Morley (1990), *Flashbacks: On Returning to Vietnam*. New York: Random House.
Schickel, Richard (11 June 1985), "Danger: Live Moral Issues," *Time*, p. 91.
Scott, Wilbur (2003), *Vietnam Veterans Since the War: The Politics of PTSD, Agent Orange, and the National Memorial*, Norman: University of Oklahoma Press.
Scranton, William W. (1970), *The Report of the President's Commission on Campus Unrest*, U.S. Government Printing Office.
Scruggs, Jan and Swerdlow, J. (1985), *To Heal a Nation*, New York: Harper & Row.

References

Shales, Tom (March 1986), "The ReDecade," *Esquire*, pp. 67–72.

Shay, Jonathan (2003), *Achilles in Vietnam: Combat Trauma and the Undoing of Character*. New York: Scribner.

Sidey, Hugh (1970), "Kent State: Four Deaths at Noon," *Life Magazine*, 15 May, p. 31.

Smith, Winnie (1992), *American Daughter Gone to War*, New York: William Morrow.

Sontag, Susan (2003), *Regarding the Pain of Others*, New York: Picador.

St. Mark, Robert and Mike White (22 May 2012), "Flooding with Love for First Blood, Son," www.projection-booth.blogspot.com/2012/5/episode-64-flooding-with-love-for-first.html, Accessed 15 August 2012.

Stasio, M. (2009), "Rambo Solo," http://www.variety.com/review/VE1117939914?refcatid=33. Accessed 20 December 2011.

Stiller, Ben (2008), *Tropic Thunder* [film].

Stone, Oliver (1993), *Heaven and Earth* [film].

Studlar, Gail and Dresser, D. (1988), "Never Having to Say You're Sorry: Rambo's Rewriting of the Vietnam War," *Film Quarterly*, 42: 1, pp. 9–16.

Sturken, Marita (1997), *Tangled Memories: The Vietnam War, The Aids Epidemic, and the Politics of Remembering*, Berkeley: University of California Press.

Tace, Stephen A., *Letters from Quantico & Vietnam: 7 July 1966–21 April 1967*.

Taylor, Stuart, P. McGovern, and R. Genthner (1971), *Violence at Kent State May 1 to 4 1970: The Students' Perspective*, New York: College Notes & Texts.

Templar, Robert (1998), *Shadows and Wind: A View of Modern Vietnam*, New York: Penguin.

To Mai Lien (19 March 2012), "Personal Interview," New York.

To Mai Lien, Pham Huong Trang, Dang Viet Ha, Doan Thi Hong Hai (2010), *Behind the Corn* [film], Hanoi University.

Tompkins, Phillip K. (1969), "The Rhetoric of Non-Oratorical Forms," *Quarterly Journal of Speech* 55: pp. 431–439.

Tompkins, Phillip K. and Elaine Anderson (1971), *Communication Crisis at Kent State: A Case Study*, New York: Gordon and Breach.

Torricelli, Randy and A. Carroll (eds) (1995), *Extraordinary Speeches of the American Century*, New York: Washington Square Press.

Tranh Thanh (1993), "Personal Interview," Hanoi.

Trillin, Calvin (2009), "Tag Along on Calvin Trillin's Downtown Eating Tour," http://www.timeout.com/newyork/the-feed-blog/tag-along-on-calvin-trillins-downtown-eating-tour. *New York Magazine*, Accessed December 3, 2012.

Turse, Nick (2013), *Kill Anything That Moves: The Real War in Vietnam*, New York: Metropolitan Books.

VanBiema, D. H. (July 1987), "With a $100 Million Gross(Out): Sly Stallone Fends Off Rambo's Army of Adversaries," *People*, pp. 34–37.

Vu, Minh Huyen, Pham Thuy Ngan, and Nguyen Ha Phuong Ninh (2010), *Floating Futures* [film], Hanoi University.

Wainwright, Loudon (1988), *The Great American Magazine: An Inside History of Life*, New York: Ballantine Books.

Waller, Gregory (1990), "Rambo: Getting to Win This Time," in Linda Dittmar and Gene Michaud (eds), *From Hanoi to Hollywood: The Vietnam War in American Film*, New Brunswick: Rutgers University Press, pp. 113–128.

Walsh, E. (23 April 1986), "Rambo Delivers Wrong Message, Author Halberstam Says," *Stanford Campus Report*.

Wang, Jennifer (2001), "A Struggle of Contending Stories: Race, Gender and Political Memory in Forrest Gump," *Cinema Journal*, 39, pp. 92–115.

Wayne, John (1968), *Green Berets* [film].

Weller, Ken (1973), "1970–1972: The Lordstown struggle and the real crisis in production," *Solidarity*, http://libcom.org/library/lordstown-struggle-ken-weller. Accessed 15 August 2009.

Wikipedia (2012), "Hanoi Traffic," http://en.wikipedia.org/wiki/Hanoi.

Wilder, Carol (1974), *The Rhetoric of Social Movements: A Critical Perspective*, Ann Arbor: University Microfilms.

—— (1977), "A Conversation with Colin Cherry," *Human Communication Research*, Summer 1977, pp. 354–362.

—— (1979), "The Palo Alto Group: Difficulties and Directions of the Interactional View for Human Communication Research," Winter: pp. 174–194.

—— (1988), "Up against the Wall: The Vietnam Veterans Memorial and the Paradox of Remembrance," *Political Culture and Public Opinion*, New Brunswick: Transaction, pp. 133–147.

—— (1990), "Wounded Warriors and the Revisionist Myth," *Media USA*, New Brunswick: Transaction, pp. 197–205.

—— (2005), "Separated at Birth: Argument by Irony in Hearts and Minds and Fahrenheit 9/11," *Atlantic Journal of Communication*, 13:56–72.

Wilder, Carol and Colby, Adam (1992), "The Rhetorical Rollercoaster to War," *Magazine*, II: 2, pp. 110–119.

Wilder, Carol and Weakland, John, eds. (1982), *Rigor and Imagination: Essays from the Legacy of Gregory Bateson*, New York: Praeger.

Willson, S. Brian (2011), *Blood on the Tracks: The Life and Times of S. Brian Willson*, Oakland: PM Press.

Wolfe, Tom (1965), "What if He's Right?," *New York Magazine*.

Wyler, William (1946), *The Best Years of our Lives* [film].

Young, Marilyn B. (1991), *The Vietnam Wars 1945–1990*, New York: Harper Collins.

—— (1997), Interviewed by Bill Moyers, http://www.pbs.org/moyers/journal/05112007/transcript3.html.

Zelizer, Barbie (2010), *About to Die: How News Images Move the Public*, New York: Oxford University Press.

Zemeckis, Robert (1994), *Forrest Gump* [film].

Zinoman, Peter (2001), *The Colonial Bastille: A History of Imprisonment in Vietnam 1886–1940*, Berkeley: University of California Press.

Zoglin, R. (24 June 1985), "An Outbreak of Ramboiana," *Time*, pp. 72–73.

Index

60 Minutes, Hung interview 7, 20, 101, 104, 121–3 *see also* Nguyen Ngoc Hung

A
Achilles in Vietnam; Combat Trauma and the Undoing of Character (Shay) 128
Adams, Lily 20
Adelman, Tama 20
Adorno, Theodor 223
age, and language 102
Agent Orange 25, 95, 97
Akers, Peggy 20
Akron Beacon Journal 187, 191
Al Jazeera 114–15
Alexander, Shana 88, 89
All Quiet on the Western Front (Milestone film) 109, 134–5
All Quiet on the Western Front (Remarque) 7
Allman, Greg 16
Alvarez, Everett 49–50
The American Century (Jennings) 103
American War 5, 22–3, 24–7 *see also* Vietnam War
Apocalypse Now (Coppola) 25, 133, 143, 152
Aristotle 17, 27, 67, 110, 175, 223
Arlen, Michael 81, 226
Arnett, Peter 226
Ashby, Hal, *Coming Home* 7, 133, 136–8, 152
Atwood, Paul 158
Ayres, Lew 134

B
Ba Dinh Square speech 63, 65–8 *see also* Ho Chi Minh

Bac Ho *see* Ho Chi Minh
Bac Ninh Province 37
Bao Dai 63
Barbato, Carole 173
Barthes, Roland 223
Bateson, Gregory 223, 224
Baudrillard, Jean 13, 223
Becker, Samuel 225
Behind the Corn (student film) 215
Beidler, Phillip 126
Berger, Albert 120
The Best Years of our Lives (Wyler) 7, 136
Biden, Jill 129
Bien Hoa 88
Blecker, Michael 20
Bliss, Ron 53
The Bombs of Pham Hong Thai (play) 43
Born on the Fourth of July (Stone) 142
Bowers, John Waite, *The Rhetoric of Agitation and Control* 230–1
Boyle, Deirdre, *Subject to Change: Guerilla Television Revisited* 230
Boyle, Kay 18
Brinkley, Alan 82
Bronson, Tom 158
Burke, Kenneth 18, 68
Burrows, Larry 79, 83, 91
Bush, George W. 25, 118, 127, 153, 155, 167

C
CAARE Project 140
Caine, Michael 116, 118–19
Cam Ne 227
Cameron, James 157
Canfora, Chic 197

capitalism 5, 26
Capps, Walter 19–20
cartography 220 see also maps
Casale, Gerald 197
censorship 64, 91, 114–15, 164, 226–8
Center for Understanding Media 17
Chicago Tribune 178–80
Chomsky, Noam 224
Chuong Chung 20
Cimino, Michael, *The Deer Hunter* 133, 152
Cinematheque 35, 106, 116
Cleveland Heights 15
Cleveland Plain Dealer 180–2, *188*, 189, 192–3
Clinton, Bill 24–5
coffee table war 81–2
cognitive therapy 144–5
Colby, Adam 232
Cold War 81, 117, 228, 231 see also Russia
Collins, Nancy 155
Collins, Sue 21
colonialism 6, 119, 206–7
    French 40, 45, 46, 113, 206–7
Coming Home (Ashby) 7, 133, 136–8, 152
Communist Party, and education 37
Concord Naval Weapons Station 20
confessions 47, 51, 55 see also prisoners
Confucius 64–5, 102–3, 110, 113, 215, 223
Coogan, John 35
Copper, Kelly 149
Coppola, Francis, *Apocalypse Now* 25, 133, 143, 152
Cosmatos, George P., *Rambo: First Blood Part II* 152, 157–9 see also Rambo films
Country Joe McDonald 20
Cox, Paul 20
Crenna, Richard 152
Crocker, Jim 17
Cronkhite, Walter 226, 227, 231
Crow, Joan, *The Media Works* 230
Cruise, Tom 142
Cu Chi 72, 73, 74

cultural difference 21, 111, 207
cultural revolution, in 1960s U.S. 16, 230

D
Da Nang 84
Daily Kent Stater 197–8
Dargis, Manohla 164
Dark Shadows (TV series) 25
Davis, Laura 173
Davis, Peter, *Hearts and Minds* 19, 106, 109
Davis, Robert Gorham 117
Debrov, Sergei 71
DeCaro, Peter 6, 63, 68, 74
The Deer Hunter (Cimino) 133, 152
Del Corso, Sylvester 175, 180
Del Signore, John 149
Dellinger, David 20
democracy 66, 111, 127, 181
Dennehy, Brian 152
Dern, Bruce 136–8
dissent 87, 92, 180, 181, 200, 230
dissidents 35, 40, 45–6, 57
Do Thi Hai Yen 118, 119, 120
Dohrn, Bernardine 197
domestic violence 139–42, 144–5
Donovan, Hedley 83, 86–7, 92, 94
Doss, Erika 81, 92
Douglas, Kirk 152
draft avoidance 16
Dresser, David 134
Druicker, William 64–7
Duc Nguyen 20
Duncan, David Douglas 79
Duong Lam 219

E
Eco, Umberto 53
education systems 7, 37, 43, 69, 105–7, 113
    see also political education
Eiffel, Gustave 207
Ellsberg, Daniel, *The Pentagon Papers* 20, 26

Index

F
Faas, Horst 83
Facebook 114
Fahrenheit 9/11 (Moore) 19
Fellman, Gordon, *Rambo and the Dalai Lama* 154
feminism 17
Fields, Sally 142
Filo, John, Kent State photograph 178, 181, 198–9
First Amendment 114–15
First Blood (Kotcheff) 133–4, 144, 149, 151–4 *see also Rambo* films
First Blood (Morrell) 8, 151
First Blood (Oberzan) 8, 154
Fitzgerald, Frances 102
Floating Futures (student film) 214
Floating Lives (student film) 214–15
Flooding With Love for the Kid (Oberzan) 7–8, 154, 165–8
The Fog of War (Morris) 72
Fonda, Jane 26, 137
Forest Hills 15
Forrest Gump (Groom) 142
Forrest Gump (Zemeckis) 142–5
France
   colonialism 40, 45, 46, 113, 206–7
   occupation 45–6, 53, 63, 113, 207
   see also colonialism
Fraser, Brendan 118, 119
Fulbright Scholarship 21, 105, 109, 203, 204
Fuldheim, Dorothy 182–4

G
Gaddis, John 130, 178, 187, 200
Gearhart, Sally 18
gender, and reporting Kent State 180
gender roles 119–21
General Motors, Lordstown 132–3
Gerry 106, 116, 120
Giap, General *see* Vo Nguyen Giap
Gitlin, Todd 230

Goldsmith, Nick 164
Grace, Thomas M. 8, 171, 172–3, 174, 176–7, 186–7, 197, 200
Graves, Ralph 87, 94
Greene, Graham 7, 116
   influence 119
   on Manckiwiez film 118
   on writing 121
   see also The Quiet American
Groom, Winston, *Forrest Gump* 142
Gulf War 167, 231–2
guns,
   at Kent State 173, 174
   and Rambo 156, 159, 161, 162

H
Ha Thanh 42
Haggis, Paul, *In the Valley of Elah* 7, 144
Hai Ba Trung Street 58
Haid, Charles 159
Haines, Harry 20
Halberstam, David, *The Making of a Quagmire* 159, 227, 231
Hallin, Daniel, *The "Uncensored War": The Media and Vietnam* 83, 84, 228–30, 232
Mme. Hang *see* Nguyen Thi Phuc Hang
Hanks, Tom 142
Hanoi,
   architecture 207
   bombing 208–10
   first visit 13
   traffic 3–5
   see also Hanoi Towers; Hanoi University; Hoa La Prison and Museum; Long Bien Bridge
Hanoi Central Prison *see* Hoa La Prison
"Hanoi Hilton" *see* Hoa La Prison
Hanoi March 51
Hanoi Towers 33–4, 38, 41, 57–9
Hanoi University 104
   media program 203, 217–18
   see also education systems

Harris, David 20
Hayslip, Le Ly, *When Earth and Heaven Changed Places* 20, 142
Hearts and Minds (Davis) 19, 106, 109
Hebrard, Ernst 207
"Hell's Hole" *see* Hoa Lo Prison
Henry 69–70
Hermann, Edward 224
Hguyen Thai Hoc 40
hierarchies 47, 102–3, 113
Ho Chi Minh 6–7, 24, 63–8
   Ba Dinh Square speech 63, 65–8
   death 69
   and education 68–9
   legacy 72, 74
   New Years Greeting 1969 52
   reputation 69–70
   speech style 67, 68–9
Ho Chi Minh Mausoleum 70–1
Ho Chi Minh Museum 22, 68
Ho Chi Minh Trail 74
Hoa Lo Prison and Museum 6, 24, *31*, 34, 41, 57–9
   American exhibits 46–52
   bookshop 57–8, 116
   conditions 44–5, 50
   construction 45
   cultural transformation 57–9
   female prisoners 38, 44–5, 53–7
   history 45–6
   "Holiday Camp" exhibit 49–52
   and political education 40, 43–6
   prison culture 43–4, 47, 51
   U.S. pilot exhibit 38, 48–9, 52
Hoffman, Abbie 144
Hong Anh 53, 54
Huet, Henry 79, 90
Hung, Professor *see* Nguyen Ngoc Hung
Huy, Mr. 34–5, 69–70, 106–8

I
identity 15
   and language 102
   and prison 40
   and war 127, 130
In Retrospect (McNamara) 72
In The Valley of Elah (Haggis) 7, 144
independence 6, 63, 64–8, 69
Indochine (Wargnier) 109
information management 231–2
Intimate Partner Violence (IPV) 142
Isherwood, Charles 149, 150, 166
Iyer, Pico 116

J
Japanese occupation 45–6, 55, 63
Jardine, Douglas 8, 205–7, 218–19
Jennings, Garth, *Son of Rambow* 154, 163–4, 166
Jennings, Peter, *The American Century* 103
Johnson, Hiram 231
Johnson, Lyndon B. 86–7, 91, 208–9, 231
   letter to 7, 79, 82–3
Jones, Tommy Lee 142
Jonestown, Guyana 18

K
Kael, Pauline 158
Keller, Ted 18
Kent State University,
   appointment at 17
   May 4th 8, 24, 28, 171–3
      guns 173, 174
      importance of accuracy 198
      maps 187–94
      memorials 174–5, 177–8, 198–9, 200
      National Guard 172–4, 180, 194–7
      numbers involved 172, 194–7
      reporting 176, 178–84
   see also May 4th Visitor Center
Kerrey, Bob 20, 25, 159
Kerry, John 25
King, Martin Luther 25, 128
kinship 102–3
Knightley, Phillip 227, 228
Kopkind, Andrew 157

Kotcheff, Ted 152
   First Blood 133–4, 144, 149, 151–4
   see also Rambo films
Kozoff, Michael 157
Krause, Allison 173, 175, *185*
Kubrick, Stanley, *Paths of Glory* 109

L
Laderman, Scott 46
"The Lady" *see* Nguyen Thi Phuc Hang
language 8–9, 31, 102–3, 105
   of Ho Chi Minh 67–8
   and politics 176
Lansdale, Edward 116
Le Duan 40, 65
Le Duc Tho 65
learning styles 111, 113, 212
Lee, David 150–1
LeMay, Curtis 208
Leow, Rachel 67–8
LeShan, Lawrence 227
letters from Vietnam 78–97
Lewis, Jerry 181
Lewis, Joe 195
Libertore, Paul 162
Liebling, A.J. 117
Life magazine 7, 20, 24, 77–8, 81–97
   circulation 81, 82
   dissent at 87, 92, 93–4
   final issue 94–5
   influence 81–2
   and movies 92
   photography 88, 90, 92–3, 94
   reporting Kent State 181
   support for government 81–2, 86–7
   war coverage 82–4, 90–1, 93–5
Lippman, Walter 224
Liska, Pavol 149
Living on Rubbish (student film) 213–14
Logan, William 39, 57, 72
Long Bien Bridge 8, 206–17
Long Bien Story (student film) 215–17
Loy, Myrna 136

Luce, Clare Booth 92
Luce, Henry 81–2, 92
Lunine, Mike 28

M
MacArthur, John 91
Maison Centrale see Hoa La Prison and Museum
The Making of a Quagmire (Halberstam) 227
Manckiwiez, Joseph, *The Quiet American* 115, 118, 119
Manning, Eli 155
maps, of Kent State shootings 187–94
   see also cartography
March, Frederic 136
The March of Time (newsreel) 92
Martin, Mary 87–8
Marx, Karl 110, 223
Maxtone-Graham, Jamie 216
M.A.S.H. (TV series) 25
Mather, Keith 20
May 4th Visitor Center, maps 187, 193–4, 197 *see also* Kent State University
McCain, John 6, 46–7, 48, 51, 52, 53
McCarthy, Mary 208
McCloskey, Jack 20
McDermid, Nancy 18, 19
McGrath, Mike 47
McGuckin, Hank 13, 18, 21, 67, 81
McGuckin, Henry E. 18
McLuhan, Marshall 7, 17, 110, 111–12
McNamara, Robert 105
   In Retrospect 72
media,
   reporting Vietnam War 225, 226, 228, 229–30, 231
   problems teaching 106–12
   and social change 17, 175, 227–8, 230
media environment 224–7
"Media Studies: History, Theory, Practice" class 109–11
The Media Works (Crow and Valdes) 230
Merrick, David 88

Mike 7, 131–3, 138–41
Milestone, Lewis, *All Quiet on the Western Front* 109, 134–5
Milgrim, Stanley 225–6
Milk, Harvey 18
Miller, Jeffrey 173, 175, 178, 181, *185*
Miller, John 143
Millner, Bill 163–4
Mintier, Tom 42
Mohr, Charles 87
Moll, Giorgia 119
Mondale, Walter 158–9
Monmonier, Mark 188
Moore, Charles 87
Moore, Michael, *Fahrenheit 9/11* 19
Morrell, David 166
   First Blood 8, 151
   Rambo: First Blood Part II 157
Morris, Errol 72
Morris-Suzuki, Tessa 24
Morrissey, Rachel 120
Moscone, George 18
movies,
   and *Life* magazine 92
   and teaching 24, 109–10, 112
   veteran portrayals 7, 24, 130–8, 142–5, 153
   see also Long Bien Bridge; *Rambo* films
Moving Wall *see* Vietnam Veterans Memorial
Moyers, Bill 15–16
Mueller, John 153
Murphy, Audie 118, 151
Muskat, Hal 20
Mutual Friendship Association 37

N
National Historic Register 8, 175, 200
Nature Theater of Oklahoma 149–50
New School Media Studies Program 17, 21
New York Magazine 111
The New York Times 79, 83, 87, 180–1
The New Yorker 226
Newsweek 79, 181
Ngo Dinh Diem 118

Nguyen Ai Quoc *see* Ho Chi Minh
Nguyen Chi Thien 57
Nguyen Ngoc Cuong 123
Nguyen Ngoc Hung (Professor Hung) 7, 20–1, 101, 103–4, 105, 121–3
Nguyen Qui Duc 20
Nguyen Sinh Cung *see* Ho Chi Minh
Nguyen Tat Thanh *see* Ho Chi Minh
Nguyen Thi Phuc Hang (Mme. Hang) 6, 34–7, *56*, *58*
   contacting 34–5
   on Ho Chi Minh's speech 63, 65
   marriage 56–7
   political activities 36–7, 56, 63
   in prison 37, 44–5, 55–6
   on Quang Thai 54–5
Nguyen Thi Quang Thai 53–5
Nguyen Xuan Tue 21
Nguyen Xuan Vang 105, 205–6
Nha Trang airbase 87–9
Niagara Falls 79
Night of the Living Dead (Romero) 25
Nixon, Richard 92, 175, 176, 180, 209
Noyce, Phillip, *The Quiet American* 115–16, 118–20, 219

O
Obama, Barak 129
Obama, Michele 129
Oberzan, Zachary 149–51
   First Blood 8, 154
   Flooding With Love for the Kid 154, 165–8
   Rambo Solo 7–8, 149–51, 154, 165, 168
objective journalism 230
Ochs, Donovan, *The Rhetoric of Agitation and Control* 230–1
OGRIP (Ohio Geographically Referenced Information Program) 191
O'Hehir, Andrew 165–6
Once Upon a Distant War (Prochnau) 81
Ong, Walter 111–12
Orality and Literacy: The Technologies of the Word 226

Operation Linebacker II 209
Operation Rolling Thunder 208
Orality and Literacy: The Technologies of the Word (Ong) 226
The Organizer's Manual (O.M. Collective) 230

P
Page, Tim 79
Palm, Edward 20
Papert, Seymour 3–4
Parenti, Michael 230
passports 5
Paths of Glory (Kubrick) 109
patriarchy 120–1
The Pentagon Papers (Ellsberg) 26
Perris, Donald 184
Peterson, Pete 50
Pham Thi Hang 122
Pham Van Dong 65
Pham Viet Ha 204
Phan Boi Chau 40
Phu Khanh ceramics village 38–40
Pike, Douglas 20
pilots 38, 48–9, 52, 57, 83
  see also veterans
Plato 110, 175, 223, 224
Platoon (Stone) 25, 143
political education 40, 43–6, 57 *see also* education systems
politics, and language 176
Pont Doumer *see* Long Bien Bridge
Poulter, Will 163–4
President's Commission on Campus Unrest (Scranton Report) 172, 175, 187, 189, 190–1
The Prison Review 43
The Prisoner's Life 43
prisoners
  confessions 47, 51, 55
  culture of 43–4, 47, 51
  female 38, 44–5, 53–7
  and identity 40
  U.S. 48–9, 52
Prochnau, William 81
pronunciation of Vietnamese 31 *see also* language
propaganda 27, 51–2, 64, 72, 81, 118, 224, 231–2
psychics 122–3
PTSD (Post Traumatic Stress Disorder) 7, 25, 128–9, 144–5
  and domestic violence 139–42
  first treatment unit 141
  in veteran movies 142
punishment in Hoa La Prison 47, 51–2

Q
Quang Duc 72
Quang Tri 7, 104, 121
"Question Authority" 13–15, 109–11
The Quiet American (Greene) 7, 24, 58, 115, 144
  critical analysis 115–21
  quoted 101, 109, 116, 117
The Quiet American (Manckiwiez 1958) 115, 118, 119
The Quiet American (Noyce 2002) 115–16, 118–20, 219

R
Radical Software (Raindance Collective) 230
Rambo and the Dalai Lama (Fellman) 154
Rambo films 7–8, 109
  box office 152, 155, 157
  First Blood (Kotcheff) 133–4, 144, 149, 151–4
  and guns 156, 159, 161, 162
  kill chart 152–4
  popularity and influence 154–7, 158–63, 167–8
  Rambo: First Blood Part II (Cosmatos) 152, 157–9
  source of name 151
  and timeshifting 166–7
  and veterans 130, 158, 162–3

Rambo Solo (Oberzan) 7–8, 149–51, 154, 165, 168
Ramirez, Richard 162
Rather, Dan 226
Reagan, Ronald 151, 155–6, 157, 158, 160, 167
The Red Prison 43
Redgrave, Michael 119
Remarque, Erich Maria, *All Quiet on the Western Front* 7, 134
Rentmeester, Co 91
representation 8, 52, 115, 130, 178–81, 187–9, 198, 200
Reser, Phil 20
Return with Honor (TV documentary) 47
The Rhetoric of Agitation and Control (Bowers and Ochs) 230–1
Rhodes, James 172
Rice, Harold 171
Riefenstahl, Leni, *Triumph of the Will* 109
Romero, George 25
Rubin, Jerry 182–3, 227–8
Rudd, Mark 197
Rumsfeld, Donald 105, 231
Russell, Harold 136
Russia 101, 113, 158 *see also* Cold War

S
Sackheim, William 157
Safer, Morley 104, 105, 121, 227
San Francisco State University 18
Sartre, Jean Paul 117, 223
Scheuer, Sandra 173, 174–5, 177, *185*
Schickel, Richard 158
Schroeder, William 173, 175, *185*
Scranton Report *see* President's Commission on Campus Unrest
Scuggs, Jan 126
SDS (Students for a Democratic Society) 17
Shales, Tom 167
"Shanghai Port" 210–11, 216

Shay, Jonathan, *Achilles in Vietnam: Combat Trauma and the Undoing of Character* 128, 133
Sinise, Gary 143, 144
Smith, Winnie 20
social change 144, 223
    and media 17, 175, 227–8, 230
social consciousness 6, 15, 84, 87, 212–13
Son of Rambow (Jennings) 8, 154, 163–4
Sonneborn, Barbara 20
Sontag, Susan 198
spelling of Vietnamese words 8–9
spheres of discourse (Hallin) 228–30
Stallone, Sylvester 152, 155, 157, 158, 166
    see also Rambo films
Stasio, Marilyn 150
Stiller, Ben, *Tropic Thunder* 143
Stockdale, William 50
Stone, Oliver
    Born on the Fourth of July 142
    Platoon 25, 143
students,
    in *All Quiet on the Western Front* 135
    short film project 205–6, 210–17
    in Vietnam 68, 69–70, 101–3, 104, 106, 212–13
    see also Hanoi University; Kent State University; Long Bien Bridge
Studlar, Gaylyn 134
Subella, Kevin 191
Subject to Change: Guerilla Television Revisited (Boyle) 230
suicides, in military 25, 129, 144–5
superstition 122–3
Swords to Plowshares 19

T
Tace, Stephen A. 7, 97
    letters home 78, 85, 89, 91, 95–6
teaching 7, 16–17, 70, 101–2
    media 106–12
    and movies 24, 109–10, 112
    short film project 205–6, 210–17

Thien Mu Pagoda 72, *73*
Third Force 116, 118
To Mai Lien 8, 34, 35, 58, 203, *204*, 217–18
Tompkins, Phillip 172
tourism 6, 26, 46
trade relations 26, 67
Tran Dang Ninh 65
Tran Din Vanh 67
Tran Do 35, 55, 56–7, 63
Tran Duy Hung 63
Tran Quoc Hoan 55, 65
Tran Thanh 68
Tran Trong Kim 55
Trillin, Calvin 26
Trinh Minh-ha 20
Triumph of the Will (Riefenstahl) 109
Tropic Thunder (Stiller) 143
Truman, Harry S. 64
trust 87, 105, 228, 231
Turse, Nick 25
twilight sleep 15–17, 27, 226, 228, 231, 232
Tye, James 158

U
The "Uncensored War": The Media and Vietnam (Hallin) 83, 84, 228–30, 232
Uncle Ho *see* Ho Chi Minh
U.S.
   1960s cultural revolution 16, 230
   dissent against War 87, 91–2
   distance from Vietnam 23
   Vietnamese visitors 20–1

V
Valdes, Jean, *The Media Works* 230
van chai (floating villages) 211
Vecchio, Mary Ann 178, 181
Veteran Speakers Alliance 18–19, 158
veterans 19, 129–31
   Mike 7, 131–3, 138–41
   in movies 7, 24, 130–8, 142–5, 153
   and Rambo 130, 158, 162–3
   suicides 25, 129, 144–5
   see also pilots
Viet Kieu 69
"Vietnam: Rhetoric and Realities" class 20–1
Vietnam,
   distance from U.S. 23
   French occupation 45–6, 53, 63, 113, 207
   independence 6, 63, 64–8, 69
   Japanese occupation 45–6, 55, 63
   resistance to U.S. 210
   Russian occupation 113
   and tourism 6, 26, 46
Vietnam in Pictures (magazine) 79
Vietnam Veterans of America 158
Vietnam Veterans Memorial 13, 26, 126
Vietnam War 6, 24–7
   "advisors" 83
   bombing 208
   combat fatalities 92, 94
   as commodity 6, 26
   dissent in U.S. 87, 91–2
   escalation 228
   legacy 25
   and media 225, 226, 228, 229–30, 231
   pilots 38, 48–9, 52, 57, 83
   reasons for 25–6, 127–8
   support 226–7
   troop numbers 16, 84, 87, 89, 129
Vietnamese, visits to U.S. 20–1
Vietnamese Language Center 101
Vildieu, Auguste-Henri 45
visa procurement 21–2
Vo Nguyen Giap (General Giap) 34, 47, 53–4, 56, 210
Voight, Jon 136–8
Vu Duc Vuong 20

W
Wainwright, Loudon 81, 93–4
Wang, Jennifer 143
war, and identity 127, 130
"War Film" class 107–9
War Resisters League 158

war rhetoric 231–2
Wargnier, Régis, *Indochine* 109
Weakland, John 141
Webb, Ralph 20
Weiner, Norbert 223
Wheeler, John 20
When Heaven and Earth Changed Places (Hayslip) 142
Wikipedia, map of Kent State shootings 187, 191–2, 197
Wilder, Carol *58, 204*
   education 13–17
   father 16, 22, 27, 107
   Fulbright Scholarship 21, 105, 109, 203–4
   in Hanoi 3, 13, 22–3, 31–5, 101–3, 105–7, 203–5
   at Kent State University 171–2, 175–6, 182, 197–8, 199–200
   and identity 15, 102
   and *Life* magazine 84–5
   and Mike 131, 138–41
   and Vietnam 5, 19, 21–3, 112, 232
Wilensky, Uri 3
Willson, S. Brian 20, 200
Wilson, Pete 20
Wilson, Woodrow 64
Wolfe, Tom 111
Wright, Robin 142
Wyler, William, *The Best Years of Our Lives* 7, 136

Y
Yen Bai 42
Young, Marilyn B. 15, 226
YouTube 115

Z
Zachurek, Stephanie 120
Zemeckis, Robert, *Forrest Gump* 142–5
Zimbardo, Phillip 225–6
Zinoman, Peter 40